Fundamentals of Network Security

For a listing of recent titles in the *Artech House Telecommunications Library*, turn to the back of this book.

Fundamentals of Network Security

John E. Canavan

Artech House
Boston • London
www.artechhouse.com

Library of Congress Cataloging-in-Publication Data
Canavan, John E.
    Fundamentals of network security / John E. Canavan.
       p.   cm. — (Artech House telecommunications library)
    Includes bibliographical references and index.
    ISBN 1-58053-176-8 (alk. paper)
    1. Computer security.   2. Computer networks—Security measures.
    I. Title.   II. Series.
QA76.9.A25 C364   2000
005.8—dc21   00-050810
                                                            CIP

British Library Cataloguing in Publication Data
Canavan, John E.
    Fundamentals of network security. — (Artech House
    telecommunications library)
    1. Computer networks — Security measures
    I. Title
    005.8

    ISBN 1-58053-176-8

Cover design by Yekaterina Ratner

Microsoft® screen shots reprinted by permission from Microsoft Corporation.

Netscape Communicator browser window © 1999 Netscape Communications Corporation. Used with permission. Netscape Communications has not authorized, sponsored, endorsed, or approved this publication and is not responsible for its content.

Permission to reproduce screen shots from the PGP and Sniffer products has been provided by Network Associates, Inc. Network Associates, PGP, Pretty Good Privacy Sniffer, and Distributed Sniffer System are registered trademarks of Network Associates, Inc. and/or its affiliates in the U.S. and/or other countries.

MIT screen shots used with permission.

Qualcomm's Eudora screen shots used with permission.

© 2001 ARTECH HOUSE, INC.
685 Canton Street
Norwood, MA 02062

International Standard Book Number: 1-58053-176-8
Library of Congress Catalog Card Number: 00-050810

10 9 8 7 6 5 4 3 2 1

To my wife Anne and my daughter April

Contents

Preface

Regarding This Book

I decided to write this book for several reasons. First, it is the culmination of 18 years of professional experience in the information technology (IT) field and my desire to learn more about the subject. It is also the result of research performed during my graduate studies. Most of all, however, this book is the result of teaching a network security class. For a number of years, I have taught a class aptly titled the "Fundamentals of Network Security Management." Most of my students are professionals employed in the IT or telecommunications fields who are attending school on a part-time basis. Some are involved in the technical side of operations, while others are more involved with the business and marketing side.

When I first started teaching the class I searched for a text that covered the topics that were pertinent to my students and that could be applied in their daily jobs. Since the course was an introductory level class, I wanted the book to cover the fundamentals of network security. Many good books covering computer or network security are available. However, most focus on a specific operating system. I needed a book to provide practical information that my students could apply on their jobs, rather than one focusing solely on UNIX security or NT security. No single book did so in a useful and easily understood format.

As a result, I began developing this book. In the process, I have tried to cover principles and concepts that are applicable to all operating systems. Whenever possible, I have also tried to provide useful examples of the practical application of those principles and concepts.

Network and computer security is critical to the financial health of every organization. If you have any doubt about that statement just read your local newspaper. Every day there is a new network security incident reported. One recent report stated that in 2000, hacking and viruses will cost companies approximately $1.6 trillion worldwide. That is a staggering amount of money with a direct effect on companies' return on investment or assets. The figure is made even more incredible by the fact that businesses and universities still do not treat the issue of computer security as a core business competency. In general, businesses spend money on computer and network security only when they have to. The fact that students can graduate from most computer science or IT programs without ever taking a single class in network, computer, or information security is evidence of a lack of understanding on the part of most universities of the critical role of security.

Intended Audience

This book is not a hacker's guide, nor is it intended for the experienced computer security professional. I don't claim to be a computer security "expert." Then again, I don't believe that many who claim that distinction are as expert as they maintain. This book is intended for those who are just beginning their journey of discovery in the area of computer and network security. It is a starting point from which one can build a foundation of knowledge.

This book, which focuses on security from a management perspective, addresses principles and methods in a real-world context. Specific topics covered include company security reviews; policy development; risk analysis; threats, vulnerabilities, and countermeasures; electronic commerce (e-commerce); encryption; and ciphers.

Contents

Chapter 1 reviews the importance of network security and presents some relevant background and history. It also introduces some basic terminology that is used throughout the book to define network, information, and computer security.

Chapter 2 focuses on threats, vulnerabilities, and various types of attacks and hacks. It also identifies useful sources of information on network and computer hacking.

Chapter 3 discusses encryption and its practical application. In addition, it details the various types of ciphers and their application. Chapter 3 also introduces digital signatures, digital certificates, and the concept of a public key infrastructure.

Chapter 4, an overview of the Kerberos security scheme, illustrates the basic technique that Kerberos employs to provide network security. It also compares the Kerberos scheme to a public key infrastructure.

Chapter 5 introduces the secure sockets layer (SSL) protocol and illustrates how some of the cipher systems introduced in Chapter 3 are employed with Microsoft Internet Explorer and Netscape Navigator. Next, Chapter 6 discusses security issues associated with sending, receiving, authenticating, and storing e-mail. Furthermore, Chapter 6 reviews the various secure e-mail protocols and different applications of encryption with e-mail and discusses the concept of e-mail as a weapon.

Chapter 7 covers general operating system security guidelines and introduces concepts that are common or applicable to most operating systems, including password guidelines and access controls. In addition, it reviews some of the techniques used to break passwords and ways to counter these techniques. Chapter 7 also reviews issues associated with modems and introduces some useful tools that can be employed to make a system more secure.

Chapter 8 covers general LAN security guidelines and introduces the concepts of policy-based network management, honeypot systems, segmentation of LAN traffic, and security issues associated with the use of dynamic host configuration protocol (DHCP). Chapter 9 introduces security issues associated with the various physical media that can be employed for a LAN installation. It also discusses security issues to consider when installing cable and when selecting WAN circuits, media, and protocols. In addition, Chapter 9 describes frame relay, xDSL, wireless local area network (LAN) and wide area network (WAN) media, and different types of circuits.

Chapter 10 examines router security issues and introduces the Cisco Internetworking Operating System. It also discusses the simple network management protocol (SNMP) and some of the risks that are inherent in using this protocol.

Chapter 11 explains the functioning of virtual private networks (VPNs) and the considerations that must be addressed before implementing a VPN. Chapter 11 also surveys the various protocols now in use and presents an example of a low-cost VPN implementation.

Chapter 12 introduces the concept of a firewall and explains how it functions. In addition, it discusses the pros and cons of firewalls and the various types of firewalls and their implementation. It also discusses some of the freeware firewalls and personal firewalls that are available to download.

Chapter 13 covers the benefits and drawbacks of biometric identification and authentication systems. In addition, it discusses the different biometric techniques employed and issues that must be considered before deploying a biometric system.

Chapter 14 provides a detailed discussion of the development, format, content, implementation, and enforcement of corporate network security policies and procedures. Chapter 14 also provides some general recommendations for policies and procedures.

Chapter 15 focuses on the role that network and system auditing and monitoring plays in a multitiered approach to network security. In addition, it discusses traditional audits, automated auditing tools, and developments in the area of intrusion detection systems.

Chapter 16 discusses the need for organizations to develop adequate plans to respond to a disaster or computer security incident. In addition, it describes disaster recovery planning and presents a case study. Chapter 16 also covers computer incident response planning and provides some general guidelines. It also lists sources of information for response planning.

Chapter 17 identifies specific risks associated with browser cookie and cache files. In addition, it discusses the risks associated with Internet Explorer's AutoComplete function.

1

Basic Security Concepts

It seems that every other day there is a story in the newspapers about a computer network being compromised by hackers. In fact, not too long ago the Department of Defense (DOD) was the victim of a successful hacker raid; hackers were able to penetrate DOD computers during a two-week period before they were detected. Fortunately, the computers contained only non-classified personnel and payroll information, so national security was not threatened.

More recently, Yahoo, Amazon.com, eBay, and some other popular World Wide Web (WWW) sites were targets of what appears to have been a coordinated "denial-of-service" attack. During a three- or four-day period, the sites were overwhelmed with massive bombardments of false traffic from multiple sites. As a result, the sites were shut down for hours at a time. These attacks illustrate how pervasive the threat from outside hackers has become.

At the same time, every organization that uses computers faces the threat of hacking from individuals within the organization. Employees or former employees with malicious intent or who want to obtain information such as employee salaries or view other employee's files are also a threat to an organization's computers and networks.

Computerworld recently ran a story about a programmer employee of a company who allegedly launched a denial-of-service attack against his own company, a provider of on-line stock trading services. Apparently, this programmer was in negotiations with the company for more compensation.

He became frustrated with the progress of the negotiations and decided to demonstrate to the company its vulnerability by launching an attack on its systems from the Internet. He was intimately familiar with the company's systems and software, and his inside knowledge enabled him to hit the firm in a manner that shut it down. In fact, the attack disrupted stock trading services at the company for three days. The U.S. Secret Service was eventually employed, and the attack was traced to the employee, who was subsequently arrested.

Every organization should monitor its systems for possible unauthorized intrusion and other attacks. This needs to be part of the daily routine of every organization's IT unit, as it is essential to safeguarding a company's information assets.

The most reliable way to ensure the safety of a company's computers is to refrain from putting them on a network and to keep them behind locked doors. Unfortunately, however, that is not a very practical solution. Today, computers are most useful if they are networked together to share information and resources, and companies that put their computers on a network need to take some simple precautions to reduce the risk of unauthorized access.

Every year, corporations, governments, and other organizations spend billions of dollars on expenditures related to network security. The rate at which these organizations are expending funds seems to be increasing. However, when companies need to find areas in which they can decrease spending, budget items such as security and business resumption planning have historically been some of the first to be cut.

Why Is Computer and Network Security Important?

It may seem absurd to ask the question, "Why is computer and network security important?" but it is crucial for organizations to define why they want to achieve computer security to determine how they will achieve it. It is also a useful tool to employ when seeking senior management's authorization for security-related expenditures. Computer and network security is important for the following reasons.

- *To protect company assets:* One of the primary goals of computer and network security is the protection of company assets. By "assets," I do not mean the hardware and software that constitute the company's computers and networks. The assets are comprised of the "information" that is housed on a company's computers and networks. Information is a vital organizational asset. Network and computer security is concerned, above all else, with the protection, integrity, and availability of information. Information can be defined as data that is organized and accessible in a coherent and meaningful manner.

- *To gain a competitive advantage:* Developing and maintaining effective security measures can provide an organization with a competitive advantage over its competition. Network security is particularly important in the arena of Internet financial services and e-commerce. It can mean the difference between wide acceptance of a service and a mediocre customer response. For example, how many people do you know who would use a bank's Internet banking system if they knew that the system had been successfully hacked in the past? Not many. They would go to the competition for their Internet banking services.

- *To comply with regulatory requirements and fiduciary responsibilities:* Corporate officers of every company have a responsibility to ensure the safety and soundness of the organization. Part of that responsibility includes ensuring the continuing operation of the organization. Accordingly, organizations that rely on computers for their continuing operation must develop policies and procedures that address organizational security requirements. Such policies and procedures are necessary not only to protect company assets but also to protect the organization from liability. For-profit organizations must also protect shareholders' investments and maximize return. In addition, many organizations are subject to governmental regulation, which often stipulates requirements for the safety and security of an organization. For example, most financial institutions are subject to federal regulation. Failure to comply with federal guidelines can result in the seizure of a financial institution by federal regulators. In some cases, corporate officers who have not properly performed their regulatory and fiduciary responsibilities are personally liable for any losses incurred by the financial institution that employs them.

- *To keep your job:* Finally, to secure one's position within an organization and to ensure future career prospects, it is important to put into place measures that protect organizational assets. Security should be part of every network or systems administrator's job. Failure to perform adequately can result in termination. Termination should not be the automatic result of a security failure, but if, after a thorough postmortem, it is determined that the failure was the result of inadequate policies and procedures or failure to comply with existing procedures, then management needs to step in and make some changes.

One thing to keep in mind is that network security costs money: It costs money to hire, train, and retain personnel; to buy hardware and software to secure an organization's networks; and to pay for the increased overhead and degraded network and system performance that results from firewalls, filters, and intrusion detection systems (IDSs). As a result, network security is not cheap. However, it is probably cheaper than the costs associated with having an organization's network compromised.

Background

While I am always wary of statistics used by various organizations to quantify or measure information security incidents, it is useful to review some recently reported numbers. In 1999, a survey conducted jointly by the American Society for Industrial Security and Pricewaterhouse-Coopers (ASIS/PWC) reported that *Fortune 1000* companies lost more than $45 billion from theft of "proprietary information." The ASIS/PWC survey of *Fortune 1000* companies received 97 responses. Also of interest, the survey reported the following:

- Forty-five percent of the respondents said that they had suffered a financial loss as a result of information loss, theft, or misappropriation.

- On average, the responding companies reported 2.45 incidents with an estimated cost of $500,000 per incident.

- The number of reported incidents per month had increased over the last 17 months.

An annual survey conducted jointly by the FBI and the Computer Security Institute (CSI) also yielded some interesting numbers. The FBI/CSI survey received 521 responses from individuals in the computer security field. Almost across the board, the numbers were up for the various types of incidents:

- Thirty percent of the respondents reported an intrusion from an outside source.

- Fifty-five percent of the respondents reported an unauthorized intrusion by a source inside the organization.

- Of those respondents that reported a loss, the average loss from the theft of proprietary information increased from $1,677,000 in 1998 to $1,847,652 in 1999.

- The average loss from financial fraud rose from $388,000 in 1998 to over $1,400,000 in 1999.

- The total financial losses due to computer-related crime for the 521 respondents amounted to more than $120 million.

It is interesting to note that most computer-related crimes are not reported. If you take the numbers being reported in these surveys and extrapolate them to account for all organizations, the potential number of incidents and associated financial loss is mind-boggling. Some estimates claim that as many as 90% of computer-related crimes are neither reported to the legal authorities nor prosecuted. Companies may leave themselves open to lawsuits, ridicule, and loss of customer confidence by admitting a computer-related loss.

I have seen estimates from various sources for the annual financial loss related to computer crime ranging from $5 billion to $45 billion. It seems clear that the annual cost related to computer crime is substantial and that it is growing every year.

History

The need for network security is a relatively new requirement. Prior to the 1980s most computers were not networked. It was not due to lack of desire to network them; it was more a result of the lack of technology. Most systems were mainframes or midrange systems that were centrally controlled and administered. Users interfaced with the mainframe through "dumb" terminals. The terminals had limited capabilities. Terminals actually required a physical connection on a dedicated port. The ports were often serial connections that utilized the RS-232 protocol. It usually required one port for one terminal. IBM, Digital Equipment, and other computer manufacturers developed variations on this architecture by utilizing terminal servers, but the basic concept was the same. There was nothing equivalent to what we experience today where hundreds if not thousands of connections can reach a system on a single network circuit.

In the 1980s, the combination of the development of the personal computer (PC), the development of network protocol standards, the decrease in the cost of hardware, and the development of new applications made networking a much more accepted practice. As a result, LANs, WANs, and distributed computing experienced tremendous growth during that period.

When first deployed, LANs were relatively secure—mainly because they were physically isolated. They were not usually connected to WANs, so their standalone nature protected the network resources.

WANs actually preceded LANs and had been around for some time, but they were usually centrally controlled and accessible by only a few individuals in most organizations. WANs utilizing direct or dedicated privately owned or leased circuits were relatively secure because access to circuits was limited. To connect two locations (points A and B) usually required a point-to-point (A-B) circuit. If you wanted to connect a third location (point C) to both A and B, it required two more circuits (A-B, A-C, B-C). Figure 1.1 illustrates this concept.

Development of packet-switched protocols such as X.25 and Transmission Control Protocol/Internet Protocol (TCP/IP) reduced the cost to deploy WANs, thus making them more attractive to implement. These protocols allowed many systems to share circuits. Many people or organizations could be interconnected over the shared network. It was no longer necessary

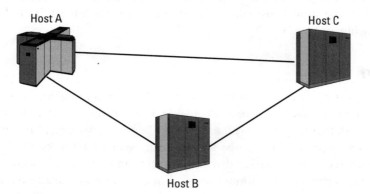

Figure 1.1 Point-to-point WAN.

to connect systems in a point-to-point configuration. Vulnerabilities were introduced with the deployment of this distributed environment utilizing shared, packet-switched networks employing protocols such as TCP/IP and the concept of trusted systems. Systems on the network "trusted" each other. This situation was frequently made worse by connecting relatively secure LANs to an unsecured WAN. Figure 1.2 illustrates the concept behind the packet-switched network. Basically, an organization's network connections enter into the cloud of the packet-switched network. Other organizations share the cloud, and on the packet-switched network one company's packets are intermixed with another organization's packets.

In this distributed environment the emphasis was on providing ease of access and connectivity. Security was an afterthought, if it was considered at all. As a result, many systems were wide open and vulnerable to threats that previously had not existed.

The Internet is the largest and best known of this type of network. The Internet utilizes TCP/IP and was primarily designed to connect computers regardless of their operating systems in an easy and efficient manner. Security was not part of the early design of TCP/IP, and there have been a number of widely publicized attacks that have exploited inherent weaknesses in its design. One well-known event was the Internet Worm that brought the Internet to its knees back in 1986. Today, security has to be more important than ease of access.

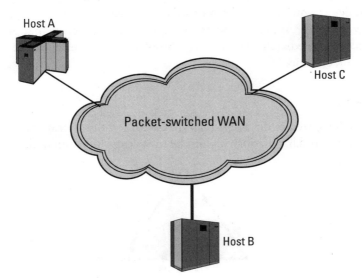

Figure 1.2 Packet-switched WAN.

The Security Trinity

The three legs of the "security trinity," prevention, detection, and response, comprise the basis for network security. The security trinity should be the foundation for all security policies and measures that an organization develops and deploys. See Figure 1.3.

Prevention

The foundation of the security trinity is prevention. To provide some level of security, it is necessary to implement measures to prevent the exploitation of vulnerabilities. In developing network security schemes, organizations should emphasize preventative measures over detection and response: It is easier, more efficient, and much more cost-effective to prevent a security breach than to detect or respond to one. Remember that it is impossible to devise a security scheme that will prevent all vulnerabilities from being exploited, but companies should ensure that their preventative measures are strong enough to discourage potential criminals—so they go to an easier target.

Detection

Once preventative measures are implemented, procedures need to be put in place to detect potential problems or security breaches, in the event preventative measures fail. As later chapters show, it is very important that problems be detected immediately. The sooner a problem is detected the easier it is to correct and cleanup.

Response

Organizations need to develop a plan that identifies the appropriate response to a security breach. The plan should be in writing and should identify who

Figure 1.3 The security trinity.

is responsible for what actions and the varying responses and levels of escalation.

Before beginning a meaningful discussion on computer and network security, we need to define what it entails. First, network security is not a technical problem; it is a business and people problem. The technology is the easy part. The difficult part is developing a security plan that fits the organization's business operation and getting people to comply with the plan. Next, companies need to answer some fundamental questions, including the following.

- How do you define network security?

- How do you determine what is an adequate level of security?

To answer these questions, it is necessary to determine what you are trying to protect.

Information Security

Network security is concerned, above all else, with the security of company information assets. We often lose sight of the fact that it is the information and our ability to access that information that we are really trying to protect—and not the computers and networks. I have a simple definition for information security:

Information security = confidentiality + integrity + availability + authentication

There can be no information security without confidentiality; this ensures that unauthorized users do not intercept, copy, or replicate information. At the same time, integrity is necessary so that organizations have enough confidence in the accuracy of the information to act upon it. Moreover, information security requires organizations to be able to retrieve data; security measures are worthless if organizations cannot gain access to the vital information they need to operate when they need it. Finally, information is not secure without authentication—determining whether the end user is authorized to have access.

Among the many elements of information security are ensuring adequate physical security; hiring proper personnel; developing, and adhering to, procedures and policies; strengthening and monitoring networks and systems; and developing secure applications. It is important to remember that information security is not just about protecting assets from outside hackers. The majority of the time threats are internal to an organization: "We have found the enemy and it is us."

Information security is also about procedures and policies that protect information from accidents, incompetence, and natural disasters. Such policies and procedures need to address the following:

- Backups, configuration controls, and media controls;
- Disaster recovery and contingency planning;
- Data integrity.

It is also important to remember that network security is not absolute. All security is relative. Network security should be thought of as a spectrum that runs from very unsecure to very secure. The level of security for a system or network is dependent on where it lands along that spectrum relative to other systems. It is either more secure or less secure than other systems relative to that point. There is no such thing as an absolutely secure network or system.

Network security is a balancing act that requires the deployment of "proportionate defenses." The defenses that are deployed or implemented should be proportionate to the threat. Organizations determine what is appropriate in several ways, described as follows.

- Balancing the cost of security against the value of the assets they are protecting;
- Balancing the probable against the possible;
- Balancing business needs against security needs.

Organizations must determine how much it would cost to have each system or network compromised—in other words, how much it would cost in dollars to lose information or access to the system or to experience information theft. By assigning a dollar value to the cost of having a system or network compromised, organizations can determine the upper limit they should be willing to pay to protect their systems. For many organizations this exercise is not necessary, because the systems are the lifeblood of the business. Without them, there is no organization.

Organizations also need to balance the cost of security against the cost of a security breech. Generally, as the investment in security increases, the expected losses should decrease. Companies should invest no more in security than the value of the assets they are protecting. This is where cost benefit analysis comes into play.

Moreover, organizations must balance possible threats against probable threats: As it is impossible to defend against every possible type of attack, it is necessary to determine what types of threats or attacks have the greatest probability of occurring and then protect against them. For example, it is possible that an organization could be subjected to van Eck monitoring[1] or a high-energy radio frequency (HERF)[2] attack, but the probability is low.

It is also important to balance business needs with the need for security, assessing the operational impact of implementing security measures. Security measures and procedures that interfere with the operation of an organization are of little value. Those types of measures are usually ignored or circumvented by company personnel, so they tend to create, rather than plug, security holes. Whenever possible, security measures should complement the operational and business needs of an organization.

Risk Assessment

The concept of *risk assessment* is crucial to developing proportionate defenses. To perform a risk analysis, organizations need to understand possible threats and vulnerabilities. Risk is the probability that a vulnerability will be exploited. The basic steps for risk assessment are listed as follows:

1. Identifying and prioritizing assets;
2. Identifying vulnerabilities;
3. Identifying threats and their probabilities;
4. Identifying countermeasures;
5. Developing a cost benefit analysis;
6. Developing security policies and procedures.

---

1. van Eck monitoring is the monitoring of the activity of a computer or other electronic equipment by detecting low levels of electromagnetic emissions from the device. It is named after Dr. Wim van Eck who published on the topic in 1985.
2. A HERF gun is a device that can disrupt the normal operation of digital equipment such as computers and navigational equipment by directing HERF emissions at them.

To identify and prioritize information assets and to develop a cost benefit analysis, it is helpful to ask a few simple questions such as the following.

- What do you want to safeguard?
- Why do you want to safeguard it?
- What is its value?
- What are the threats?
- What are the risks?
- What are the consequences of its loss?
- What are the various scenarios?
- What will the loss of the information or system cost?

Prioritize assets and systems by assigning a dollar value to the asset. The dollar value can be the replacement cost, the cost to not have the asset available or the cost to the organization to have the asset, such as proprietary information, obtained by a competitor. It is also necessary to include more obscure costs, such as loss of customer confidence. Weed out the probable threats from the possible. Determine what threats are most likely, and develop measures to protect against those threats.

Security Models

There are three basic approaches used to develop a network security model. Usually, organizations employ some combination of the three approaches to achieve security. The three approaches are security by obscurity, the perimeter defense model, and the defense in depth model.

Security by Obscurity

Security by obscurity relies on stealth for protection. The concept behind this model is that if no one knows that a network or system is there, then it won't be subject to attack. The basic hope is that hiding a network or at least not advertising its existence will serve as sufficient security. The problem with this approach is that it never works in the long term, and once detected, a network is completely vulnerable.

The Perimeter Defense

The perimeter defense model is analogous to a castle surrounded by a moat. When using this model in network security, organizations harden or strengthen perimeter systems and border routers, or an organization might "hide" its network behind a firewall that separates the protected network from an untrusted network. Not much is done to secure the other systems on the network. The assumption is that perimeter defenses are sufficient to stop any intruders so that the internal systems will be secure.

There are several flaws in this concept: First, this model does nothing to protect internal systems from an inside attack. As we have discussed, the majority of attacks on company networks are launched from someone internal to the organization. Second, the perimeter defense almost always fails eventually. Once it does, the internal systems are left wide open to attack.

The Defense in Depth

The most robust approach to use is the defense in depth model. The defense in depth approach strives for security by hardening and monitoring each system; each system is an island that defends itself. Extra measures are still taken on the perimeter systems, but the security of the internal network does not rest solely on the perimeter systems. This approach is more difficult to achieve and requires that all systems and network administrators do their part. With this model, however, the internal network is much less likely to be compromised if a system administrator on the network makes a mistake like putting an unsecured modem on the system. With the defense in depth approach, the system with the modem may be compromised, but other systems on the network will be able to defend themselves. The other systems on the network should also be able to detect any attempted hacks from the compromised system. This approach also provides much more protection against an internal intruder. The activities of the internal intruder are much more likely to be detected.

Basic Terminology

Threats

A threat is anything that can disrupt the operation, functioning, integrity, or availability of a network or system. There are different categories of threats. There are natural threats, occurrences such as floods, earthquakes, and storms. There are also unintentional threats that are the result of accidents and stupidity. Finally, there are intentional threats that are the result of malicious indent. Each type of threat can be deadly to a network.

Vulnerabilities

A vulnerability is an inherent weakness in the design, configuration, or implementation of a network or system that renders it susceptible to a threat. Most vulnerabilities can usually be traced back to one of three sources:

1. *Poor design:* Hardware and software systems that contain design flaws that can be exploited. In essence, the systems are created with security holes. An example of this type of vulnerability would be the "sendmail" flaws in early versions of Unix. The sendmail flaws allowed hackers to gain privileged "root" access to Unix systems. These flaws were exploited on numerous occasions.

2. *Poor implementation:* Systems that are incorrectly configured, and therefore vulnerable to attack. This type of vulnerability usually results from inexperience, insufficient training, or sloppy work. An example of this type of vulnerability would be a system that does not have restricted-access privileges on critical executable files, thereby allowing these files to be altered by unauthorized users.

3. *Poor management:* Inadequate procedures and insufficient checks and balances. Security measures cannot operate in a vacuum; they need to be documented and monitored. Even something as simple as the daily backup of a system needs to be verified. There also needs to be delineation of responsibility for some functions and dual custody for others. In this manner, an organization can ensure that procedures are being followed and that no one person has total control of a system.

While there are only three sources of vulnerabilities, they can manifest themselves in many ways.

Physical Vulnerabilities

Canavan's first rule of security is to physically safeguard systems and networks. Are your systems, communications equipment, and media located in a secure facility? Central hosts and servers should be kept in secure rooms that can only be entered by authorized personnel. Routers and communications equipment should also be kept in secure locations with restricted access.

In addition, critical removable media, such as backups, should be stored in a secure area to which only authorized personnel have access.

As part of this process, organizations need to take into consideration the physical and natural environment in which they operate. They should consider the probability of earthquakes, fires, floods, and other "acts of God" and plan accordingly. Proper planning of physical facilities can mitigate many of the effects of natural disasters. For instance, organizations in an earthquake zone need to bolt their equipment to the building's structure so that they don't bounce off the walls or out of the windows during a big quake. Organizations located in flood plains shouldn't place their computer rooms in their buildings' basements. It's really nothing more than common sense.

Hardware and Software

Design flaws in hardware or software can render systems vulnerable to attack or affect the availability of systems. For example, the sendmail flaw in earlier versions of UNIX enabled hackers to gain privileged access to systems.

Media Vulnerabilities

Disks, tapes, and other media can be stolen, lost, or damaged. Information can be copied and removed from an organization's facilities without detection. Accordingly, companies need to ensure the safety of all media that contains or stores vital information assets.

Transmission and Emanation Vulnerabilities—Interception of Information

Signal emissions from electrical equipment can be remotely intercepted and monitored using sophisticated devices in a process sometimes referred to as van Eck monitoring. Organizations also need to be concerned about the interception of most forms of communication. Communication is the sharing of information on a medium. As such, it is inherently vulnerable to interception, monitoring, forgery, alteration, and interruption. Every medium used for transmission of information can be "tapped." Network "sniffers" or packet sniffers are common hacker tools that can read traffic as it passes on a network—although backhoes probably do more damage than hackers do when it comes to the interruption of communication.

Human Vulnerabilities

Human stupidity, carelessness, laziness, greed, and anger represent the greatest threats to networks and systems and will do more damage than the rest of the others combined. Moreover, human vulnerabilities and the risks associated with them are the most difficult to defend against.

It is important to keep in mind that every network or system designed, configured or implemented has vulnerabilities. There is no such thing as a totally secure network or system. It does not exist!

Countermeasures

Countermeasures are the techniques or methods used to defend against attacks and to close or compensate for vulnerabilities in networks or systems.

More Basic Terminology

Before embarking on a meaningful discussion of network security, it is first necessary to define some fundamental terms relating to network security. These terms are the foundation for any discussion of network security and are the elements used to measure the security of a network. To be considered sufficiently advanced along the spectrum of security, a system must adequately address identification, authentication, access control or authorization, availability, confidentiality, integrity, accountability, and nonrepudiation, each of which is defined in the following sections.

Identification

Identification is simply the process of identifying one's self to another entity or determining the identity of the individual or entity with whom you are communicating.

Authentication

Authentication serves as proof that you are who you say you are or what you claim to be. Authentication is critical if there is to be any trust between parties. Authentication is required when communicating over a network or logging onto a network. When communicating over a network you should ask yourself two questions: 1) With whom am I communicating? and 2) Why do I believe this person or entity is who he, she, or it claims to be? If you don't have a good answer for question 2, then chances are you are wrong on question 1.

When logging onto a network, three basic schemes are used for authentication. Very often networks will use a combination of more than one of the schemes—something you know, something you have, and something you are—which are described as follows.

- *Something you know:* The most commonly employed scheme is "something you know." Typically, the something you know that authenticates your identity is a password, code, or sequence. The security is predicated on the idea that if you know the secret password or code then you must be who you claim to be and be authorized to access the network. Even though this scheme is the most widely implemented, it is not very secure. It is easy to circumvent or compromise.

- *Something you have:* "Something you have" requires a key, badge, or token card, some device or "thing" that provides you with access. Security is predicated on the concept that only authorized individuals or entities will have access to the specific device. The drawback to this scheme is that the "thing" can be lost or stolen.

- *Something you are:* "Something you are" authentication relies upon some physical or behavioral characteristic. It is referred to as *biometric authentication.* Biometrics can authenticate one's identity based on fingerprints, a voice print, or an iris scan. Even keystrokes (along with almost any physical or behavioral trait) can be used. These systems, when designed properly, can be extremely difficult to circumvent or compromise. The trick is finding one that works correctly.

Access Control (Authorization)

This refers to the ability to control the level of access that individuals or entities have to a network or system and how much information they can receive. Your level of authorization basically determines what you're allowed to do once you are authenticated and allowed access to a network, system, or some other resource such as data or information. Access control is the determination of the level of authorization to a system, network, or information (i.e., classified, secret, or top-secret).

Availability

This refers to whether the network, system, hardware, and software are reliable and can recover quickly and completely in the event of an interruption in service. Ideally, these elements should not be susceptible to denial of service attacks.

Confidentiality

This can also be called privacy or secrecy and refers to the protection of information from unauthorized disclosure. Usually achieved either by restricting access to the information or by encrypting the information so that it is not meaningful to unauthorized individuals or entities.

Integrity

This can be thought of as accuracy. This refers to the ability to protect information, data, or transmissions from unauthorized, uncontrolled, or accidental alterations. The term integrity can also be used in reference to the functioning of a network, system, or application.

When used in reference to information or data there are several requirements for integrity. First, data must be consistent with internal requirements. For example, arithmetic calculations must be accurate; all of the numbers in a column representing the deposits to a company's bank account should equal the total stored for that column of deposits. Second, data must also be consistent with external requirements. The total representing the sum of the deposits should match what was actually deposited to the bank account. Data must also be timely and complete. If data is a day or a week behind, then its integrity is in question. Similarly, if not all of the data is being recorded, its integrity is doubtful.

Data integrity is achieved by preventing unauthorized or improper changes to data, ensuring internal and external consistency, and ensuring that other data attributes (such as timeliness and completeness) are consistent with requirements.

Integrity can be used in reference to the proper functioning of a network, system, or application. For example, when the term integrity is used in reference to a system it means that the system behaves according to design, specifications, and expectations even under adverse circumstances such as an attack or disaster. System integrity remains high under duress.

Accountability

This refers to the ability to track or audit what an individual or entity is doing on a network or system. Does the system maintain a record of functions performed, files accessed, and information altered?

Nonrepudiation

The ability to prevent individuals or entities from denying (repudiating) that information, data, or files were sent or received or that information or files were accessed or altered, when in fact they were. This capability is crucial to e-commerce. Without it an individual or entity can deny that he, she, or it is responsible for a transaction and that he, she, or it is, therefore, not financially liable.

The concepts and terms introduced in this chapter will appear in later chapters, and readers may find it useful to refer back to them. We will explore how the concepts have been implemented in real-world applications. Recent developments such as public key cryptography and digital signatures have been crucial to enabling confidentiality, integrity, authentication, nonrepudiation, and even, to a certain degree, availability. As we go forward we will see how applied cryptography has been used to address many of these concepts. We will also explore the limitations of technology in providing security.

2

Threats, Vulnerabilities, and Attacks

Before we begin our discussion of threats, vulnerabilities, and attacks, it is important to review TCP/IP basics and the seven-layer OSI model. This review is important because many of the attacks that are utilized today take advantage of some of the inherent vulnerabilities designed into the TCP/IP protocol suite. The attacks actually use the functioning of TCP/IP to defeat the protocol.

Protocols

Protocols are nothing more than a set of formal rules or standards that are used as a basis for communication. Protocols are designed to facilitate communications. We'll use the example of a protocol officer at an embassy to describe how protocols function. The job of a protocol officer is to ensure proper communication between the embassy and the host country. A network protocol functions much in the same manner, only it ensures communications between network devices. Before network devices are able to exchange data, it is necessary for the devices to agree on the rules (protocol) that will govern a communication session.

The OSI Reference Model

The OSI reference model is a seven-layer model that was developed by the International Standards Organization (ISO) in 1978. The OSI model is a framework for international standards that can be used for implementing a heterogeneous computer network architecture. The OSI architecture is split into seven layers. Figure 2.1 illustrates the seven layers of the OSI model. Each layer uses the layer immediately below it and provides a service to the layer above. In some implementations a layer may itself be composed of sublayers.

The physical layer addresses the physical link and is concerned with the signal voltage, bit rate, and duration. The data link layer is concerned with the reliable transmission of data across a physical link. In other words, getting a signal from one end of a wire to the other end. It handles flow control and error correction. The network layer handles the routing of data and ensures that data is forwarded to the right destination. The transport layer provides end-to-end control and constructs the packets into which the data is placed to be transmitted or "transported" across the logical circuit. The session layer handles the session set-up with another network node. It handles the initial handshake and negotiates the flow of information and termination of connections between nodes. The presentation layer handles the conversion of data from the session layer, so that it can be "presented" to the application layer in a format that the application layer can understand. The application layer is the end-user interface. This includes interfaces such as browsers, virtual terminals, and FTP programs.

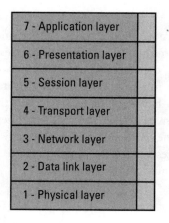

Figure 2.1 OSI model.

TCP/IP Protocol Suite

TCP/IP is a suite of protocols that can be used to connect dissimilar brands of computers and network devices. The largest TCP/IP network is the Internet. The Internet was developed by the U.S. DOD under the auspices of the Defense Advanced Research Project Agency (DARPA) when DOD scientists were faced with the problem of linking thousands of computers running different operating systems. The Defense Advanced Research Project Agency (DARPA) is a small organization within the Pentagon, but its impact on technology in general and on data communications in particular has been huge. For all practical purposes, DARPA's programs and funding created the Internet. You can think of the TCP/IP suite as the lifeblood of the Internet. The TCP/IP suite has become widely adopted, because it is an open protocol standard that can be implemented on any platform regardless of the manufacturer. In addition, it is independent of any physical network hardware. TCP/IP can be implemented on Ethernet, X.25, and token ring, among other platforms.

Although there are different interpretations on how to describe TCP/IP within a layered model, it is generally described as being composed of fewer than the seven used in the OSI model. The TCP/IP protocol suite generally follows a four-layer architecture.

The IP portion of TCP/IP is the connectionless network layer protocol. It is sometimes called an "unreliable" protocol, meaning that IP does not establish an end-to-end connection before transmitting datagrams and that it contains no error detection and recovery code. The datagram is the packet format defined by IP. IP operates across the network and data link layers of the OSI model and relies on the TCP protocol to ensure that the data reaches its destination correctly.

The heart of the IP portion of TCP/IP is a concept called the Internet address. This is a 32-bit number assigned to every node on the network. IP addresses are written in a dotted decimal format that corresponds to the 32-bit binary address. Each octet is assigned a number between 0 and 255. An example of an IP address in dotted decimal format is 12.31.80.1. This IP address translated into a 32-bit binary number is:

```
00001100 00011111 01010000 00000001
```

An IP address is divided into two parts, a network ID and a host ID, but the format of these parts depends on the class of the address. There are three main address classes: class A, class B, and class C. The formats differ in the number of bits allocated to the network ID and host ID and are distinguished by the first three bits of the 32 bit address.

The TCP portion of TCP/IP comes into operation once a packet is delivered to the correct Internet address. In contrast to IP, which is a connectionless protocol, TCP is connection-oriented. It establishes a logical end-to-end connection between two communicating nodes or devices. TCP operates at the transport layer of the OSI model and provides a virtual circuit service between end-user applications, with reliable data transfer, which is lacking in the datagram-oriented IP.

Software packages that follow the TCP standard run on each machine, establish a connection to each other, and manage the communications exchanges. TCP provides the flow control, error detection, and sequencing of the data; looks for responses; and takes the appropriate action to replace missing data blocks.

The end-to-end connection is established through the exchange of control information. This exchange of information is called a three-way handshake. This handshake is necessary to establish the logical connection and to allow the transmission of data to begin.

In its simplest form, host A would transmit to host B the *synchronize sequence number* bit set. This tells host B that host A wishes to establish a connection and informs host B of the starting sequence number for host A. Host B sends back to host A an acknowledgment and confirms its starting sequence number. Host A acknowledges receipt of host B's transmission and begins the transfer of data. Later, in this chapter, I will explain how this three-way handshake can be exploited to disrupt the operation of a system.

Another important TCP/IP protocol is the user datagram protocol (UDP). Like TCP, UDP operates at the transport layer. The major difference between TCP and UDP is that UDP is a connectionless datagram protocol. UDP gives applications direct access to a datagram delivery service—like the service IP provides. This allows applications to exchange data with a minimum of protocol overhead. Figure 2.2 illustrates the hierarchical relationship between IP and TCP/UDP and the applications that rely upon the protocols.

The UDP protocol is best suited for applications that transmit small amounts of data, where the process of creating connections and ensuring delivery may be greater than the work of simply retransmitting the data. Another situation where UDP would be appropriate is when an application provides its own method of error checking and ensuring delivery.

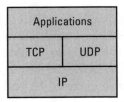

Figure 2.2 TCP/IP model.

Threats, Vulnerabilities, and Attacks

Intro

Now that we have reviewed some of the TCP/IP basics, we can proceed in our discussion of threats, vulnerabilities, and attacks. It is important to understand the difference between a threat, a vulnerability, or an attack in the context of network security.

Threats

A threat is anything that can disrupt the operation, functioning, integrity, or availability of a network or system. This can take any form and can be malevolent, accidental, or simply an act of nature.

Vulnerabilities

A vulnerability is an inherent weakness in the design, configuration, implementation, or management of a network or system that renders it susceptible to a threat. Vulnerabilities are what make networks susceptible to information loss and downtime. Every network and system has some kind of vulnerability.

Attacks

An attack is a specific technique used to exploit a vulnerability. For example, a threat could be a denial of service. A vulnerability is in the design of the operating system, and an attack could be a "ping of death." There are two general categories of attacks, passive and active. Passive attacks are very difficult to detect, because there is no overt activity that can be monitored or detected. Examples of passive attacks would be packet sniffing or traffic analysis. These types of attacks are designed to monitor and record traffic on the network. They are usually employed for gathering information that can be used later in active attacks.

Active attacks, as the name implies, employ more overt actions on the network or system. As a result, they can be easier to detect, but at the same time they can be much more devastating to a network. Examples of this type of attack would be a denial-of-service attack or active probing of systems and networks.

Networks and systems face many types of threats. There are viruses, worms, Trojan horses, trap doors, spoofs, masquerades, replays, password cracking, social engineering, scanning, sniffing, war dialing, denial-of-service attacks, and other protocol-based attacks. It seems new types of threats are being developed every month. The following sections review the general types of threats that network administrators face every day, including specific descriptions of a few of the more widely known attacks.

Viruses

According to Computer Economics, Inc. (www.computereconomics.com), a computer research and analysis group, over $12 billion was spent worldwide in 1999 as a result of computer viruses. A virus, a parasitic program that cannot function independently, is a program or code fragment that is self-propagating. It is called a virus, because like its biological counterpart, it requires a "host" to function. In the case of a computer virus the host is some other program to which the virus attaches itself. A virus is usually spread by executing an infected program or by sending an infected file to someone else, usually in the form of an e-mail attachment.

There are several virus scanning programs available on the market. Most are effective against known viruses. Unfortunately, however, they are incapable of recognizing and adapting to new viruses.

In general, virus scanning programs rely on recognizing the "signature" of known viruses, turning to a database of known virus signatures that they use to compare against scanning results. The program detects a virus when a match is found. If the database is not regularly updated the virus scanner can become obsolete quickly. As one would expect, there is usually some lag time between the introduction of a new virus and a vendor updating its database. Invariably, someone always has the dubious distinction of being one of the early victims of newly released virus.

Worm

A worm is a self-contained and independent program that is usually designed to propagate or spawn itself on infected systems and to seek other systems via available networks. The main difference between a virus and a worm is that a virus is not an independent program. However, there are new breeds of computer bugs that are blurring the difference between viruses and worms. The Melissa virus is an example of this new hybrid. In 1999 the Melissa virus attacked many users of Microsoft products. It was spread as an attachment, but the virus spread as an active process initiated by the virus. It was not a passive virus passed along by unsuspecting users.

One of the first and perhaps the most famous worms was the Internet Worm created and released by Robert Morris. In 1986, Morris wrote his worm program and released it onto the Internet. The worm's functioning was relatively benign, but it still had a devastating effect on the Internet. The worm was designed to simply reproduce and infect other systems. Once released, the program would spawn another process. The other process was simply another running copy of the program. Then the program would search out other systems connected to the infected system and propagate itself onto the other systems on the network. The number of processes running grew geometrically. Figure 2.3 illustrates how the Internet worm grew and spread: One process spawned to become two processes. Two processes spawned to become four processes. Four processes spawned to become eight. It didn't take very long for the spawning processes to consume all the CPU and memory resources until the system crashed. In addition, each time the processes spawned another, the processes would seek outside connections. The worm was designed to propagate, seek out other systems to infect them, and then repeat the process.

Stopping the processes from growing was a simple matter of rebooting the system. However, system administrators found that they would reboot their systems and get them functioning again only to find them being reinfected by another system on the Internet. To stop the worm from reinfecting systems on the network, all of the systems had to be shut down at the same time or taken off-line. The cost to clean up the Internet worm was estimated to be in the tens of millions of dollars. Morris was arrested, prosecuted, and convicted for his vandalism.

Trojan Horses

A Trojan horse is a program or code fragment that hides inside a program and performs a disguised function. This type of threat gets its name from

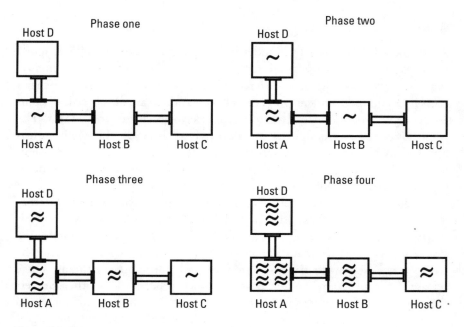

Figure 2.3 Internet worm.

Greek mythology and the story of the siege of Troy. The story tells of how Odysseus and his men conquered Troy by hiding within a giant wooden horse. A Trojan horse program hides within another program or disguises itself as a legitimate program. This can be accomplished by modifying the existing program or by simply replacing the existing program with a new one. The Trojan horse program functions much the same way as the legitimate program, but usually it also performs some other function, such as recording sensitive information or providing a trap door.

An example would be a *password grabber* program. A password grabber is a program designed to look and function like the normal login prompt that a user sees when first accessing a system. For example, in the screen depicted in Figure 2.4, the user has entered the username john and the correct password. However, the system tells the user that the login is incorrect. When the user tries again it works and he or she is able to log on.

In this example a Trojan horse designed to steal passwords is actually controlling the interaction. The standard login.exe has been replaced with a Trojan horse program. It looks like the standard login prompt, but what is actually occurring is that the first login prompt is the Trojan horse. When the username and password is entered that information is recorded and

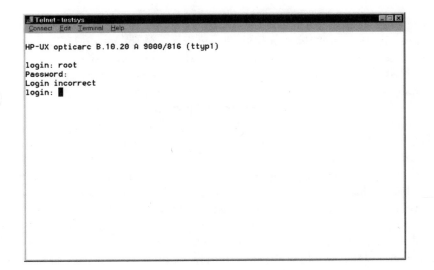

Figure 2.4 Trojan horse login.

stored. Then the Trojan horse program displays the "login incorrect" message and passes the user off to the real login program, so that he or she can actually log on to the system. The user simply assumes that he or she mistyped the password the first time never knowing that her or his username and password have just been stolen.

Trap Doors

A trap door or back door is an undocumented way of gaining access to a system that is built into the system by its designer(s). It can also be a program that has been altered to allow someone to gain privileged access to a system or process.

There have been numerous stories of vendors utilizing trap doors in disputes with customers. One example is the story of a consultant who was contracted to build a system for a company. The consultant designed a trap door into the delivered system. When the consultant and the company got into a dispute over payment, the consultant used the trap door to gain access to the system and disable the system. The company was forced to pay the consultant to get its system turned back on again.

Logic Bombs

A logic bomb is a program or subsection of a program designed with malevolent intent. It is referred to as a logic bomb, because the program is triggered when certain logical conditions are met. This type of attack is almost always perpetrated by an insider with privileged access to the network. The perpetrator could be a programmer or a vendor that supplies software.

As an example, I once heard a story about a programmer at a large corporation who engineered this type of attack. Apparently, the programmer had been having some trouble at the company at which he worked and was on probation. Fearing that he might be fired and with vengeance in mind, he added a subroutine to another program. The subroutine was added to a program that ran once a month and was designed to scan the company's human resources employee database to determine if a termination date had been loaded for his employee record. If the subroutine found that a termination date had been loaded, then it was designed to wipe out the entire system by deleting all files on the disk drives. The program ran every month and so long as his employee record did not have a termination date then nothing would happen. In other words, if he were not fired the program would do no damage.

Sure enough this stellar employee was fired, and the next time the logic bomb that he created ran it found a termination date in his employee record and wiped out the system. This is an example of how simple it can be, for one with privileged access to a system, to set up this type of attack.

Port Scanning

Like a burglar casing a target to plan a break-in, a hacker will often case a system to gather information that can later be used to attack the system. One of the tools that hackers often use for this type of reconnaissance is a port scanner. A port scanner is a program that listens to well-known port numbers to detect services running on a system that can be exploited to break into the system.

There are several port-scanning programs available on the Internet at various sites. They are not difficult to find. Organizations can monitor their system log files to detect port scanning as a prelude to an attack. Most intrusion detection software monitors for port scanning. If you find that your system is being scanned you can trace the scan back to its origination point and perhaps take some pre-emptive action. However, some scanning programs take a more stealthy approach to scanning that is very difficult to detect. For example, some programs use a SYN scan, which employs a SYN packet to create a half-open connection that doesn't get logged. SYN packets and half-open connections will be detailed later in this chapter.

Spoofs

Spoofs cover a broad category of threats. In general terms, a spoof entails falsifying one's identity or masquerading as some other individual or entity to gain access to a system or network or to gain information for some other unauthorized purpose. There are many different kinds of spoofs, including, among many others, IP address spoofing, session highjacking, domain name service (DNS) spoofing, sequence number spoofing, and replay attacks.

IP Address Spoofing

Every device on a TCP/IP network has a unique IP address. The IP address is a unique identification of the device, and no two devices on the network can have the same IP address. IP addresses are formatted as four decimal numbers separated by dots (e.g., 147.34.28.103). IP address spoofing takes advantage of systems and networks that rely on the IP address of the connecting system or device for authentication. For example, packet-filtering routers are sometimes used to protect an internal network from an external untrusted network. These routers will only allow specified IP addresses to pass from the external network to the internal network. If a hacker is able to determine an IP address that is permitted access through the router, he or she can spoof the address on the external network to gain access to the internal network. The hacker in effect masquerades as someone else.

Sequence Number Spoofing

TCP/IP network connections use sequence numbers. The sequence numbers are part of each transmission and are exchanged with each transaction. The sequence number is based upon each computer's internal clock, and the number is predictable because it is based on a set algorithm.

By monitoring a network connection, a hacker can record the exchange of sequence numbers and predict the next set of sequence numbers. With this information, a hacker can insert himself or herself into the network connection and, effectively, take over the connection or insert misinformation.

The best defense against sequence number spoofing is to encrypt a connection. Encrypting a connection prevents anyone who may be monitoring the network from being able to determine the sequence numbers or any other useful information.

Session Highjacking

Session highjacking is similar to sequence number spoofing. In this process, a hacker takes over a connection session, usually between a client user and a server. This is generally done by gaining access to a router or some other network device acting as a gateway between the legitimate user and the server and utilizing IP spoofing. Since session highjacking usually requires the hacker to gain privileged access to a network device, the best defense to take is to properly secure all devices on the network.

DNS

Domain Name Service (DNS) is a hierarchical name service used with TCP/IP hosts that is distributed and replicated on servers across the Internet. It is used on the Internet and on intranets for translating IP addresses into host names. The host names can be used in URLs. DNS can be thought of as a lookup table that allows users to specify remote computers by host names rather than their IP addresses. The advantage of DNS is that you don't have to know the IP addresses for all the Internet sites to access the sites. DNS can be configured to use a sequence of name servers, based on the domains in the name being sought, until a match is found. The most commonly deployed DNS server software on the Internet is BIND. DNS is subject to several different spoofs. Two common ones are the man in the middle (MIM) and DNS poisoning. Redirects, another less common attack, rely on the manipulation of the domain name registry itself to redirect a URL.

Man in the Middle Attack (MIM)

In a MIM attack, a hacker inserts himself or herself between a client program and a server on a network. By doing so the hacker can intercept information entered by the client, such as credit card numbers, passwords, and account information. Under one execution of this scheme, a hacker would place himself or herself between a browser and a Web server. The MIM attack, which is also sometimes called Web spoofing, is usually achieved by DNS or hyperlink spoofing.

There are several ways a hacker can launch a MIM attack. One way is to register a URL that is very similar to an existing URL. For example, a hacker could register a URL like www.micrisoft.com. When someone who wants to go to the Microsoft Web site at www.microsoft.com mistakenly types in www.micrisoft.com they would be brought to a Web site set up by the hacker to look like the Microsoft Web site. Figure 2.5 illustrates how the process works.

To Web surfers everything would look normal. They would interact with the counterfeit Web site just as they would with the real site. As the Web surfer enters in choices and information the hacker's Web site can even pass it onto the real site and pass back to the Web surfer the screens that the real site returns.

Browser   www.micrisoft.com   www.microsoft.com

Figure 2.5 MIM.

DNS Poisoning

Another method that can be used to launch this attack is to compromise a DNS server. One method for doing so is known as DNS poisoning. DNS poisoning exploits a vulnerability in early versions of the Berkeley Internet Name Daemon (BIND). BIND, the most commonly deployed DNS software on the Internet, was developed for BSD UNIX. A network of Internet BIND servers translates native Internet IP addresses to the commonly used names such as www.ggu.edu for Golden Gate University. Prior to version 8.1 of BIND, it was possible to "poison" the table entries of a DNS server with false information.

The information could include a false IP address for a DNS entry in the server's table. The result could be that when someone used that DNS server to "resolve" the URL name, he or she would be directed to the incorrect IP address.

By compromising a DNS server, a hacker can make a legitimate URL point to the hacker's Web site. The Web surfer might enter in www.amazon.com expecting to go to the Amazon.com Web site to purchase a book. The URL www.amazon.com normally points to xxx.xxx.xxx.xxx, but the hacker has compromised a DNS server to point that URL to his or her server. As a result, the Web surfer is brought to the hacker's site and not to Amazon.com.

Redirects

Under another method of DNS attack, hackers compromise a link on someone else's page or set up their own page with false links. In either case, the link could state that it is for a legitimate site, but in reality the link brings the Web surfer to a site set up and controlled by the hacker that looks like the site the Web surfer was expecting.

If all other attempts fail, a hacker can try manipulating the domain name registry system originally maintained by the InterNIC. In 1999, on at least three occasions, hackers were able to transfer domain names or redirect Internet surfers to sites other than the ones they were attempting to access. In one case Network Solutions' own DNS entry was altered, so that when users entered in the Network Solutions URL they were redirected to another site.

In at least three other cases hackers were able to transfer ownership of domain names to other IP addresses. Once the ownership was transferred and the NSI database altered, anyone attempting to access those domains would be redirected to the new sites. In one case the domain for excite.com was transferred to an unsuspecting site that found itself inundated with the millions of hits that excite.com normally receives. In other cases the ownership of the domains for the Ku Klux Klan and another site opposed to homosexuality called godhatesfags.com were transferred. Ownership of the Ku Klux Klan site was transferred to a site dedicated to fighting bigotry. Ironically, the godhatesfags.com domain was transferred to a site with the domain godlovesfags.com, a site that went on-line to appeal for tolerance. No individuals from the sites to which the domain were redirected were involved with the manipulation of the domain name registry system.

When employing the MIM attack, a hacker's false or counterfeit site can actually pass the client's requests onto the real site and return to the client the requested pages from the real site. All the while the hacker is monitoring and recording the interaction between the client and the server.

There is really no effective countermeasure to MIM. This attack can even be successful when encryption, such as SSL, is being employed. It only requires the hacker to obtain a valid digital certificate to load on his or her server, so that SSL can be enabled. Web surfers need only to be careful about where they are browsing, confirming links and only trusting links from a secure and trusted site.

Note that there are other methods to execute a redirect or MIM attack. For example, certain operating systems such as Microsoft's Windows 95, 98, and 2000 and Sun's Solaris have an inherent vulnerability in their implementation of the Internet Control Message Protocol (ICMP) Router Discovery Protocol (IRDF); ICMP is an integral part of the TCP/IP suite protocols. Hackers can exploit this vulnerability by rerouting or modifying outbound traffic as they choose. A key limitation on an attack using this vulnerability is that the attacker must be on the same network as the targeted system.

Replay Attack

A hacker executes a replay attack by intercepting and storing a legitimate transmission between two systems and retransmitting it at a later time. Theoretically, this attack can even be successful against encrypted transmissions.

The best defense to this attack is to use session keys, check the time stamp on all transmissions, and employ time-dependent message digests. This will be discussed further in Chapters 3 and 4.

Password Cracking

Password cracking is sometimes called a dictionary-based attack. Password crackers are programs that decipher password files. Password-cracking programs are available for most network and computer operating systems. They are able to decipher password files by utilizing the same algorithm used to create the encrypted password. They generally employ a dictionary of known words or phrases, which are also encrypted with the password algorithm. The password crackers compare each record in the password file against each record in the dictionary file to find a match. When a match is found, a password is found.

The source code for password-cracking programs for most computer and network operating systems (NOSs) is easily available on the Web at sites such as www.L0pht.com. Some of the programs available on the Web include Brute, CrackerJack, John The Ripper, and NewHack. Chapter 6 details passwords and password cracking.

Social Engineering

Social engineering, which refers to the nontechnical methods hackers employ to gain access to systems, can be amazingly effective. Social engineering usually refers to the process of convincing a person to reveal information (such as a password) that enables the hacker to gain access to a system or network.

Under the typical scenario, hackers obtain a company phone directory and call an unsuspecting employee, claiming to be calling from the company IS department. The hacker, who may even use the name of someone in the IS department, might say that there is a problem and ask the employee to enter in a long series of obscure commands to check the problem. The employee enters the commands, which do not seem to work, while the phony IS employee pretends to get increasingly exacerbated with the employee. The targeted employee feels pressured in his or her seeming failure to enter the commands correctly, and finally, the phony IS employee says something like, "Just give me your password so that I can check it myself and we can get this problem resolved." Subsequently, the employee reveals his or her password to the hacker thinking the hacker is a company IS employee. As simple as that, the hacker now has a username and password and access to the company system. It is amazing how many times I have heard of this approach being successful.

It is important for every organization to have a policy regarding the disclosure of passwords. Generally that policy should state that passwords are not to be disclosed to anyone, including IS personnel. That policy should be communicated to all company employees.

Another method commonly employed by hackers is referred to as dumpster diving. Dumpster diving may not officially fall under the category of social engineering, but it certainly is low-tech. Dumpster diving refers to the process of gathering information by going through garbage. Computer printout is of particular value in dumpster diving. Hackers look for information such as system account names, source code (particularly if it has passwords hardcoded), or customer account numbers (for financial institutions). It is important that an organization has proper controls for the disposal of hardcopy records and files. The controls should be codified in a formal policy.

Sniffing

Network sniffing or packet sniffing is the process of monitoring a network in an attempt to gather information that may be useful in an attack. With the proper tools a hacker can monitor the network packets to obtain passwords or IP addresses. Many vendors manufacture hardware and software for legitimate purposes that can be abused by hackers. The only comforting fact about these products is that hackers usually can't afford them. They can, however, steal them. There are also some common utilities available and programs that can be downloaded from hacker sites such as tcpmon, tcpdump, or gobbler. Network Associates' Sniffer Pro is an example of a commercially available product.

Password sniffing is particularly a threat for users who log into Unix systems over a network. Telnet or rlogin is usually employed when logging onto a Unix systems over a network. Telnet and rlogin do not encrypt passwords. As a result, when a user enters in his or her password, it is transmitted in the clear, meaning anyone monitoring the network can read it. In contrast, both Novel and Windows NT workstations encrypt passwords for transmission.

There are many tools available to reduce the risk of packet sniffing. Chapters 7, 8, and 11 discuss some of them, including secure shell (ssh) and VPNs. However, useful information can still be discerned from a network that is completely encrypted. Sometimes even simple traffic analysis can provide useful information. Being able to identify the systems that have the most activity can be of great value. Employing network switches instead of traditional hubs is another method to reduce the risk of network sniffing. Chapter 8 discusses this topic in more detail.

There are also tools available that purport to detect unauthorized packet sniffers on a network. One example, AntiSniff, is available from L0pht Heavy Industries on its Web site www.l0pht.com. Typically, these products detect the characteristics of a network interface card (NIC) configured for promiscuous mode, which can be used to packet sniff a network. However, these systems can be countered by simply cutting the send wire on the NIC's cable. By doing so the NIC cannot send packets onto the network. Therefore, the sniffer detection programs will not be able to detect the NIC configured for promiscuous mode.

Web Site Defacement

I'm not sure that this really deserves to be categorized by itself. However, it occurs so frequently that it is worth noting. Every week some organization's Web site is defaced by hackers, who post some message protesting something or other. Web site defacements are usually achieved by exploiting some incorrect configuration or known vulnerability of the Web server software, or by exploiting some other protocol-based vulnerability of the server's operating system.

An organization's best defense against Web site defacement is to maintain the most recent versions of its Web server software and the server's operating system. Also, an organization should ensure that its Web administrator is properly trained to install and maintain the software. Some organizations have taken more creative approaches to ensuring the integrity of their Web sites by deploying network cache servers that update the Web servers. The cache server mirrors a particular Web site and periodically refreshes the Web server with the original image of the system. If the Web site is defaced by a hacker, the cache server will overwrite the hackers' changes when it pushes the Web site refresh out to the Web server.

War Dialing

War dialing is a brute-force method of finding a back door into an organization's network. It is particularly effective against a perimeter defense. Most organizations have telephone numbers that are within a specified range and begin with the same prefix. For example, let's consider a fictitious company called Acme Networks. All of the company's telephone numbers begin with 895; there are 4,000 extensions; and the first extension is 1000. The range of telephone numbers for Acme Networks begins at 595-1000 and ends at 595-5000. War dialing usually employs an automated dialing system (a program) to call every telephone number for the organization, searching for modem connections.

The program logs a telephone number whenever it finds a modem. Later after the program has called every extension, the hacker can review the log for modems and go back and attempt to break into the system to which the modem is connected to gain access to the network.

This method almost always works for large organizations. When dealing with a company with several thousand telephone numbers, the odds are with the hacker that some of them are connected to modems. I worked for a large company that hired one of the big consulting firms to test the company's network security. The consulting firm was unsuccessful at penetrating the corporate firewall. However, it employed war dialing and identified several telephone numbers that were connected to modems. One of the modems was connected to a PC running PC AnyWhere, which had been enabled to allow someone to dial into the office from home. The consultants were able to gain access to the network by exploiting a flaw in an early version of PC AnyWhere that allowed a user to bypass the password protection. Once on the network the consultant was able to compromise almost every system it hit, and no one detected the illicit activity. The one exception was my group; we detected the activity on the systems for which we were responsible and made inquiries into the source of the activity. It was then that we were told that it had been a test of the corporate network security.

The source code for war dialing programs may be obtained easily at many hacker sites. Some of the programs available are ToneLoc, PhoneTap, and BlueDeep. If you are a programmer, you may be interested in viewing the code, but I do not recommend using these programs. A word of warning is necessary here: You should always be careful when downloading programs on the Web, but when downloading from hacker sites you need to be especially careful. To understand why simply reread the section on Trojan horses.

Denial of Service

Denial-of-service attacks are designed to shut down or render inoperable a system or network. The goal of the denial-of-service attack is not to gain access or information but to make a network or system unavailable for use by other users. It is called a denial-of-service attack, because the end result is to deny legitimate users access to network services. Such attacks are often used to exact revenge or to punish some individual or entity for some perceived slight or injustice. Unlike real hacking, denial-of-service attacks do not require a great deal of experience, skill, or intelligence to succeed. As a result, they are usually launched by nerdy, young programmers who fancy themselves to be master hackers.

There are many different types of denial-of-service attacks. The following sections present four examples: ping of death, "synchronize sequence number" (SYN) flooding, spamming, and smurfing. These are examples only and are not necessarily the most frequently used forms of denial-of-service attacks.

Ping of Death

The ping-of-death attack, with its melodramatic name, is an example of how simple it can be to launch a denial-of-service attack once a vulnerability has been discovered. Those who originally discover a vulnerability deserve credit, but it takes no great skill or intelligence to exploit it.

To better understand how the ping of death worked or works we need to once again review some TCP/IP basics. The ping of death exploited a flaw in many vendors' implementations of ICMP. ICMP is part of the IP of TCP/IP and operates at the Internet layer using the IP datagram to deliver messages; ping is a TCP/IP command that simply sends out an IP packet to a specified IP address or host name to see if there is a response from the address or host. It is often used to determine if a host is on the network or alive. The typical ping command syntax would be

```
ping 145.34.35.56
or
ping www.acme.net
```

Many operating systems were or are vulnerable to larger-than-normal ICMP packets. As a result, specifying a large packet in a ping command can cause an overflow in some systems' internals that can result in system crashes. The command syntax would vary depending on the operating system you were using. Below are two examples, one for Windows and the other for Sun Solaris.

```
Windows: ping -l 65527 -s 1 hostname
Solaris: ping -s hostname 65527
```

Normally it requires a flood of pings to crash a system. Moreover, from firsthand experience I have found that you are just as likely to crash the system from which you are launching the attack as you are to crash the system you are targeting. Nevertheless, the ping-of-death approach may still constitute an effective denial-of-service attack. Once this vulnerability was discovered, most vendors issued operating system patches to eliminate the problem.

SYN Flooding

SYN flooding is a denial-of-service attack that exploits the three-way handshake that TCP/IP uses to establish a connection. Basically, SYN flooding disables a targeted system by creating many half-open connections. Figure 2.6 illustrates how a typical TCP/IP connection is established.

In Figure 2.6, the client transmits to the server the SYN bit set. This tells the server that the client wishes to establish a connection and what the starting sequence number will be for the client. The server sends back to the client an acknowledgment (SYN-ACK) and confirms its starting sequence number. The client acknowledges (ACK) receipt of the server's transmission and begins the transfer of data.

With SYN flooding a hacker creates many half-open connections by initiating the connections to a server with the SYN number bit. However, the return address that is associated with the SYN would not be a valid address. The server would send a SYN-ACK back to an invalid address that would not exist or respond. Using available programs, the hacker would transmit many SYN packets with false return addresses to the server. The server would respond to each SYN with an acknowledgment and then sit there with the connection half-open waiting for the final acknowledgment to come back. Figure 2.7 illustrates how SYN flooding works.

The result from this type of attack can be that the system under attack may not be able to accept legitimate incoming network connections so that users cannot log onto the system. Each operating system has a limit on the number of connections it can accept. In addition, the SYN flood may exhaust system memory, resulting in a system crash. The net result is that the system is unavailable or nonfunctional.

One countermeasure for this form of attack is to set the SYN relevant timers low so that the system closes half-open connections after a relatively

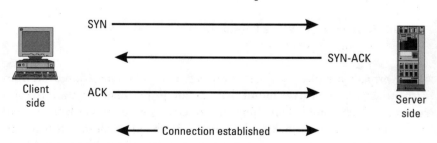

Figure 2.6 Normal TCP/IP handshake.

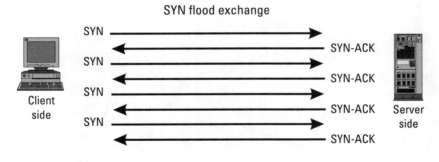

Figure 2.7 SYN flooding exchange.

short period of time. With the timers set low, the server will close the connections even while the SYN flood attack opens more.

SPAM

SPAM is unwanted e-mail. Anyone who has an e-mail account has received SPAM. Usually it takes the form of a marketing solicitation from some company trying to sell something we don't want or need. To most of us it is just an annoyance, but to a server it can also be used as a denial-of-service attack. By inundating a targeted system with thousands of e-mail messages, SPAM can eat available network bandwidth, overload CPUs, cause log files to grow very large, and consume all available disk space on a system. Ultimately, it can cause a system to crash.

SPAM can be used as a means to launch an indirect attack on a third party. SPAM messages can contain a falsified return address, which may be the legitimate address of some innocent unsuspecting person. As a result, an innocent person, whose address was used as the return address, may be spammed by all the individuals targeted in the original SPAM.

E-mail filtering can prevent much unwanted e-mail from getting through. Unfortunately, it frequently filters out legitimate e-mail as well.

Smurf Attack

The smurf attack is named after the source code employed to launch the attack (smurf.c). The smurf attack employs forged ICMP echo request packets and the direction of those packets to IP network broadcast addresses. The attack issues the ICMP ECHO_REQUEST to the broadcast address of another network. The attack spoofs as the source address the IP address of the system it wishes to target. Figure 2.8 illustrates how a smurf attack works.

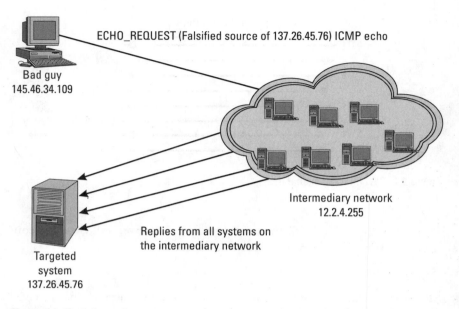

ECHO_REQUEST (Falsified source of 137.26.45.76) ICMP echo

Bad guy
145.46.34.109

Intermediary network
12.2.4.255

Replies from all systems on
the intermediary network

Targeted
system
137.26.45.76

Figure 2.8 Smurf attack.

When the systems on the network to whose broadcast address the ECHO_REQUEST is sent receive the packet with the falsified source address (i.e., the return address), they respond, flooding the targeted victim with the echo replies. This flood can overwhelm the targeted victim's network. Both the intermediate and victim's networks will see degraded performance. The attack can eventually result in the inoperability of both networks.

There are steps that the intermediate network can take to prevent from being used in this way. The steps include configuring network devices not to respond to ICMP ECHO_REQUESTs and disabling IP directed broadcasts from passing the network routers. There are really no steps that the targeted victim can take to prevent this kind of attack. The only defense is contacting the intermediate network to stop the ECHO_REQUESTs from being relayed, once an organization determines that it is the victim of an attack.

Denial-of-service attacks are the most difficult to defend against, and, of the possible attacks, they require the least amount of expertise to launch. In general, organizations should monitor for anomalous traffic patterns, such as SYN-ACK but no return ACKs. Since most routers filter incoming and outgoing packets, router-based filtering is the best defense against denial-of-service attacks. Organizations should use packet filters that filter based on destination and sender address. In addition, they should always use SPAM/sendmail filters.

Keep in mind there is a tradeoff with packet and mail filtering. The filtering that is performed to detect denial-of-service attacks will slow network performance, which may frustrate an organization's end users and slow its applications. In addition, mail filtering will bounce some e-mails that really should be allowed through, which may also aggravate end users.

Useful Web Sites

One of the best places to find information on network security is the WWW. There are numerous Web sites offering information on the latest threats and the how-tos of hacking and providing a forum in which to learn from others. They provide in-depth descriptions of attacks and hacks and list source codes for many useful tools that can be used to monitor, strengthen, and test the security of networks or individual systems. Some of the sites also provide source codes for tools used to attack or hack other systems. The Smurf source code, war dialers, or password crackers for practically every known operating system can be downloaded from some sites. Several sites are dedicated to phreaking, or the hacking of phone systems. Different sites provide different information, and the choice for the best site to access is dictated by the type of information for which one is searching.

There are several sites that I categorize as institutional or governmental. These sites are maintained and sponsored by formal, institutionalized organizations. They can be a very good resource of reliable information. In addition, the fact that they are maintained by known, reputable organizations tends to make me more comfortable about downloading source code from these sites.

The sites that fall under this category include the Department of Energy's Computer Incident Advisory Capability (CIAC). With the URL www.ciac.org, this site has information on the latest attacks, hoaxes, tools, and other resources.

Another site that falls under this category is the Computer Emergency Response Team (CERT). CERT is associated with Carnegie-Mellon University and can be found at www.cert.org. Just like CIAC, CERT has information on the latest attacks, hoaxes, tools, and other resources.

CERT is perhaps the best known organization that is concerned with computer security. It is the organization that is most often referenced or quoted in the media. It is also the organization to whom more people report new threats or vulnerabilities. For that reason, CERT is often the first to broadly distribute information.

Another institutional site is the System Administration, Networking, and Security (SANS) Institute located at www.sans.org. The SANS Web site is designed by and for system administrators and has a great deal of useful information.

SANS also offers printed publications and organizes conferences throughout the United States and around the world. The focus of the conferences is system administration and network security. I highly recommend them to anyone interested in learning more about system and network security.

Another useful site is the Computer Operations, Audit, and Security Technology (COAST) Web page. The URL for the COAST homepage is www.cerias.purdue.edu/coast/. COAST is now part of Purdue University's Center for Education and Research in Information Assurance and Security (CERIAS) program.

There are many other sites on the Web that fall under the "institutional" category. Many companies, government agencies, and universities have sites that can act as a resource for system and network security. However, my space is limited, so I cannot possibly list all of them.

Other sites can be categorized as counterculture or hacker sites. They can be considered black hat or white hat sites depending on your point of view.

One of the best sites is L0pht Heavy Industries at the URL www.l0pht.com. Two quotes on the L0pht Heavy Industry home page describe the philosophy of the site: The first quote is from Microsoft in reference to one of the many vulnerabilities of their software that have been uncovered throughout the years. It reads, "That vulnerability is completely theoretical." The second is the L0pht motto: "Making the theoretical practical since 1992."

In addition to the usual advisories and tools, the L0pht Heavy Industry site has a wealth of hacker tools and references. If you want to learn how hackers operate and what tools they use, this is a good place to start. There are password crackers, sniffers, war dialers, and other hacker tools that can be downloaded from the site. You can also find instructions and directions on how to hack particular systems. This information is not just limited to computer and network systems.

Another interesting site is Digital Information Society's site, which focuses more on phreaking, or telephony hacking. The information available on this site includes the how-tos of cellular telephony and hacking of cell phones. The URL for the site is www.phreak.com, but much of its useful information is reserved for members.

Another interesting site, run by *The Hacker Quarterly,* a print publication, provides information on what is happening in the hacker community; its URL is www.2600.com. The site contains information on hacker gatherings and links to similar sites, such as that run by *Phrack.*

The Hackers Network is another hacker site located at www.hack-net.com. Like many of the other sites, it has resources for the would-be hacker. There is also a members-only section, which I have never been privy to.

A point of interest for the person just beginning to learn the ways of the hacker, the Hackers Network site, has a newbie section. As the name implies, this section is designed as a resource for those who want to learn to become a hacker.

Another hacker site of interest is the Chaos Computer Club at the URL www.ccc.de/index.html. Most of this site's text is in German.

I list these hacker sites only as a reference. I do not necessarily recommend that you use the sites, nor do I condone, or in any way support, the activities of the members of the various sites. You should also be cautious about downloading any files from these or any other sites. You can never be sure about what you are actually downloading. Some other useful sites are listed as follows:

- The DOE Information Security Server: http://doe-is.llnl.gov/;
- The Root Shell Web site: www.rootshell.com;
- The National Security Institute: www.nsi.org;
- The Computer Security Institute: www.gocsi.com;
- ICSA: www.icsa.net;
- NT Bug Traq: www.ntbugtraq.org;
- Internet Security Systems: http://xforce.iss.net/.

Search Engines

Finally, the various Internet search engines can be a great resource when looking for information on network and system security. There are literally thousands of sites on the Internet that provide useful information. The nice thing about using the search engines is that you can tailor your search to a specific topic. If you want information on Windows NT IIS, you don't what to have to wade through pages about Unix security or Netscape Enterprise

Server. There is plenty of information out there on the Internet; the only problem with much of the information is that you have no way of determining its quality or the reliability of the source.

Mailing Lists

Other useful resources are the various mailing lists that cover specific topics relating to network and system security. For example, there are mailing lists that focus on firewalls, Windows NT, viruses, and Linux. There are probably hundreds of such lists available for almost any imaginable aspect of network and system security. The mailing lists are a forum in which users can ask questions regarding a particular topic or seek advice from knowledgeable colleagues. Table 2.1 lists some of the many available mailing lists.

The BugTraq mailing list, for example, covers discussions and announcements of computer security vulnerabilities in terms of what they are, how to exploit them, and how to fix them. The NTBugtraq mailing list is similar to the BugTraq mailing list but concerned with specific

Table 2.1
Network and System Security Mailing Lists

List	URL
Best of Security List	best-of-security-request@cyber.com.au
Bugtraq Full Disclosure List	listserv@netspace.org
NTBugtraq	listserv@listserv.ntbugtraq.com
CERT Advisories	cert-advisory-request@cert.org
CIAC Advisories	Majordomo@rumpole.llnl.gov
COAST Security Archive	coast-request@cs.purdue.edu
Firewall Digest	majordomo@lists.gnac.net
IDSs	majordomo@uow.edu.au
Linux Security	linux-security-request@RedHat.com
Legal Aspects of Computer Crime	majordomo@suburbia.net
NT Security Issues (ntsecurity)	majordomo@iss.net
WWW Security (www-security-new)	majordomo@nsmx.rutgers.edu
The Virus Lists	LISTSERV@lehigh.edu
Security maillists	http://xforce.iss.net/maillists/

Windows NT issues. NTBugtraq covers security exploits and security bugs in Windows NT and its related applications.

To subscribe to most of the mailing lists, it is only necessary to send an e-mail to the mail server (i.e. majordomo@lists.gnac.net) with "subscribe" in the subject box or in the body of the text.

I have a few words of warning regarding the mailing lists: Most of them are designed to forward all e-mail sent to the mail server to the subscribers of the mailing list. As a result, once you subscribe to one of these lists you may find you are inundated with e-mail. When I subscribed, I found that it was not unusual to receive 50 to 100 e-mails a day from a single mailing list. If you subscribe to more than one mailing list you will receive more e-mail than is humanly possible to read. In fact, it is a common ploy of pranksters to subscribe other individuals or e-mail servers to mailing lists as a sort of denial-of-service attack. Once subscribed to multiple mailing lists, the target is flooded with unwanted e-mail. You may want to limit the number of mailing lists to which you subscribe or use an e-mail filter.

One of the reasons there may be a high volume of e-mail from a mailing list is because of the flaming debates that sometimes rage. These discussions tend to flare up fairly regularly, and over time you may find that the same individuals seem to monopolize the discussion. One mailing list to which I subscribed suffered so greatly from this problem that I eventually unsubscribed from the list.

Another thing to keep in mind is that with certain mailing lists the subscribers do not have much patience for newbies. As a result, if you are a newbie and submit a question, be sure it is appropriate for the mailing list (i.e., no NT questions on a firewall mailing list) and be prepared for a certain amount of patronization.

3

Encryption, Digital Signatures, and Certification Authorities

For the exchange of information and commerce to be secure on any network, a system or process must be put in place that satisfies requirements for confidentiality, access control, authentication, integrity, and nonrepudiation. The key to the securing information on a network is cryptography. Cryptography can be used as a tool to provide privacy, to authenticate the identities of communicating parties, and to ensure message integrity. Confidentiality, access control, authentication, integrity, and nonrepudiation are terms that were introduced in Chapter 1, but they are defined again in Table 3.1.

Traditionally, cryptography conjures up thoughts of spies and secret codes. In reality, cryptography and encryption have found broad application in society. Every time you use an ATM machine to get cash or a point-of-sale machine to make a purchase, you are using encryption. Encryption is the process of scrambling the contents of a file or message to make it unintelligible to anyone not in possession of the "key" required to unscramble it.

Civilizations have been using various cryptosystems for at least 4,000 years. A cryptosystem or algorithm is the process or procedure to turn plaintext into cryptotext. A crypto algorithm is also known as a "cipher." There are several key elements that go into making an effective cryptosystem. First and foremost it must be reversible. A crypto algorithm is of no practical use if

Table 3.1

Cryptography Terms

Term	Definition
Confidentiality	The ability to encrypt or encode a message to be transmitted over an insecure network
Access control	The ability to control the level of access that an individual or entity can have to a network or system and how much information they can receive
Authentication	The ability to verify the identity of individuals or entity on the network
Integrity	The ability to ensure that a message or data has not been altered in transit from the sender to the recipient
Nonrepudiation	The ability to prevent individuals or entities from denying that they sent or received a file, when in fact they did

once you have scrambled your information, you cannot unscramble it. The security of the cryptosystem should be dependent on the secrecy and length of the key and not on the details of the algorithm. In other words, knowing the algorithm should not make it significantly easier to crack the code (restricted versus unrestricted). If security is dependent on keeping the algorithm secret, then it is considered a "restricted" algorithm. It is also important that the algorithm has been subjected to substantial cryptoanalysis. Only those algorithms that have been analyzed completely and at length are trustworthy. The algorithm should contain no serious or exploitable weakness. Theoretically, all algorithms can be broken by one method or another. However, an algorithm should not contain an inherent weakness that an attacker can easily exploit.

Below is an example of a cipher; to scramble a message with this cipher, simply match each letter in a message to the first row and convert it into the number or letter in the second row. To unscramble a message, match each letter or number in a message to the corresponding number or letter in the second row and convert it into the letter in the first row.

A	B	C	D	E	F	G	H	I	J	K	L	M	N	O	P	Q	R	S	T	U	V	W	X	Y	Z
1	2	3	4	5	6	A	B	C	D	E	F	G	H	I	J	K	L	M	N	O	P	Q	R	S	T

To illustrate how this works, see the following where the cipher is used to scramble the message "Little green apples."

- Cipher text: FCNNF5 AL55H 1JJF5M;
- Clear text: LITTLE GREEN APPLES.

This rudimentary cipher would not be effective at keeping a message secret for long. It does not comply with one of the qualities of a truly effective cipher, where knowing the algorithm should not make it significantly easier to crack the code. This is an example of a restricted algorithm. In this case, the cipher is the code. Once you know the cipher, you can unscramble any message. Ciphers usually fall into one of two categories: block ciphers or stream ciphers.

Stream Ciphers

Stream cipher algorithms process plaintext to produce a stream of ciphertext. The cipher inputs the plaintext in a stream and outputs a stream of ciphertext. Figure 3.1 illustrates the concept of the stream cipher's function.

Stream ciphers have several weaknesses. The most crucial shortcoming of stream ciphers is the fact that patterns in the plaintext can be reflected in the ciphertext. To illustrate this weakness we can use the rudimentary cipher introduced earlier in the chapter. Below, I have scrambled the plaintext message "Let us talk one to one" into ciphertext to compare the two patterns:

A	B	C	D	E	F	G	H	I	J	K	L	M	N	O	P	Q	R	S	T	U	V	W	X	Y	Z
1	2	3	4	5	6	A	B	C	D	E	F	G	H	I	J	K	L	M	N	O	P	Q	R	S	T

- Plaintext: Let us talk one to one.
- Ciphertext: F5n om n1fe ih5 ni ih5.

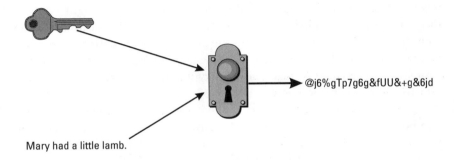

@j6%gTp7g6g&fUU&+g&6jd

Mary had a little lamb.

Figure 3.1 Stream cipher.

Patterns in the plaintext are reflected in the ciphertext. Words and letters that are repeated in the plaintext are also repeated in the ciphertext. Knowing that certain words repeat makes breaking the code easier. In addition, certain words in the English language appear with predictable regularity. Letters of the alphabet also appear in predictable regularity. The most commonly used letters of the alphabet in the English language are E, T, A, O, N, and I. The least commonly used letters in the English language are J, K, X, Q, and Z. The most common combination of letters in the English language is "th." As a result, if a code breaker is able to find a "t" in a code, it doesn't take long to find an "h." It is not hard for a trained code breaker to break this type of code.

Another weakness of stream ciphers is that they can be susceptible to a substitution attack even without breaking the code. This is a type of replay attack where someone can simply copy a section of an old message and insert it into a new message. You don't need to break the code to insert the old section into a new message.

Examples of stream ciphers include the Vernam cipher, Rivest cipher #4 (RC4), and one-time pads.

Block Ciphers

Block ciphers differ from stream ciphers in that they encrypt and decrypt information in fixed size blocks rather than encrypting and decrypting each letter or word individually. A block cipher passes a block of data or plaintext through its algorithm to generate a block of ciphertext. Ideally, a block cipher should generate ciphertext roughly equivalent in size (in terms of number of blocks) to the cleartext. A cipher that generates a block of ciphertext that is significantly larger than the information it is trying to protect is of little practical value. Think about it in terms of network bandwidth: If the ciphertext block was twice the size of the plaintext, the net effect is that your bandwidth would be cut in half. This would also have an impact on files stored in an encrypted format. An unencrypted file 10 MB in size would be 20 MB in size when encrypted.

Another requirement of block ciphers is that the ciphertext should contain no detectable pattern. Figure 3.2 illustrates how block ciphers function. Examples of well-known block ciphers include the Data Encryption Standard (DES), the International Data Encryption Algorithm (IDEA), and SKIPJACK.

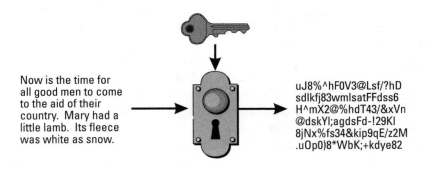

Now is the time for all good men to come to the aid of their country. Mary had a little lamb. Its fleece was white as snow.

uJ8%^hF0V3@Lsf/?hD
sdlkfj83wmlsatFFdss6
H^mX2@%hdT43/&xVn
@dskYl;agdsFd-!29Kl
8jNx%fs34&kip9qE/z2M
.uOp0)8*WbK;+kdye82

Figure 3.2 Block cipher.

Breaking Ciphers

For as long as ciphers have existed, there have been people trying to break them. There are many methods employed to break cipher. Some methods are ingenious. Some are sophisticated and technical in nature, while others are more crude in nature. The following sections describe some of the more widely used techniques employed in breaking ciphers.

Known Plaintext Attack

This method relies on the code breaker knowing in advance the plaintext content of a ciphertext message. Having both the plaintext and the ciphertext the code breaker reengineers the cipher and the key used to create the ciphertext.

Chosen Plaintext Attack

This method relies on the ability of the code breaker to somehow get a chosen plaintext message encrypted. During World War II the United States used a variation of this method to ascertain the plans of the Japanese navy in the Pacific.

Right after Pearl Harbor the U.S. Pacific Fleet was forced to fight what was primarily a defensive war. The U.S. Pacific Fleet had been devastated by the Japanese surprise attack on Pearl Harbor, and all that was left of the fleet were three aircraft carriers and a handful of supporting ships.

The United States had some success in breaking the Japanese codes. The U.S. Navy had determined that the Japanese were planning to attack a location referred to in their transmissions as "AF." The United States suspected that site AF was Midway Island. To determine if AF was, in fact, Midway, the United States ordered that a message be transmitted from Midway stating that the island's water condenser had broken down. The message was to be sent in the clear so that there would be no chance that the Japanese could not intercept it. Sure enough the Japanese took the bait. A few days later, the United States intercepted a Japanese coded message stating that AF's water condenser had failed.

From that message the United States knew that the Japanese were going to attack Midway. As a result, the United States was able to send what was left of the Pacific Fleet to Midway where they ambushed the Japanese carrier task force. The United States sank four of the Japanese' frontline aircraft carriers. It was a strategic victory for the United States in the Pacific from which the Japanese navy never recovered. From that point on, it was the Japanese Navy that was forced to fight a defensive war.

Cryptanalysis

Technically, any method employed to break a cipher or code is cryptanalysis. However, when I refer to cryptanalysis I am specifically talking about employing mathematical analysis to break a code. This method requires a high level of skill and sophistication. It is usually only employed by academics and governments. Today it relies very heavily on the use of ultrafast super computers.

Probably the most active and successful organization in the world, dedicated to breaking codes, is the National Security Agency (NSA). This is the largest and most secret spy agency in the United States. It is sometimes referred to as the Puzzle Palace, because the group spends so much time and energy on codes and cipher. The NSA employs tens of thousands of people. The only comparable organization in the world ever to have existed in terms of size is the former Soviet Union's KGB. But with the breakup of the Soviet Union, the NSA is now left without peers.

Brute Force

The brute force method tries every possible combination of keys or algorithms to break a cipher. Doing so can require tremendous resources. Usually, this type of attack requires computer assistance. If the algorithm is simple or the key is small, then the CPU resources required could be provided by a simple PC. If the algorithm is sophisticated or the key is large, then advanced computing power might be required.

Social Engineering

This method relies on breaking a cipher by getting someone knowledgeable about the cipher to reveal information on how to break it. Bribing someone, tricking him or her into divulging information, or threatening him or her with harm can reveal information. When the threat of harm is employed it is sometimes referred to as rubber-hose cryptanalysis.

Other Types of Attacks

Some other types of attacks are discussed as follows.

- *Substitution:* This is a type of replay attack where a previous message, in part or in whole, is inserted into a legitimate message. An attacker does not need to break the cipher for this type of attack to be effective.

- *Timing attacks:* Some cryptosystems can be broken if an outsider is able to accurately measure the time required to perform the encryption and decryption of a known ciphertext. The known ciphertext and the timing provide enough information to deduce fixed exponents and factors of some systems. This vulnerability is mostly theoretical. If an attacker has enough access to a network to be able to accurately measure the time required to encrypt and decrypt information, then you have other and bigger problems to worry about.

Encryption

Encryption is the process of scrambling the contents of a file or message to make it unintelligible to anyone not in possession of the "key" required to unscramble the file or message. There are two types of encryption: symmetric (private/secret) key and asymmetric (public) key encryption.

Symmetric Key Encryption

When most people think of encryption it is symmetric key cryptosystems that they think of. Symmetric key, also referred to as private key or secret key, is based on a single key and algorithm being shared between the parties who are exchanging encrypted information. The same key both encrypts and decrypts messages. This concept is illustrated in Figure 3.3.

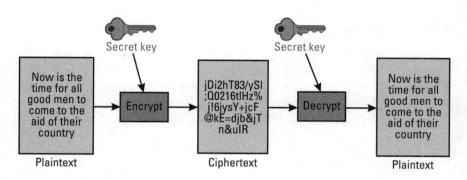

Figure 3.3 Symmetric key encryption.

The strength of the scheme is largely dependent on the size of the key and on keeping it secret. Generally, the larger the key, the more secure the scheme. In addition, symmetric key encryption is relatively fast.

The main weakness of the system is that the key or algorithm has to be shared. You can't share the key information over an unsecured network without compromising the key. As a result, private key cryptosystems are not well suited for spontaneous communication over open and unsecured networks. In addition, symmetric key provides no process for authentication or nonrepudiation. Remember, nonrepudiation is the ability to prevent individuals or entities from denying (repudiating) that a message was sent or received or that a file was accessed or altered, when in fact it was. This ability is particularly important when conducting e-commerce. Table 3.2 lists the advantages and disadvantages of symmetric key cryptosystems. Examples of widely deployed symmetric key cryptosystems include DES, IDEA, Blowfish, RC4, CAST, and SKIPJACK.

Table 3.2

The Advantages and Disadvantages of Symmetric Key Cryptography

Advantages	Disadvantages
Fast	Requires secret sharing
Relatively secure	Complex administration
Widely understood	No authentication
	No nonrepudiation

Data Encryption Standard (DES)

DES is one of the oldest and most widely used algorithms. DES was developed by IBM with the encouragement of the NSA. It was originally deployed in the mid 1970s. DES consists of an algorithm and a key. The key is a sequence of eight bytes, each containing eight bits for a 64-bit key. Since each byte contains one parity bit, the key is actually 56 bits in length. According to author James Bamford in his book *The Puzzle Palace*, IBM originally intended to release the DES algorithm with a 128-bit key, but the NSA convinced IBM to release it with the 56-bit key instead. Supposedly this was done to make it easier for the NSA to decrypt covertly intercepted massages.

DES is widely used in automated teller machine (ATM) and point-of-sale (POS) networks, so if you use an ATM or debit card you are using DES. DES has been enhanced with the development of triple DES. However, DES has been broken. It is gradually being phased out of use.

International Data Encryption Algorithm (IDEA)

IDEA is a symmetric key block cipher developed at the Swiss Federal Institute in the early 1990s. IDEA utilizes a 128-bit key. Supposedly, it is more efficient to implement in software than DES and triple DES. Since it was not developed in the United States, it is not subject to U.S. export restrictions.

CAST

The CAST algorithm supports variable key lengths, anywhere from 40 bits to 256 bits in length. CAST uses a 64-bit block size, which is the same as the DES, making it a suitable drop-in replacement. CAST has been reported to be two to three times faster than a typical implementation of DES and six to nine times faster than a typical implementation of triple DES. The CAST algorithm was developed by Carlisle Adams and Strafford Travares and patented by Entrust Technologies, but a version of the CAST algorithm is available for free commercial and noncommercial use. CAST is employed in Pretty Good Privacy (PGP).

Rivest Cipher #4 (RC4)

Developed by Ron Rivest of RSA fame, RC4 is a stream cipher that uses a variable size key. However, when used with a key of 128 bits it can be very effective. Until recently, the approved export version only used a 40-bit key. RC4 is used in Netscape Navigator and Internet Explorer.

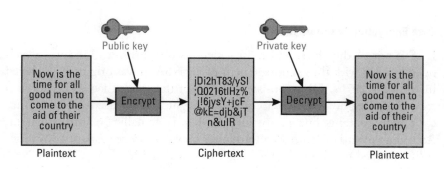

Figure 3.4 Asymmetric key encryption.

Asymmetric Key Encryption

For centuries, all cryptography was based on the symmetric key cryptosystems. Then in 1976, two computer scientists, Whitfield Diffe and Martin Hellman of Stanford University, introduced the concept of asymmetric cryptography. Asymmetric cryptography is also known as public key cryptography. Public key cryptography uses two keys as opposed to one key for a symmetric system. With public key cryptography there is a public key and a private key. The keys' names describe their function. One key is kept private, and the other key is made public. Knowing the public key does not reveal the private key. A message encrypted by the private key can only be decrypted by the corresponding public key. Conversely, a message encrypted by the public key can only be decrypted by the private key. This process is illustrated in Figure 3.4.

With the aid of public key cryptography, it is possible to establish secure communications with any individual or entity when using a compatible software or hardware device. For example, if Alice wishes to communicate in a secure manner with Bob, a stranger with whom she has never communicated before, Alice can give Bob her public key. Bob can encrypt his outgoing transmissions to Alice with Alice's public key. Alice can then decrypt the transmissions using her private key when she receives them. Only Alice's private key can decrypt a message encrypted with her public key. If Bob transmits to Alice his public key, then Alice can transmit secure encrypted data back to Bob that only Bob can decrypt. It does not matter that they exchanged public keys on an unsecured network. Knowing an individual's public key tells you nothing about his or her private key. Only an individual's private key can decrypt a message encrypted with his or her public key. The security breaks down if either of the parties' private keys is compromised.

While symmetric key cryptosystems are limited to securing the privacy of information, asymmetric or public key cryptography is much more versatile. Public key cryptosystems can provide a means of authentication and can support digital certificates. With digital certificates, public key cryptosystems can provide enforcement of nonrepudiation. Unlike symmetric key cryptosystems, public key allows for secure spontaneous communication over an open network. In addition, it is more scalable for very large systems (tens of millions) than symmetric key cryptosystems. With symmetric key cryptosystems, the key administration for large networks is very complex. Table 3.3 summarizes the advantages and disadvantages of the public key cryptosystems.

Public Key Cryptosystems

There are three public key algorithms in wide use today—Diffie-Hellman; RSA; and the Digital Signature Algorithm (DSA). They are described in the following sections.

Diffie-Hellman

The Diffie-Hellman algorithm was developed by Whitfield Diffie and Martin Hellman at Stanford University. It was the first usable public key algorithm. Diffie-Hellman is based on the difficulty of computing discrete logarithms. It can be used to establish a shared secret key that can be used by two parties for symmetric encryption. Diffie-Hellman is often used for IPSEC key management protocols.

For spontaneous communications with Diffie-Hellman, two communicating entities would each generate a random number that is used as their private keys. They exchange public keys. They each apply their private keys

Table 3.3
The Advantages and Disadvantages of Public Key Cryptography

Advantages	Disadvantages
No secret sharing necessary	Slower or computationally intensive
Authentication supported	Certificate authority required
Provides nonrepudiation	
Scalable	

to the other's public key to compute identical values (shared secret key). They then use the shared secret key to encrypt and exchange information.

Rivest, Shamir, Adelman (RSA)

The RSA public key algorithm was developed by Ron Rivest, Adi Shamir, and Len Adelman at MIT. RSA multiplies large prime numbers together to generate keys. Its strength lies in the fact that it is extremely difficult to factor the product of large prime numbers. This algorithm is the one most often associated with public key encryption. The RSA algorithm also provides digital signature capabilities. I will discuss digital signatures later in this chapter. They are used in SSL to set up sessions and with privacy-enhanced mail (PEM) and PGP. SSL is discussed in Chapter 5. PEM and PGP are discussed in Chapter 6.

Digital Signature Algorithm

DSA was developed as part of the Digital Signature Standard (DSS). (A more detailed discussion of DSS and DSA is provided later in this chapter.) Unlike the Diffie-Hellman and RSA algorithms, DSA is not used for encryption but for digital signatures.

A Slight Digression

For many years it was believed that Whitfield Diffie and Martin Hellman were the first to conceive of asymmetric cryptography and that Ron Rivest, Adi Shamir, and Len Adelman were the first to develop the RSA algorithm. However, it is now claimed that neither collaborative was the first and that the concept of asymmetric cryptography, the Diffie-Hellman algorithm, and the RSA algorithm were all discovered years earlier in England by the Government Communications Headquarters (GCHQ), which is the British equivalent of the NSA. The GCHQ claims that it conceived of the concept years before anyone else but never released information on the work for national security reasons.

Message Integrity

To attain a high level of confidence in the integrity of a message or data, a process must be put in place to prevent or detect alteration during transit. One technique employed is called a hash function. A hash function takes a message of any length and computes a product value of fixed length. The product is referred to as a "hash value." The length of the original message does not alter the length of the hash value. Hash functions are used to ensure the integrity of a message or file. Using the actual message or file, a hash function computes a hash value, which is a cryptographic checksum of the message. This checksum can be thought of as a fingerprint for that message. The hash value can be used to determine if the message or file has been altered since the value was originally computed.

Using e-mail as an example, the hash value for a message is computed at both the sending and receiving ends. If the message is modified in anyway during transit, the hash value computed at the receiving end will not match the value computed at the sending end. Hash functions must be one way only. In other words, there should be no way to reverse the hash value to obtain information on the message. Obviously, this would represent a risk.

Another requirement of an effective one-way hash function is that the possibility of "collisions" is very limited, if nonexistent. A collision occurs when the same hash value is computed for two or more unique messages. If the messages are different the hash values should be different. No two unique messages should compute the same hash value. Table 3.4 lists some of the more widely implemented hashing algorithms.

MD4

MD4 was developed by Ron Rivest of RSA. MD4 is a one-way hash function that takes a message of variable length and produces a 128-bit hash value or message digest. MD4 has been proven to have weaknesses. Analysis has shown that at least the first two rounds of MD4 are not one-way (there are three rounds in MD4) and that the algorithm is subject to collisions.

MD5

MD5 was also created by Ron Rivest as an improvement on MD4. Like MD4, MD5 creates a unique 128-bit message digest value derived from the

Table 3.4
Widely Used Hashing Algorithms

Message digest #4 (MD4) from RSA
Message digest #5 (MD5) from RSA
Secure hash algorithm-1 (SHA-1)
RACE Integrity Primitives Evaluation (RIPE) MD-160 (RIPEMD-160)

contents of a message or file. This value, which is a fingerprint of the message or file content, is used to verify the integrity of the message's or file's contents. If a message or file is modified in any way, even a single bit, the MD5 cryptographic checksum for the message or file will be different. It is considered very difficult to alter a message or file in a way that will cause MD5 to generate the same result as was obtained for the original file.

While MD5 is more secure than MD4, it too has been found to have some weaknesses: Analysis has found a collision in the compression function of MD5, although not for MD5 itself. Nevertheless, this attack casts doubts on the whether MD5 is truly a collision-resistant hash algorithm.

The MD5 algorithm is intended for digital signature applications, where a large file must be "compressed" in a secure manner before being encrypted with a private (secret) key under a public-key cryptosystem such as RSA.

Secure Hash Algorithm-1 (SHA-1)

SHA-1 is a one-way hash algorithm used to create digital signatures. SHA-1 is derived from SHA, which was developed in 1994 by the NIST. SHA-1 is similar to the MD4 and MD5 algorithms developed by Ron Rivest. SHA-1 is slightly slower than MD4 and MD5, but it is reported to be more secure.

The SHA-1 hash function produces a 160-bit hash value or message digest. I am aware of no known cryptographic attacks against SHA-1 that have been successful. Since it produces a 160-bit message digest it is more resistant to brute force attacks than MD4 and MD5, which produce a 128-bit message digest.

RIPEMD

RIPEMD is a hash function that was developed through the European Community's project RIPE. There are several extensions to RIPEMD1RIPEMD-128, RIPEMD-160, and RIPEMD-256. Each extension is a reference to the length of the hash value or message digest. For example, RIPEMD-160 is a 160-bit cryptographic hash function, designed by Hans Dobbertin, Antoon Bosselaers, and Bart Preneel.

Authentication

To have a high level of confidence and trust in the integrity of information received over a network, the transacting parties need to be able to authenticate each other's identity. In the example involving Alice and Bob, it was demonstrated how they could transmit secure information between each party using encryption by exchanging public keys. While confidentiality was ensured with the use of public key cryptography, there was no authentication of the parties' identities. Bob may not really have been Bob. For that matter, Bob doesn't really know if Alice was Alice. In addition, how does Alice know that when she was sending her public key to Bob, that Jack did not intercept it and use it to send his public key to her and masquerade as Bob. To ensure secure business transactions on unsecured networks like the Internet, both parties need to be able to authenticate their identities. Authentication in a digital setting is a process whereby the receiver of a message can be confident of the identity of the sender. The lack of secure authentication has been a major obstacle in achieving widespread use of the Internet for commerce. One process used to authenticate the identity of an individual or entity involves digital signatures.

Digital Signatures

A digital signature allows a receiver to authenticate (to a limited extent) the identity of the sender and to verify the integrity of the message. For the authentication process, you must already know the sender's public key, either from prior knowledge or from some trusted third party. Digital signatures are used to ensure message integrity and authentication. In its simplest form, a digital signature is created by using the sender's private key to hash the entire contents of the message being sent to create a message digest. The recipient uses the sender's public key to verify the integrity of the message by recreating the message digest. By this process you ensure the integrity of the message and authenticate the sender. Figure 3.5 illustrates the process.

To sign a message, senders usually append their digital signature to the end of a message and encrypt it using the recipient's public key. Recipients decrypt the message using their own private key and verify the sender's identity and the message integrity by decrypting the sender's digital signature using the sender's public key.

Once again we will use Alice and Bob to illustrate how digital signatures work. Alice has a pair of keys, her private key and her public key. She sends a message to Bob that includes both a plaintext message and a version of the plaintext message that has been encrypted using her private key. The encrypted version of her text message is her digital signature. Bob receives the message from Alice and decrypts it using her public key. He then compares the decrypted message to the plaintext message. If they are identical, then

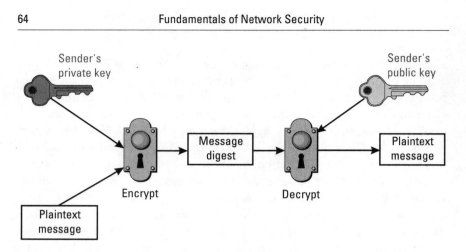

Sender's private key

Sender's public key

Message digest

Plaintext message

Encrypt

Decrypt

Plaintext message

Figure 3.5 Digital signature.

he has verified that the message has not been altered and that it came from Alice. He can authenticate that the message came from Alice because he decrypted it with Alice's public key, so it could only have been encrypted with Alice's private key, to which only Alice has access.

The strengths of digital signatures are that they are almost impossible to counterfeit and they are easily verified. However, if Alice and Bob are strangers who have never communicated to each other before, and Bob received Alice's public key, but had no other means to verify who Alice was, other than Alice's assertion that she was who she claimed to be, then the digital signature is useless for authentication. It will still verify that a message has arrived unaltered from the sender, but it cannot be used to authenticate the identity of the sender. In cases where the parties have no prior knowledge of one another, a trusted third party is required to authenticate the identity of the transacting parties.

Competing Standards

There are two competing standards for digital signature technology. Both systems are based on the International Telecommunications Union's X.509 standard for public key certification. The one that has been around the longest is the RSA Data Security's public key encryption standard, which has become a de facto standard in the industry. RSA Data Security uses the RSA public key algorithm, for both encryption and authentication, invented by Ron Rivest, Adi Shamir, and Leonard Adleman in 1977. The more recently developed standard is the U.S. government's DSS, which specifies a DSA. It was selected by the National Institute of Standards and Technology (NIST) in 1994.

Many have questioned the wisdom of the NIST's decision to select DSS. Not surprisingly, one of the most vocal opponents has been RSA Data Security and companies associated with RSA. However, many others have questioned the choice of DSS. The DSS cryptosystem is relatively new and has not been fully tested. For that reason alone, many believe that it is not as secure as the RSA standard, which has been subjected to rigorous testing for the past 19 years. Some have even questioned the NIST's motives for selecting DSS. The decision was made in cooperation with the NSA. The process was secretive and conducted with very little public participation or debate. Some have gone so far as to suggest that DSS was selected because the NSA has a back door into the system. While the competing standards do not represent an obstacle to implementing digital signatures within a large multinational organization, they can result in the inability to exchange digital signatures between organizations.

Digital Certificate

Digital signatures can be used to verify that a message has been delivered unaltered and to verify the identity of the sender by public key. The problem with authenticating a digital signature, however, is that you must be able to verify that a public key does in fact belong to the individual or entity that claims to have sent it and that the individual or entity is in fact who or what it claims to be.

A digital certificate issued by a certification authority (CA) utilizing a hierarchical public key infrastructure (PKI) can be used to authenticate a sender's identity for spontaneous, first-time contacts. Digital certificates provide a means for secure first-time spontaneous communication. A digital certificate provides a high level of confidence in the identity of the individual or entity with which you are communicating. A digital certificate is a means to authenticate identity.

A digital certificate is usually issued by a trusted/known third party (CA) to bind an individual or entity to a public key. The digital certificate is digitally signed by the CA with the CA's private key. This provides independent confirmation that an individual or entity is in fact who it claims to be. The CA issues digital certificates that vouch for the identities of those to whom the certificates were issued.

Using Alice and Bob as our example, Alice can send Bob her public key. Bob will be able to verify her digital signature using Alice's public key.

Given such a key, how does he verify that it actually belongs to Alice and does not really belong to Jack who is masquerading as Alice? If he has no other means available to him, he cannot. However, if Alice's public key is presented as part of a digital certificate signed by a known CA, Bob can have a high level of confidence that Alice is who and what she claims to be.

A digital certificate is a method of binding an individual or entity to a public key. The certificate is digitally signed by a CA providing independent confirmation that individuals or entities are in fact who they claim to be and that the public key provided by them does in fact belong to that party. The CA and the CA's public key must be widely known for the digital certificate to be of practical value. The CA's public key must be widely known so that there is no need to authenticate the CA's digital signature. You are relying on the CA's digital signature to authenticate the certificate owner's identity and to bind that identity to their public key.

Table 3.5 illustrates possible contents of a digital certificate. In its simplest form, a digital certificate would include the name and address of the individual/entity, certificate expiration date, serial number for the certificate, and the individuals' or entities' public key. Most importantly, it would be digitally signed by the issuing CA using the CA's private key. A digital certificate could contain other information as well. Depending on the type of certificate, it could include information on access privileges, geographic location of the owner, or the age of the owner. When fully implemented, digital certificates will most likely take several forms.

Each person's digital certificate could contain a mini-database on the owner, which includes the authorizations, access privileges, and the owner's public key. Digital certificates cannot be forged and are expected to be legally acceptable as handwritten notarized signatures. The International Chamber of Commerce is exploring the creation of a "cybernotary," a lawyer able

Table 3.5
Digital Certificate Example

Name: Individual, organization, entity
Owner's public key
Certificate expiration date
Certificate's serial number
Name of issuing CA
Issuing CA's digital signature

to demonstrate that he or she can issue certificates from a secure computer environment.

A digital signature used in concert with a digital certificate potentially possesses greater legal authority than a handwritten signature. The inability to forge a digital signature, the fact that the digital signature can verify that the document has not been altered since it was signed, and the certificate verifying the identity of the signer make a digitally signed document irrefutable. The signer cannot repudiate his or her signature at a later date.

Limitations of Digital Certificates

There are still a number of issues that need to be addressed, such as how to handle expired certificates; there is the risk that a long-term document could be signed with a digital certificate with a two-year expiration date. What is the legality of the document once the digital certificate expires? Another issue that needs to be addressed is how to handle revocation of certificates.

The certificate revocation process is cumbersome: How do you revoke a certificate once it has been issued? Once a digital certificate is issued, it is valid until it expires. That is usually at least a year. No process exists for immediate revocation of a certificate should it be compromised or should the CA withdraw its certification. CAs will have to periodically issue certificate revocation lists (CRL). All participants utilizing the PKI will have to maintain up-to-date CRLs. CRLs will eventually become very large. In addition, there are a number of issues concerning the legal responsibilities and liabilities of CAs and their issuing of digital certificates that still need to be addressed.

What is most crucial to the success of the digital certificate is the role of the CA. With the CA, the trust is no longer dependent on the individual's or entity's digital signature. Instead, the trust is transferred to the CA.

Certificate Authorities

As stated previously, a CA is a body, either public or private, that seeks to fill the need for a trusted third party in e-commerce. The CA issues digital certificates that vouch for the identities of those to whom the certificates were issued. For this process to be secure, the CA's public key must be trustworthy and well-known. When I say it must be trustworthy, I am referring to the reputation and reliability of the CA as an entity. A digital certificate issued by "Sam's Digital Certificates and Deli" would lack trustworthiness to another party on the Internet. A CA must also perform the necessary due diligence to verify that individuals or entities are in fact who they say they are, before a digital certificate is issued to an individual or entity. The CA public key must be widely known to be effective. A digital certificate signed by a CA is worthless if you do not know the CA's public key or if you have no independent means of verifying that the public key provided is in fact bound to the CA. For that reason, a CA's public keys need to be easily accessible and verifiable.

There will be a number of entities that issue digital certificates. VeriSign, Inc., which was formed by RSA Data Security and several other major corporations, is the one main issuers. Other companies that issue digital certificates include GTE, AT&T, and Microsoft. There are many others. The process of obtaining a digital certificate is relatively simple for any legitimate individual or entity.

Once again, using Alice and Bob for our example, Alice generates her own key pair from her X.509-compliant software or device. She then sends the public key to a CA with proof of who and what she is. In our example, Alice sends her public key to a CA. If the digital certificate is for her company, the CA might request a copy of the articles of incorporation, copies of the latest financial statements, and other items that establish that the company is what it claims to be and is in good standing. If the certificate is for Alice personally, the CA could request a birth certificate and perhaps take her fingerprints. The verification process is largely dependent on the level of the certificate. Once the CA has done its due diligence and is satisfied that Alice is who she claims to be, the CA sends her a digital certificate to load in her software or device. This certificate will be signed by the CA with its private key. The digital certificate will attest to the fact the CA has determined that Alice is who she says she is and binds to Alice her public key. Alice can now present that certificate to Bob to authenticate her identity and her public key.

When Bob receives Alice's signed message, he will need Alice's public key to verify her digital signature and to ensure that the message has arrived unaltered. Since he already knows the CA's public key (it will be published everywhere), he can decrypt the digital certificate or certify that the digital certificate is signed by the CA, verify the integrity of the certificate, and obtain Alice's public key and then decrypt her signed message.

The need for CAs is clear, but the duties and responsibilities of the CAs are not so clear. There are still many issues that need to be addressed with CAs. Many of these are legal, not technical, in nature: What are the CA's responsibilities when issuing digital certificates? What if the CA makes a mistake and issues one to the wrong individual or entity? CAs may be open to tremendous liability should that mistake result in fraud or some financial loss.

As we move closer to paperless commerce and a paperless society, the concept of CAs becomes increasingly important. They will have a major impact on the future of e-commerce. That impact will affect our day-to-day lives: It means the development of a whole new set of business relationships that will be necessary to function daily. Perhaps, one day, without a digital certificate you may not be able to purchase milk at the corner store. Will CAs become the future's credit agencies, rating everyone as a good or bad "risk"?

Public Key Infrastructure

As part of the future implementation of digital certificates, a movement is under way to develop a PKI. The infrastructure will be necessary to authenticate digital certificates and CAs. A PKI is a hierarchical network of CAs. A "root certificate" authority certifies subordinate CAs. The hierarchy is recognized as trusted by all entities that trust the hierarchical CA. Not every entity needs to trust the other, just the hierarchy. Some plans envision a hierarchy of CAs, where one CA certifies the identity of the previous CA. The top-level root CA in the United States could be the U.S. government. Others envision a more horizontal scheme of cross-certification with only a few layers. In either case, a certificate-based PKI can provide a process to establish trust relationships. Figure 3.6 illustrates how a theoretical PKI might be structured.

The difficult part will be developing the standards and infrastructure for certifying digital signatures and certificates between organizations using different schemes. At the same time, the NIST is working on the development of a federal PKI. While there are many challenges to developing a national PKI, the most daunting task will be the development of the global infrastructure. When we discuss a global or international PKI we open a Pandora's box of "national security" issues.

The Future

Introduction

It is stating the obious to say that developments in the field of cryptography are occurring all the time. Two of the more important changes involve the Advanced Encryption Standard and developments in the area of Elliptic Curve Cryptography.

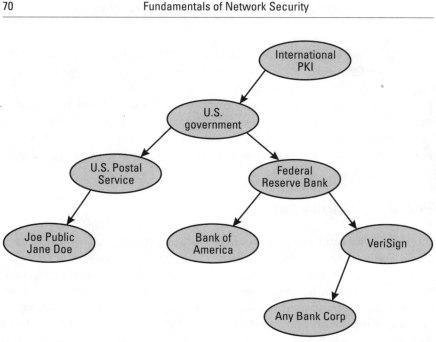

Figure 3.6 Theoretical PKI.

Advanced Encryption Standard (AES)

For decades the encryption standard in the United States has been DES. However, the DES algorithm is no longer as secure as it once was and needs to be replaced. As a result, the NIST is in the process of selecting a new algorithm to use as the new standard into the next century. This new standard is being called the Advanced Encryption Standard (AES). The goal of AES is to select an unclassified, block algorithm that will be available worldwide free of royalty fees.

As of this writing, there are five algorithms that have been selected as finalists for the AES. The five finalists are listed as follows.

- MARS developed by IBM;

- RC6, developed by RSA, which also developed RC4 and RC5;

- Rijndael developed by Vincent Rijmen and Joan Daemen;

- Serpent developed by Ross Anderson, Eli Buham, and Lars Knudsen;

- Twofish developed by Bruce Schneier, Niels Ferguson, Chris Hall, John Kelsey, Doug Whiting, and David Wagner. Incidentally, Bruce Schneier is the author of the book *Applied Cryptography* and developer of the Blowfish block algorithm.

One or more of these algorithms will eventually be selected as the AES. How long it will remain secure will largely depend on the developments in the fields of computer technology and cryptanalysis.

Elliptic-Curve Cryptography (ECC)

Another up and coming development in cryptography appears to be elliptic-curve cryptography (ECC). ECC, which is widely expected to be the next-generation algorithm, has been proposed for use as a public key cryptosystem. EEC's strength comes from the fact that it is computational very difficulty to solve the elliptic curve discrete logarithm problem.

The appeal of ECC algorithms is the fact that they hold the possibility of offering security comparable to the RSA algorithms using smaller keys. Smaller keys mean that less computation is required. Less time and CPU resources would be required to implement this technology on the network. Less time and CPU translates into less cost associated with using these algorithms. As a result, interest in these algorithms is keen.

It has also been said that ECC is more difficult to break than RSA. While both RSA with a 512-bit key and ECC with a 97-bit key have been broken, it has been stated that the ECC algorithm is more difficult to break. In 1999 a team of 195 volunteers in 20 countries using 740 computers took 40 days to recover the 97-bit ECC private key.

Although ECC holds great promise, I am not aware of any practical implementation of the technology in any product now on the market. No matter what algorithm you employ, it is important to be cognizant of the fact that as computing power increases and becomes less expensive, the cryptographic key sizes will have to increase to ensure security. Not too far in the future, a 2,024-bit key will not be sufficient to ensure security.

The Limitations of Encryption

Communications are not necessarily secure simply because they are encrypted. It is important to remember that useful information can even be discerned from encrypted communications. I like to use an example from the book *Blind Man's Bluff.* In the book, authors Sherry Sontag and Chistopher

and Annette Drew tell the story of U.S. submarine espionage during the
Cold War. In the 1970s and 1980s, Soviet missile subs were using effective
cryptosystems in conjunction with sophisticated transmitters that compressed their encrypted communications into microsecond bursts. While the
United States was not able to break the Soviet transmission code, America
was able to gather a great deal of information from the transmissions themselves. U.S. analysis of the transmission patterns revealed almost as much
information as the actual content of the transmissions would have revealed.
For example, the United States was able to determine that the messages were
coming from Soviet subs on their way to and from patrol. They were also
able to distinguish one sub from another by slight variations in the frequen-
cies of the transmissions and that the Soviet subs sent transmissions at regular
points or milestones in their patrols. Consequently, the United States was
able to determine Soviet subs' location, when they reached their patrol sec-
tor, the halfway point or a particular landmark. The analysis of the transmission patterns enabled the United States to track Soviet subs on patrol
without ever breaking the transmissions' code. It is important to understand
that simply using encryption is no guarantee of confidentiality or secrecy.

In addition, studies have shown that the randomness of the data for
encrypted files stored on media can be used to distinguish the files from other
stored data. Generally, operating systems do not store data in a random manner. Data is normally stored in a manner that optimizes retrieval, space, or
speed. Encrypted files and algorithm keys by their nature must be random
data. As a result, when large encrypted files and public/private key sets
are stored on a disk drive their randomness stands out against the normally
organized data on the drive. There are programs available that purport to be
able to find keys and encrypted files on a disk drive. If true, this could potentially mean that someone could steal key pairs if he or she had access to the
drive on which the keys were stored.

Meanwhile, however, it is also important to understand that developments in the field of cryptography and digital signature technology are the
enabling force behind the recent explosion in e-commerce on the Internet.
Without these technologies, Internet e-commerce would not be possible.
As a result, those who want to participate in this new world of e-commerce,
either as an entrepreneur or a consumer, need to understand the essential
technology that is enabling its development.

4

Kerberos Key Exchange

Chapter 3 discusses how digital certificates and a PKI can be employed for the purpose of authenticating users on a network. Another method that can be employed is the Kerberos key exchange. Like a PKI, the Kerberos key exchange process relies upon public key cryptography and digital signature technology.

Kerberos

Kerberos key exchange is a network authentication protocol developed at MIT. It is designed to provide strong authentication for client/server applications by using a combination of both secret key and public key cryptography. Kerberos utilizes a single central server, referred to as a trusted server, to act as a trusted third party to authenticate users and control access to resources on the network. The basic premise behind the Kerberos security is that it is not possible to ensure security on all network servers. This concept assumes that server security breaches are inevitable in a distributed computing environment with multiple servers. The premise is that it is impossible to secure all the servers, so one shouldn't even attempt to. The Kerberos model proposes, however, that it *is* possible to truly secure a single server. Therefore, it holds that it is more secure to control all network access from one central secure server.

The Kerberos key exchange process is really quite simple, but at the same time quite eloquent. Kerberos never transmits passwords on the network, regardless of whether they are encrypted or not. Kerberos utilizes cryptographic keys referred to as "tickets" to control access to network server resources. Tickets are encrypted passes or files issued by the "trusted" server to users and processes to determine access level. There are six types of tickets: initial, invalid, pre-authenticated, renewable, forwardable, and postdated. Figures 4.1–4.6 illustrate the Kerberos key exchange process.

In Figure 4.1 the client creates a request to send to the Kerberos server. The request is digitally signed by the client using the client's own private key. In this example the request is to access the payroll server. In Figure 4.2, the

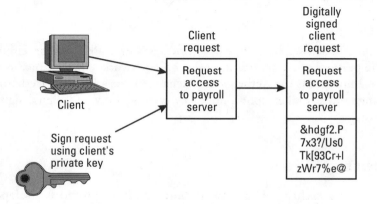

Figure 4.1 Kerberos key exchange, step one.

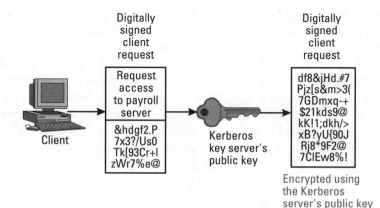

Figure 4.2 Kerberos key exchange, step two.

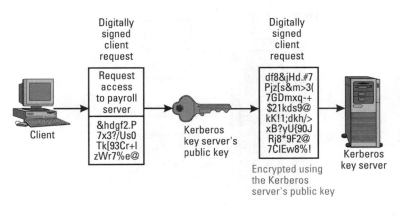

Figure 4.3 Kerberos key exchange, step three.

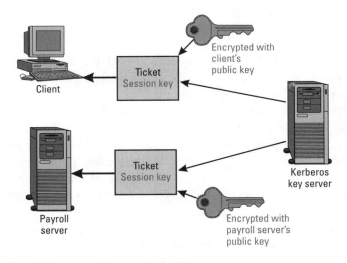

Figure 4.4 Kerberos key exchange, step four.

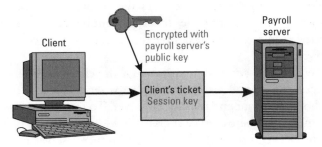

Figure 4.5 Kerberos key exchange, step five.

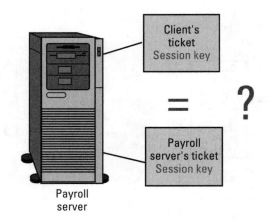

Figure 4.6 Kerberos key exchange, step six.

client takes the digitally signed request and encrypts it using the Kerberos server's public key. In Figure 4.3, the client sends the digitally signed and encrypted request to the Kerberos server.

The Kerberos server decrypts the request using its private key and then authenticates the originator of the request by verifying the digital signature of the sender. The request was digitally signed using the sender's private key, which the Kerberos server verifies by using the sender's public key.

The Kerberos server maintains a database of all the public keys of authorized users, so it does not have to rely upon the sender or a trusted third party to verify the sender's public key. If the Kerberos server does not have the sender's public key in its database, then the digital signature cannot be verified. Similarly, if the Kerberos server does not have the sender's public key, then the sender is not an authorized user of the network, and the request will be denied.

Once the Kerberos server receives the request and authenticates the sender's identity, the server verifies that the client has authorization to access the requested resource. In this example the resource requested is access to the payroll server.

If the Kerberos server determines that the client does have authorization to access the payroll server, the Kerberos server sends identical session tickets to both the client and the payroll server. To transmit the session ticket to the client, the Kerberos server encrypts it with the client's public key. To transmit the ticket to the payroll server the Kerberos server uses the payroll server's public key. Figure 4.4 depicts this process. When the encrypted session key is received, both the client and the payroll server decrypt it using their respective private keys.

The tickets could also be digitally signed by the Kerberos server to avoid the possibility of counterfeit tickets being sent to a client or network resource.

The client then sends a copy of its ticket to the payroll server. Before transmitting the ticket, the client encrypts the ticket using the payroll server's public key. Figure 4.5 illustrates this process.

When the payroll server receives the encrypted ticket from the client the server decrypts the ticket using the server's own private key. The payroll server then compares the ticket that it received from the client to the ticket that it received from the Kerberos server. If the client's ticket matches the server's ticket then the client will be allowed to connect to the server. If they don't match, the connection is refused. Figure 4.6 illustrates this process. Once the connection is established, the systems can encrypt the communication using either the session key or the client's public key, or they can use no encryption at all.

One advantage that Kerberos has over other schemes, such as using digital certificates and a PKI, is that revocation of authorization and authentication can be done immediately. The PKI relies upon CRLs to remove authorization for an individual or entity. Access to network resources may not be terminated until the CRL works its way through the PKI or the original digital certificate expires. In either case, the original certificate will provide access to network resources long after the time period you want access terminated. With Kerberos, every time an individual or entity requests access to a network resource, the Kerberos server is queried. As a result, once access is terminated at the Kerberos server, the change is effective immediately.

Kerberos' Limitations

The primary limitation of the Kerberos concept is that if the Kerberos server is down, one cannot access network resources, since access to all network resources must be authorized through the Kerberos server. As a result, the Kerberos design is particularly vulnerable to denial-of-service attacks. If you target the Kerberos server you can prevent legitimate users from gaining access to the network. You don't even have to completely crash the server to prevent others from gaining network access. Simply overwhelming the server with requests or flooding the network with traffic would be enough to prevent the server from responding to queries.

Organizations can build in back-up Kerberos servers into the design of their networks, but doing so introduces vulnerability into their network. Back-up servers deviate from one of the fundamental principles of Kerberos, which is that it is difficult to provide absolute security for multiple servers. The Kerberos concept relies on a single absolutely secure server. If the Kerberos server is compromised, then the integrity of the entire system is compromised.

Kerberos also can be susceptible to replay attacks. Someone on the network could sniff and record requests going to and from the Kerberos server. The transmission of tickets to network resources could also be copied to be retransmitted at a later time as new requests. This vulnerability can be, and usually is, mitigated by the use of a timestamp on tickets.

The other major drawback to the Kerberos concept is that its scalability is limited since the Kerberos server is communicated with every time access to a resource is requested. The more workstations and resources an organization has on its network the greater its network traffic, because each request to access a network resource will generate multiple exchanges. As the network grows, so too does the number of requests to the Kerberos server.

In addition, a network could grow to the point where a single server could not handle all of the requests to access network resources. The server would eventually become overwhelmed with requests. At that point, an organization would either have to get a greater capacity server or limit the size of its network. Ultimately, in fact, the organization would reach a point where its server capacity could no longer grow. Therefore, there is a limit on how large a Kerberos-based network can grow.

As a result of this lack of scalability, Kerberos is not a feasible authentication solution for a very large network such as the Internet. Using a PKI with digital certificates is much more scalable and therefore better suited for the Internet.

5

Encryption on the World Wide Web

The World Wide Web (WWW)

Chapter 3 covers the theories and principles behind cyptosystems and encryption. This chapter provides examples of the practical application of encryption. We have already discussed how DES is employed by most ATM and POS networks to encrypt information for transit on the network. To provide confidentiality, critical portions of each transaction are encrypted with DES at the ATM machine or POS terminal prior to the transaction being transmitted to the financial institution.

Another area where encryption has been widely deployed is on the Internet or the Web as it has come to be known. Much of the Internet's success and popularity lies in the fact that it is an open global network. At the same time, the fact that it is open and global makes it not very secure. The unique nature of the Internet makes exchanging information and transacting business over it inherently dangerous. The faceless, voiceless, unknown entities and individuals that share the Internet may or may not be who or what they profess to be. In addition, because the Internet is a global network, it does not recognize national borders and legal jurisdictions. As a result, the transacting parties may not be where they say they are and may not be subject to the same laws or regulations.

As stated in earlier chapters, for the exchange of information and for commerce to be secure on any network, especially the Internet, a system or process must be put in place that satisfies requirements for confidentiality, access control, authentication, integrity, and nonrepudiation. These requirements are achieved on the Web through the use of encryption and by employing digital signature technology. There are many examples on the Web of the practical application of encryption. One of the most important is the SSL protocol.

Secure Sockets Layer

SSL was developed by Netscape to provide security when transmitting information on the Internet. Netscape recognized the need to develop a process that would ensure confidentiality when entering and transmitting information on the Web. Without such a process very few individuals would feel comfortable entering information like credit card numbers on a Web site. Netscape recognized that e-commerce on the Web would never get off the ground without consumer confidence. As a result, SSL was developed to address the security needs of Web surfers.

It is somewhat ironic that we require such a high level of security for transactions on the Web. Most knowledgeable individuals would never enter their Visa or Mastercard number on a site that did not employ SSL for fear of having the information intercepted. However, those same individuals would not hesitate to give that same information over the phone to an unknown person when ordering flowers, nor would they fear giving their credit cards to a waiter at a restaurant. Consider that this involves handing a card over to someone you have never met who inevitably disappears for 10 minutes. Where is the security in that exchange? For some reason we hold transactions on the Web to a higher standard of security than we do most other types of transactions.

The risk that a credit card number will be stolen in transit on the Internet is very small. A greater risk is that the credit card number will be stolen from a system on which it is stored. That is precisely what happened to me: A while back I received an e-mail from my Internet service provider (ISP) informing me that a computer, which had been stolen from the ISP, may have contained credit card information for a number of its customers. The e-mail went on to state that it was possible that my credit card information was on the stolen machine. The company said that the file containing the credit card numbers was encrypted, so it did not believe that there was any real risk. Nevertheless, the firm said that it was advising its customers of this incident so they could take appropriate action. The original transaction with the ISP in which I gave the company my credit card information was not over the Internet. It was a traditional low-tech transaction. Like most companies, the ISP stored the user account information, including credit card numbers, in a database on a network. That is where the real risk lies.

SSL utilizes both asymmetric and symmetric key encryption to set up and transfer data in a secure mode over an unsecured network. When used with a browser client, SSL establishes a secure connection between the client browser and the server. Usually, it's the HTTP over SSL (HTTPS). It sets up an encrypted tunnel between a browser and a Web server over which data packets can travel. No one tapping into the connection between the browser and the server can decipher the information passing between the two. Integrity of the information is established by hashing algorithms. Confidentiality of the information is ensured with encryption. Figure 5.1 illustrates basically how the process works.

To set up an SSL session both sides exchange random numbers. The server sends its public key with a digital certificate signed by a recognized CA attesting to the authenticity of the sender's identity and binding the sender to the public key. The server also sends a session ID. The browser client creates a pre_master_secret key. The client browser encrypts the pre_master_secret key using the server's public key and transmits the encrypted pre_master_secret key to the server. Then both sides generate a session key using the pre_master_secret and random numbers.

The SSL session set-up begins with asymmetric encryption. The server presents the browser client with its public key, which the client uses to encrypt the pre_master_secret. However, once the client sends the encrypted pre_master_secret key back to the server, it employs a session key to establish a secure connection. The initial setup uses asymmetric encryption, but the two parties switch over to symmetric encryption. This is done because symmetric encryption creates much less overhead. Less overhead means better throughput and a faster response time. Asymmetric cryptosystems are much

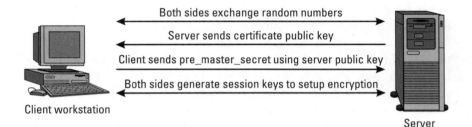

Both sides exchange random numbers

Server sends certificate public key

Client sends pre_master_secret using server public key

Both sides generate session keys to setup encryption

Client workstation

Server

Figure 5.1 SSL session handshake.

more CPU-intensive and would significantly slow the exchange of information. As a result, for spontaneous exchanges, asymmetric encryption is used initially to establish a secure connection and to authenticate identities (using digital certificates). Once identities are established and public keys are exchanged, the communicating entities switch to symmetric encryption for efficiency.

Even with the use of symmetric encryption, network throughput is significantly diminished with SSL. Cryptographic processing is extremely CPU-intensive. Web servers that would normally be able to handle hundreds of connections may only be able to handle a fraction of that when employing SSL. In 1999, *Internet Week* reported on a test of a Sun 450 server and the effects of SSL. At full capacity, the server could handle about 500 connections per second of normal HTTP traffic. However, the same server could only handle about three connections per second when the connections employed SSL.

The fact that SSL can have such a hindering effect on network performance has to be included in any capacity planning for e-commerce sites. There are SSL accelerators available that can enhance the performance of Web servers that employ SSL. Products from Hewlett-Packard, Compaq, nCipher, and others offer solutions that speed up the cryptographic processing. Usually, these products are separate boxes that interface with a server and off-load the SSL process from the server's CPU. They can also take the form of accelerator boards that are installed in the server.

Secure HTTP (SHTTP)

An alternative to HTTPS is secure HTTP (SHTTP). SHTTP is an extension of the HTTP protocol developed by Enterprise Integration Technologies. SHTTP is similar in function to HTTPS in that it is designed to secure transactions and messages on the Web. There are, however, several differences: SSL is connection-oriented and operates at the transport level. SSL creates a secure connection over which transactions are transmitted. SHTTP, on the other hand, is transaction-oriented and operates at the application level. Each individual message is encrypted to be transmitted securely. No secure pipe is established between the parties. SSL can be used for other TCP/IP protocols such as FTP and TELNET. SHTTP is specifically designed for HTTP and not for other protocols. HTTPS enjoys wide acceptance, while SHTTP's use is very limited. In fact, not all Web browsers support SHTTP.

Meanwhile, both Netscape Navigator and Internet Explorer support HTTPS. Most Web server software supports HTTPS, and most e-commerce Web sites use the protocol when obtaining confidential user information. The server is usually authenticated to the client through a digital certificate. The strength of the encryption employed can be set by the server but is usually chosen based on the capability of the client browser. Until relatively recently, there were two types of encryption employed in browsers, depending on whether the browser would be sold in the United States or overseas. The overseas version used weak encryption, while the domestic version used strong encryption. When one refers to weak encryption with SSL and browsers, it usually means 40-bit or 56-bit encryption. Strong encryption refers to 128-bit encryption. The difference in strength between 40-bit encryption and 128-bit encryption is not just 88 bits. In other words, 128-bit encryption is not just 88 times stronger than 40-bit encryption. In fact, 128-bit encryption is more than 300,000,000,000,000,000,000,000,000 times stronger than 40-bit encryption.

Browsers used to employ two different strengths of encryption because of federal regulations. There were export restrictions on most software, hardware or firmware that included encryption technology. While the export restrictions have been relaxed somewhat, there are still significant rules in place. To export their browsers, companies such as Microsoft and Netscape had to offer versions of their software that employed weak encryption. Even with the recent changes to U.S. laws regulating the export of cryptographic technology many of the browsers installed today use weak encryption.

In the past, the domestic version of Netscape's Navigator was capable of strong encryption, while its export version was only capable of weak encryption. Microsoft did not really make any distinction between the domestic or export versions of Internet Explorer. Internet Explorer by default was set to weak encryption; it was necessary to load a patch to set it to strong encryption.

Web server software can also be set to use 40-bit or 128-bit encryption. A Web server can be configured to reject browser clients that use a browser set for weak encryption. Web servers can also be configured for strong encryption but still be able to accept browsers that use weak encryption. Therefore, there is really no reason to configure the Web server software to default to 40-bit encryption.

There are several ways to tell if a site uses encryption and the strength of the encryption employed. The things to look for vary depending on whether you are using Netscape's Navigator or Microsoft's Internet Explorer and which version of either software you are using.

Microsoft's Internet Explorer

Figure 5.2 illustrates a Web page employing SSL with Internet Explorer 5.0 (IE5). The first indication of SSL is that the URL is preceded by HTTPS instead of the normal HTTP. The example depicts a fictitious Internet banking system offered by Any Bank Corporation. The digital certificate is real, but the name of the financial institution has been changed.

In addition to HTTPS being displayed in the URL, when encryption is employed there is also a closed lock at the bottom of the browser's screen on the right-hand side. I have circled the closed lock at the bottom of the screen. Normally, the lock is open, which is an indication that encryption is not employed.

Viewing Digital Certificates With Internet Explorer

Normally, to activate SSL on a Web server, a digital certificate must be installed. A digital certificate is generally obtained from a known CA and installed on the Web server. When visiting a Web site that employs encryption, it is possible to view information on the server's digital certificate. To

Figure 5.2   IE5 employing SSL.

view this information with Internet Explorer, simply click on File and then Properties. When you click on the Properties option the properties window pops up.

Figure 5.3 illustrates the properties pop-up window. Viewing the Properties window, we can see that the connection uses SSL 3.0 and RC4 with 128 bit encryption for strong (High) encryption. As you will recall from Chapter 3, RC4 is a symmetric stream cipher that uses a variable size key. When used with a key of 128 bits it can be very effective. The connection is also using RSA with 1,024-bit exchange.

More detailed information can be obtained on the digital certificate by clicking on the certificate button on the properties window. This is illustrated in Figure 5.4.

By clicking on the details tab, information can be obtained on the serial number of the certificate, the issuer, and the subject. It is also possible to view the public key for the certificate. Looking at Figure 5.4 we can see that the third field listed is the signature algorithm. In this case it is RSA's MD5.

As you may recall from Chapter 3, MD5 is used to ensure that the message has not been altered in transit. MD5 creates a unique 128-bit message

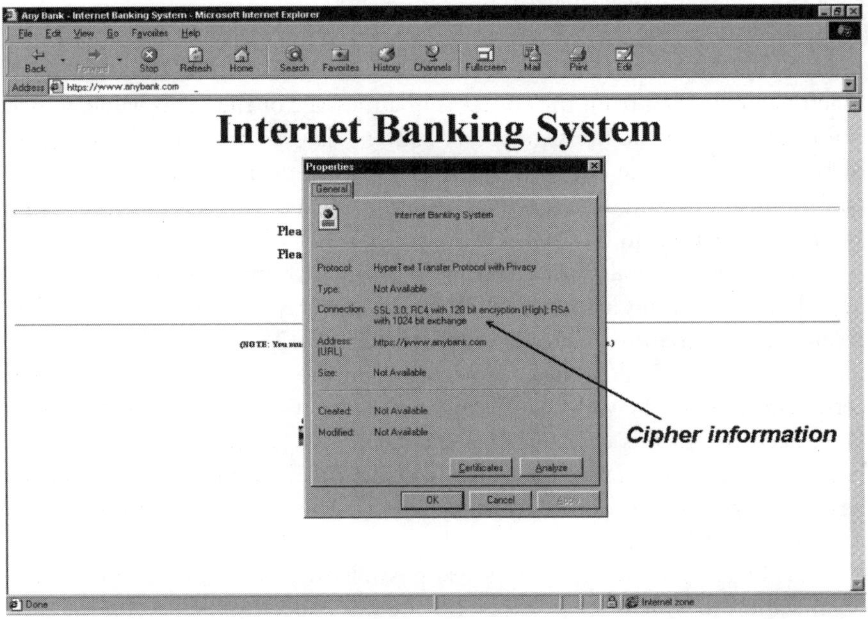

Figure 5.3 IE5 cipher information.

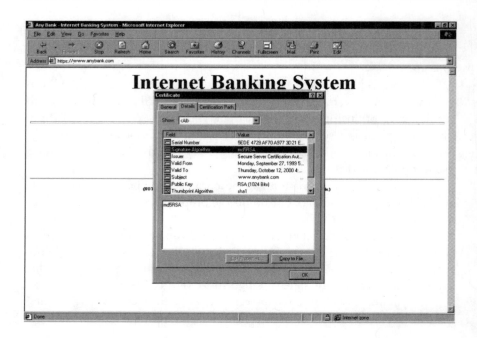

Figure 5.4 IE5 signature algorithm.

digest value derived from the contents of a message or file. This value, which is a fingerprint of the message or file content, is used to verify the integrity of the message or file content. MD5 is used to ensure the integrity of the communication, and RC4 is used to establish a secure connection using symmetric encryption.

The certificate also uses SHA-1 to create a thumbprint for the public key. As discussed in Chapter 3, SHA-1 is a one-way hash algorithm used to create digital signatures. SHA-1 is similar to the MD4 and MD5 algorithms.

As Figure 5.5 illustrates, information on the issuer (CA) of the digital certificate can also be viewed. We can see that certificate was issued by RSA Data Security. In this case the RSA certificate was issued through VeriSign. Figure 5.5 also reveals that the public key algorithm employed for the initial key exchange was the RSA algorithm. The RSA asymmetric cryptosystem is used for the exchange of public keys.

As Figure 5.6 illustrates, it is also possible to obtain information on the organization to which the digital certificate was issued by clicking on the subject line. In this example we can see that the digital certificate was issued to Any Bank Corporation in San Francisco.

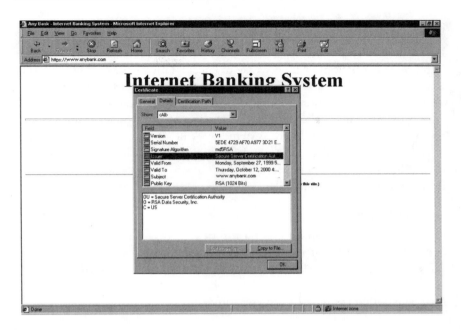

Figure 5.5 IE5 certificate authority.

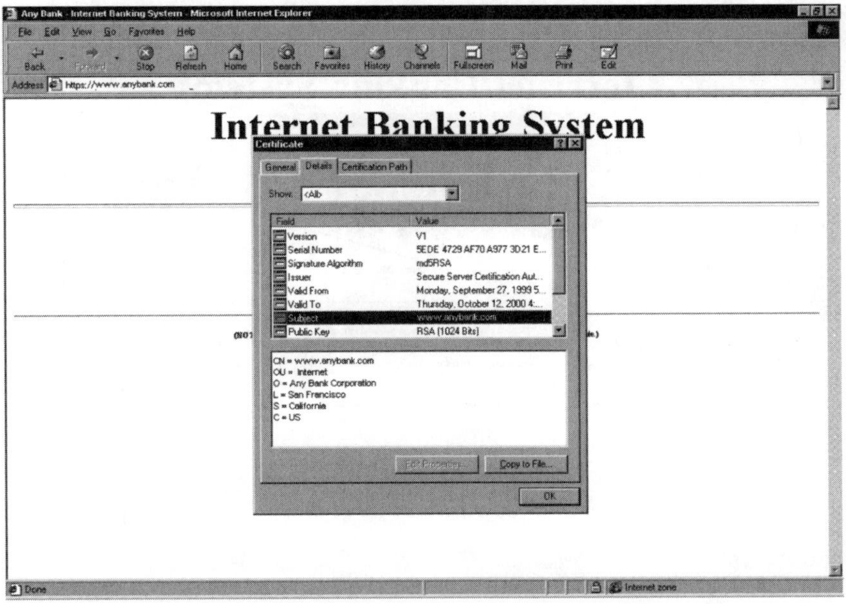

Figure 5.6 IE5 certificate owner.

Viewing the Encryption Strength of IE5

If you don't already know the encryption strength for which your Internet Explorer is configured, it is very easy to check. This works for both Internet Explore 4.X (IE4) and IE5. Chances are that if you are using IE4 then you are using weak encryption. Figure 5.7, based on IE5, illustrates how to check your browser: Simply click on Help at the top of the browser and then click on About Internet Explorer. A window will pop up that lists, among other things, the cipher strength. In Figure 5.7, the cipher strength is set to 128 bits or strong encryption. This is the strength of encryption that the browser is configured to handle.

View CAs With IE5

One of the most important criteria for a CA is that the CA must be a recognized entity and that its public key must be widely known. One of the ways in which this is achieved is by configuring software and hardware to recognize a prescribed group of CAs. This is precisely what Microsoft and Netscape both do with their browser software.

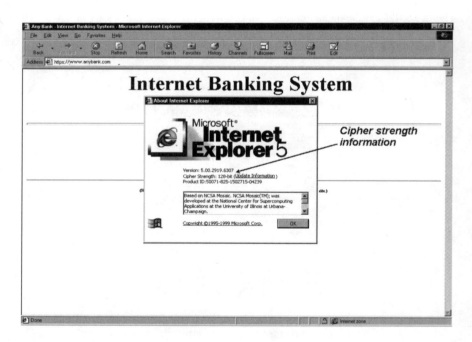

Figure 5.7 Viewing the browser's encryption strength. (Microsoft IE5 screen shot reprinted by permission of Microsoft Corporation.)

Figures 5.8 and 5.9 illustrate how to view the preconfigured CAs in IE5. The information is available under Tools/Internet Options. To view the recognized CAs click on the certificates button. Figure 5.9 displays CAs listed under the Trusted Root Certification Authorities tab. There are several digital certificate levels listed for the various CAs.

Information can also be obtained about the certificates and the CAs. Figure 5.10 shows that the certificate is issued by Versign and displays the level of guarantee provided by the certificate. Different certificates have different levels of guarantee. Information on the signature algorithm, hashing algorithm, public key algorithm, and even proposed usage can be obtained by clicking on the details tab (Figure 5.11).

As discussed in Chapter 3, a CA is a public or private entity that seeks to fill the need for a trusted third party in e-commerce. The CA issues digital certificates that vouch for the identities of those to whom the certificates are issued. For this process to be secure, the CA's public key must be well-known, and the CA's public key must be widely recognized. A digital certificate signed by a CA is worthless if you do not know the CA's public key, or you have no independent means of verifying that the public key provided is

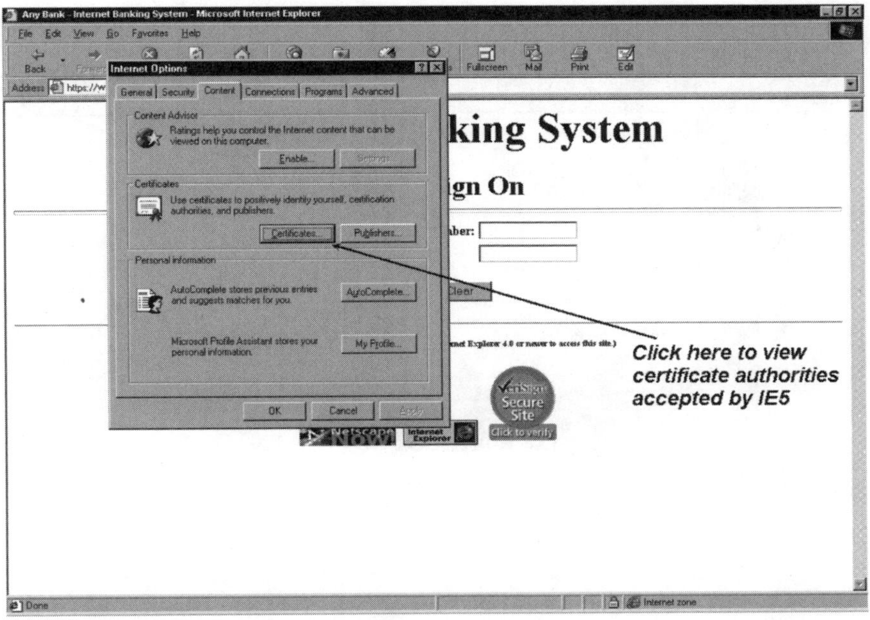

Figure 5.8   IE5-recognized CAs.

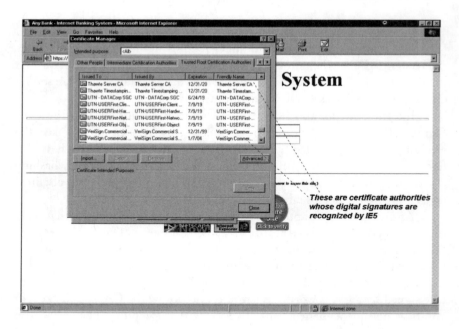

Figure 5.9 IE5-recognized CAs.

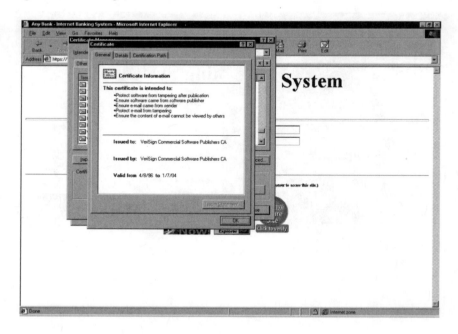

Figure 5.10 Certificate information.

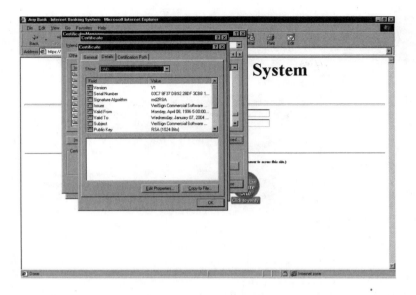

Figure 5.11 Certificate information.

in fact bound to the CA. For that reason, a CA's public key needs to be easily accessible and verifiable.

Figure 5.12 is an example of a digital certificate that is signed by an unknown CA. When I say "unknown" I mean that the software, in this case IE5, does not recognize the digital signature or public key of the CA that signed the digital certificate. In this example the digital certificate is installed on and signed by the Chaos Computer Club (CCC). The signature is unrecognized by IE5 because the CCC is not listed in Figure 5.9 as one of the recognized CAs.

Figure 5.12 illustrates the security alert message that IE5 provides when it encounters a certificate signed by an unknown CA. The message in the pop-up window states that the browser does not recognize or "trust" the CA. Basically, IE5 is asking, "Do you really want to trust this site?" Clicking on view certificate reveals that the certificate was issued to and by the same entity, in this case the CCC. This is depicted in Figure 5.13. Basically, the CCC uses a self-certifying certificate on their server.

Netscape Navigator

Since Netscape was the original developer of SSL it is only logical that Netscape's Navigator would support the protocol. IE5 and Navigator are

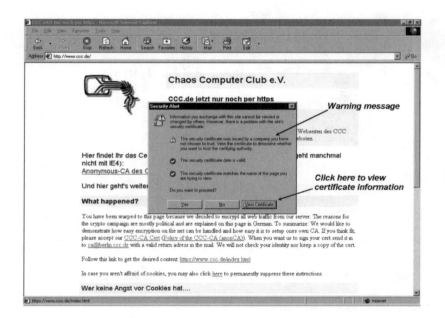

Figure 5.12 Unrecognized certification authority. (*Source:* The CCC. Reprinted with permission.)

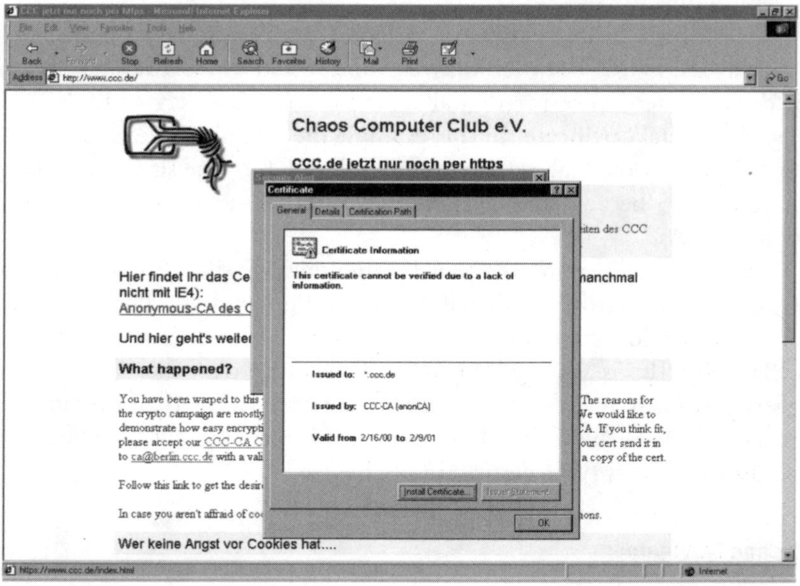

Figure 5.13 Self-signed certificate. (*Source:* The CCC. Reprinted with permission.)

similar in the way that they handle SSL in that the URL will be preceded by HTTPS instead of the normal HTTP. In addition, when encryption is employed, there is a closed lock at the bottom of the browser's screen on the left-hand side. Figure 5.14 depicts the Navigator browser when connected to the fictitious Any Bank Internet banking system. I have circled the closed lock at the bottom of the screen. Normally, the lock is open, which is an indication that encryption is not employed.

Just as with Internet Explorer, information on a server's digital certificate can be obtained using Navigator. To view the information, click on the Security button, identified by the icon of a lock, in the Navigator toolbar at the top of the browser. Figure 5.15 depicts the security information pop-up window.

Figure 5.16 is an example of the type of information that can by viewed by clicking on the Open Page Info button on the security pop-up window. This screen provides you with information on URL, the encryption strength, the subject, and the issuer of the digital certificate. The bottom of the depicted page states that the page uses high-grade encryption RC4 with a 128-bit key. In addition, it lists the owner of the certificate as Any Bank Corporation and the issuer as RSA Data Security. Similar information can be obtained by clicking on the View Certificate button on the security pop-up

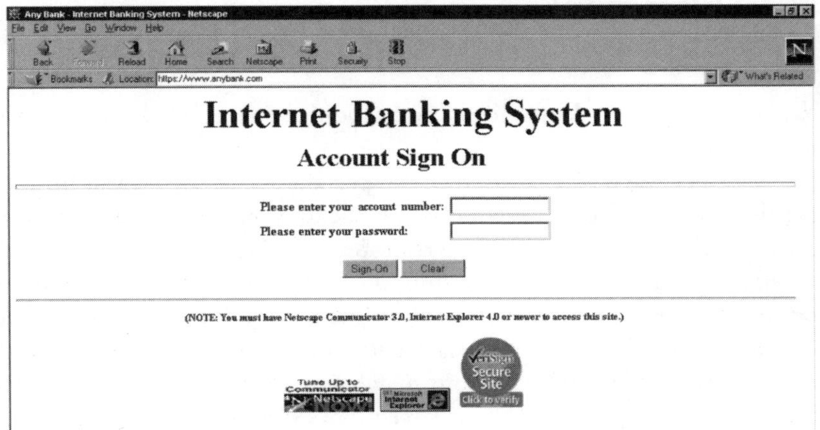

Figure 5.14 Netscape Navigator employing SSL. (Netscape Communicator browser window; © 1999, Netscape Communications Corporation. Used with permission.)

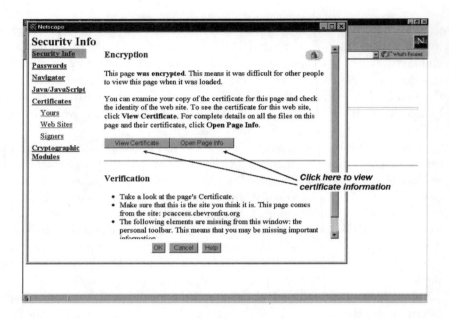

Figure 5.15 Viewing certificate information with Navigator. (Netscape Communicator browser window; © 1999, Netscape Communications Corporation. Used with permission.)

window. Figure 5.17 depicts the information obtained by clicking on that button.

With Netscape Navigator, the recognized CAs can be viewed from the security information pop-up window by clicking on the Signers option on the left-hand side just under the Certificates link. Figure 5.18 illustrates the information that is displayed regarding the recognized CAs. There is almost no difference between the CAs loaded in Internet Explorer and those loaded in Navigator. The only difference is between older and newer versions of the browser software. The older versions may have certificates that have expired, while the more recent versions may have new CAs and certificates.

Authenticode Certificates

Another example of how digital certificates are employed on the Web is Authenticode certificates. An Authenticode certificate is a security feature in Microsoft Internet Explorer that provides the end user with a high level of confidence of the source and authenticity of software components that are

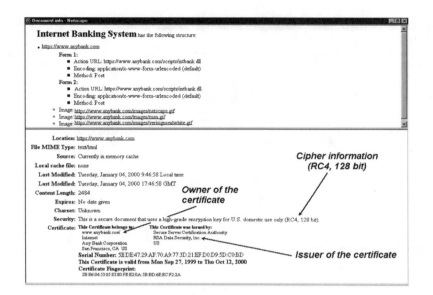

Figure 5.16 Viewing certificate information with Navigator. (Netscape Communicator browser window; © 1999, Netscape Communications Corporation. Used with permission.)

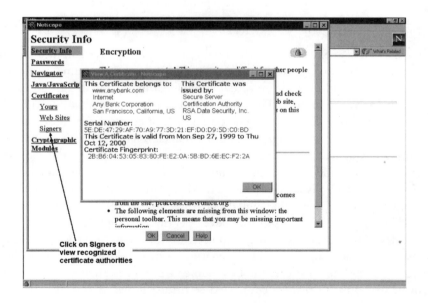

Figure 5.17 CAs recognized by Navigator. (Netscape Communicator browser window; © 1999, Netscape Communications Corporation. Used with permission.)

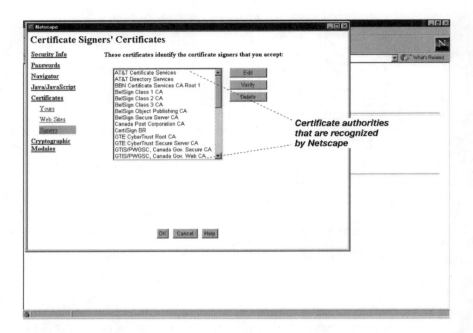

Figure 5.18 CAs recognized by Navigator. (Netscape Communicator browser window; © 1999, Netscape Communications Corporation. Used with permission.)

downloaded over the Internet. Essentially, Internet Explorer employs digital signature technology to authenticate the source of the program. Authenticode alerts an end user before actually downloading executable files from a Web site onto a computer. The purpose is to provide individuals downloading software from the Web with a certain level of comfort that they are not installing Trojan horse programs or other malicious code on their systems. If a program is signed, Authenticode presents the certificate so that the end user knows that the code has not been tampered with and so that the end user can see the code's publisher and the CA. Microsoft's Authenticode supports strong 128-bit cryptographic digital signatures and X.509 digital certificates.

The process entails a software developer digitally signing .exe, .cab, and .ocx files. The file signing assures end users of the source of the software that they are downloading. The digital signature is then endorsed through a digital certificate. The certificate can be obtained from a CA, such as VeriSign or can be issued by a privately controlled certificate server. A certificate issued by a privately controlled certificate server does not carry the same authority as one issued by a recognized CA. When a digital signature is accompanied by a digital certificate issued by a known CA, the end user is assured of the integrity of the software developer's signature and, therefore, of the integrity of software that is downloaded.

Figure 5.19 illustrates the Authenticode warning message that pops up when downloading programs using Internet Explorer. In Figure 5.19, the window shows that the program that Internet Explorer wants to download is signed by Microsoft Corporation and that Microsoft's signature is authenticated by VeriSign. In this example, VeriSign is acting as the CA.

Internet Explorer checks the information in the certificate when downloading software and ensures that the certificate is signed by a recognized CA and that the certificate is still valid. If the CA is not recognized or if the certificate has expired, Internet Explorer displays a warning message.

Downloading a Program With an Invalid Certificate

Figure 5.20 is an example of the security warning message that displays when a user attempts to download a program that does not contain a valid Authenticode signature or a digital certificate from a recognized CA. This tells the end user downloading the program that the program does not contain a certificate that verifies that the software program is genuine. As a result, the end

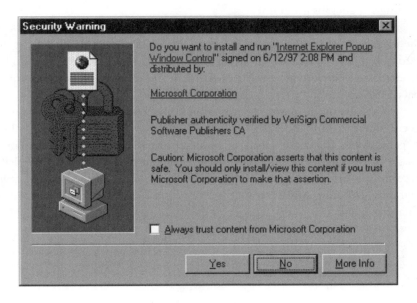

Figure 5.19 Authenticode. (Screen shot reprinted by permission from Microsoft Corporation.)

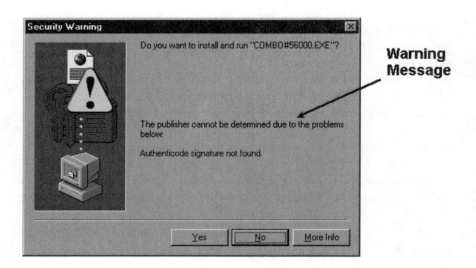

Figure 5.20   Authenticode. (Screen shot reprinted by permission from Microsoft Corporation.)

user should be careful before proceeding because he or she could be downloading a malicious program.

In Figure 5.20, Internet Explorer warns that it cannot authenticate the identity of the source of the program, either because the signature is not recognized or because there is no signature. In other words, the program has a certificate that cannot be verified. As such, the software represent a potential danger to the end user's computer and network.

The custom of signing programs or applets is not yet universally practiced. However, it is another good example of how cryptographic technology in general and digital signature technology in particular is being employed on the Web. Digital certificates and digital signature technology are quickly becoming a ubiquitous part of the WWW. Other examples of how cryptography is being applied on networks, such as VPNs, are discussed in Chapters 6 and 11.

6

E-Mail

In 1998, a *Computerworld* reader poll showed that the volume of e-mail received by users had increased by more than 58% over the 1997 volume: The survey indicated that users on average received 24 messages per day, compared with 14 messages per day for the previous year. The poll also indicated that in 1998 users sent on average about 11 messages per day, compared with eight e-mail messages per day for the previous year. Also in 1998, the *Electronic Mail & Messaging Systems* newsletter reported that the number of e-mail accounts was growing at an annualized rate of 45% and that the number of e-mail accounts could be expected to reach 400,000,000 in 1999. More recently, *Computerworld* reported that the Bureau of Business Practices is predicting that on-line users will receive more than seven *trillion* e-mail messages in 2000.

These statistics underscore the fact that e-mail is becoming as common a medium for communication as the telephone. As a result, an organization needs to factor e-mail into any security measures put into place. The management and monitoring of e-mail are becoming increasingly important to organizations. Chapter 14 discusses the policies and procedures that need to be put into place to address e-mail issues. This chapter discusses some of the more "technical" aspects of e-mail.

E-Mail Issues

The issues associated with e-mail go far beyond the problem of getting a message from one point to another. When discussing e-mail, one needs to take into consideration issues associated with the sender, the recipient, the medium, and the effect the process can have on the network.

As a sender and a recipient of e-mail you must be concerned about the disclosure of sensitive or proprietary information, either in transit or in storage. You also have to be concerned about the modification of information during transit. In addition, the identification process is a critical issue for all users of e-mail. Recipients of e-mail should be concerned about the authentication of a sender's identity. E-mail users need to be concerned about someone counterfeiting their identity, and some may actually be concerned about obscuring their identify, out of fear of reprisal or with malicious intent when sending e-mail. Finally, there is the concern of e-mail as a weapon and the effects it can have on an organization's users and network. Whether an organization is the victim of a straightforward SPAM attack or some redirect/spoofing process, the effects can be disabling. E-mail has also been proven to be a most effective delivery system for viruses.

As with most aspects of information and network security, cryptography plays a crucial role in e-mail security. We will begin with a discussion of what constitutes secure e-mail and the various standards that are being developed to achieve it.

E-Mail Security

The most important thing to remember about standard e-mail is that it is very unsecure. E-mail is almost always vulnerable to disclosure in one way or another. Very often, e-mail by necessity must traverse many networks to reach its destination. During transit, an e-mail message may pass through many mail servers. As a result, it is vulnerable to interception, replication, disclosure, or modification anywhere along its prescribed path. It can be copied and stored to be retrieved at a later date. In fact, each mail server an e-mail message passes through may be making a copy of the message before it is forwarded. Whether you use your corporation's e-mail system or an e-mail account provided by an ISP, your e-mail messages reside on an e-mail server. Even if you download your e-mail to your local disk drive, those messages probably have already been backed up and stored on some other media. If your corporation uses an e-mail portal to the Internet, then your e-mails are being copied there before being forwarded onto the appropriate Internet address. The point that I'm trying to make is that if you think your e-mail is secure and confidential, then you are greatly mistaken.

In addition to disclosure, e-mail messages are vulnerable to alteration. Anywhere along the path, an e-mail message can be intercepted and modified before being forwarded. Common e-mail provides no method of detecting messages that have been modified in transit. Messages that have been copied and stored can also be modified and retransmitted at a later time.

Another vulnerability lies in the fact that e-mail identities are very easy to forge. With common e-mail, there is no built-in process to ensure that the sender of a message is who he or she claims to be. E-mail headers are easy enough to spoof, and most individuals do not know what to look for when receiving an e-mail.

One solution to these problems is to use secure e-mail. The basic requirements of secure e-mail are described as follows:

- *Nondisclosure of the contents of the e-mail message:* This is usually achieved by employing some encryption technology.

- *Message integrity:* In other words, secure e-mail ensures that the message has not been altered during transit and provides a method to certify the message's integrity. This is usually achieved by employing some hashing or message digest algorithm.

- *Verification of sender:* Secure e-mail provides some method to ensure the identity of the sender with a high degree of confidence. This is usually achieved by employing digital signature technology.

- *Verification of recipient:* This can be achieved by employing public key encryption.

The following sections offer a very brief overview of just some of the options available for secure e-mail. Some are more popular than others. In fact, some are downright obscure. Most use encryption of some kind to varying degrees to provide message confidentiality. They also use different methods to provide sender authentication. Some use an informal process, while others depend on a more formal hierarchy that does not exist yet and may never exist.

Secure E-Mail Protocols

When it comes to secure e-mail standards there is no lack of standards. In fact, that is the problem. There are several competing standards and products from which you can choose. Some of the standards and products that are available are listed as follows:

- PGP;
- PEM;
- Secure multipurpose Internet mail extension (MIME) (S/MIME);
- MIME object security service (MOSS);
- Message security protocol (MSP).

These competing standards and products are one of the primary reasons that secure e-mail has not been widely implemented. The standards are not interoperable. If you use PGP to send someone a secure e-mail, but the recipient employs S/MIME then the recipient will not be able to open and read the message, let alone authenticate the sender of the message.

Pretty Good Privacy (PGP)

PGP is an encryption program that was developed by Phil Zimmerman in the early 1990s. It can be used to encrypt not only e-mail but also files. There is even a special version of PGP available for encrypting telephone conversations. There is also a commercial PGP VPN client available from Network Associates, which is advertised as being fully IPSec compliant and supporting X.509 digital certificates.

Basically, Zimmerman's idea behind PGP was to offer encryption capabilities to the masses. When Zimmerman made the PGP program available free of charge on the Internet for anyone to download, he got into a great deal of trouble with the U.S. government for violating restrictions on the export of encryption technology. For a while, it appeared that the government was going to press its case against Zimmerman, but reason eventually prevailed and an agreement was reached.

There was also some trouble in that the earlier version of PGP used proprietary technology owned by RSA. As a result, later versions had to be modified so that the RSA copyright was not affected, and some earlier versions of PGP may not be compatible with the later versions.

PGP uses public key cryptography to ensure confidentiality. It also uses digital signatures to authenticate the sender's identity, ensure message integrity, and provide nonrepudiation. In addition, PGP can be used to encrypt files on storage media to ensure confidentiality of stored files.

Network Associates markets PGP. It is available for purchase, but in keeping with Zimmerman's original intent, PGP is also available as freeware. It can be downloaded at a number of sites. One of the best resources for PGP is the MIT's Web site (www.mit.edu). You can download PGP at the URL web.mit.edu/network/pgp.html. Figure 6.1 illustrates the MIT PGP distribution Web page. The MIT Web site is also a great resource for information related to PGP. It provides links to other resources as well; one of those links is to a PGP key ring. Another resource is the international PGP page at www.pgpi.com.

PGP employs a combination of symmetric and asymmetric encryption to speed up the encryption process. As discussed in Chapter 3, asymmetric is CPU-intensive. As a result, it could place a substantial burden on many PCs. To avoid this, PGP was designed to encrypt and decrypt a message with symmetric key encryption but to use asymmetric key encryption to encrypt the key that was used to encrypt the message using symmetric key encryption.

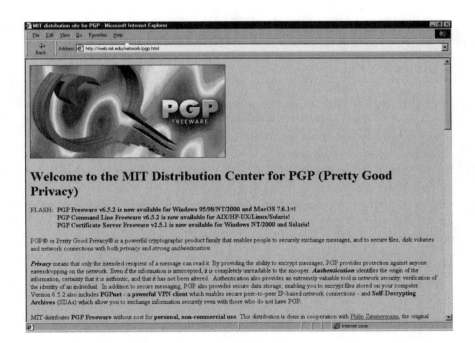

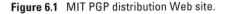

Figure 6.1 MIT PGP distribution Web site.

The process works something like this: Alice wants to send Bob an encrypted message; Alice already knows Bob's public key. Alice encrypts her message using CAST, tripleDES (3DES), or IDEA. She then encrypts the key used to encrypt the message using either the RSA or Diffie-Hellman algorithm. She can also digitally sign the message using RSA and her private key. If Diffie-Hellman is employed then she would need to use some other mechanism, such as DSS, to sign the message.

When Bob receives the message, he verifies the signature using Alice's public key, assuming the message is signed. This also assumes that Bob has access to Alice's public key. Then using his private key, he decrypts the key that was encrypted by Alice using his public key. This is the key that Alice used to encrypt the message using a symmetric key algorithm such as CAST, 3DES, or IDEA. With that key, Bob decrypts and reads the original message. As with most encryption, for the encryption and decryption process to work the decryption must be done in reverse order of the encryption. Think of it in terms of layers: The last layer on has to be the first layer off; otherwise the process does not work.

PGP relies upon an informal web of trust for public key authentication. The web of trust consists of the key rings that are maintained by various organizations. The key rings are postings of the public keys that belong to individual PGP users. If you need to authenticate the public key used to digitally sign a PGP message, you can go to a key ring to verify the sender's public key.

Figure 6.2 shows the MIT PGP certificate server. This is a key ring Web site at which you can look up someone's public key or load in your own public key, so that it can be viewed by others. In Figure 6.2, I have entered my own name to search for my public key. Figure 6.3 illustrates the information that is returned by the search.

Figure 6.3 displays my public key. From this, someone can actually cut and paste my public key into his or her own database of public keys. They can use my public key to encrypt messages to me or to authenticate messages I have digitally signed. There is a version of PGP available for most every operating system. PGP also works with most every e-mail package.

Figures 6.4–6.6 illustrate using PGP with the e-mail program Eudora 4.0 from Qualcomm. In Figure 6.4 I've typed a message that I encrypted and signed by clicking on the buttons indicated in the example. The left-hand button depicts a locked envelope representative of an encrypted message. The button on the right is a quill representing a signed message.

Figure 6.5 shows the encrypted and signed message as it looks when it is received. If you already have the sender's public key loaded into your

Figure 6.2 The MIT PGP certificate server.

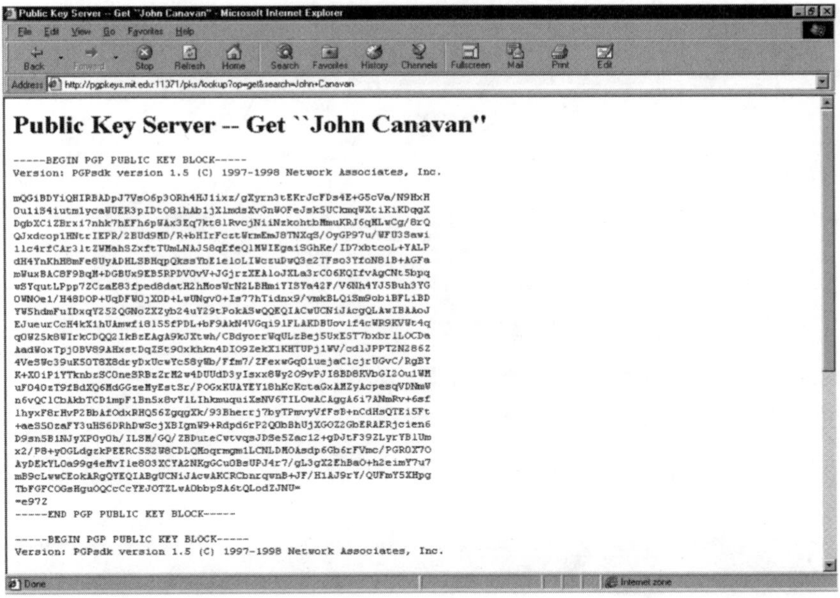

Figure 6.3 J. Canavan's public key.

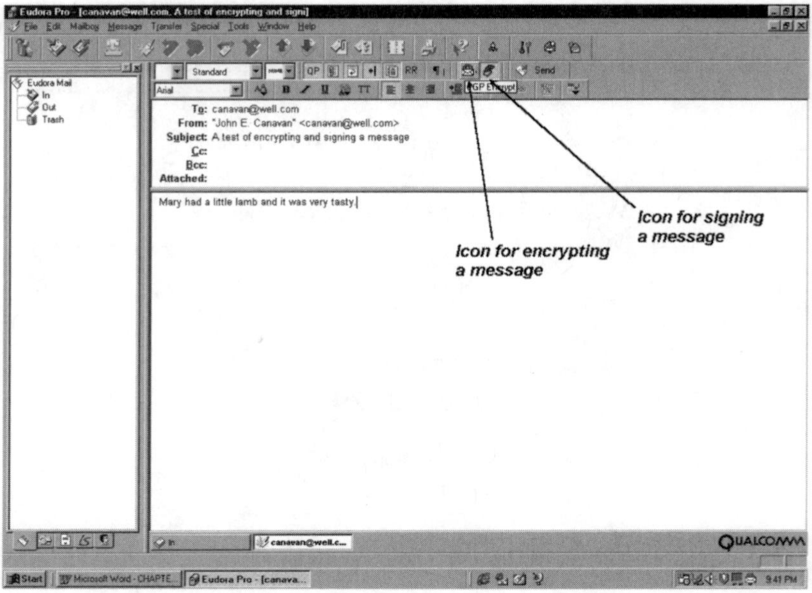

Figure 6.4 Eudora with PGP.

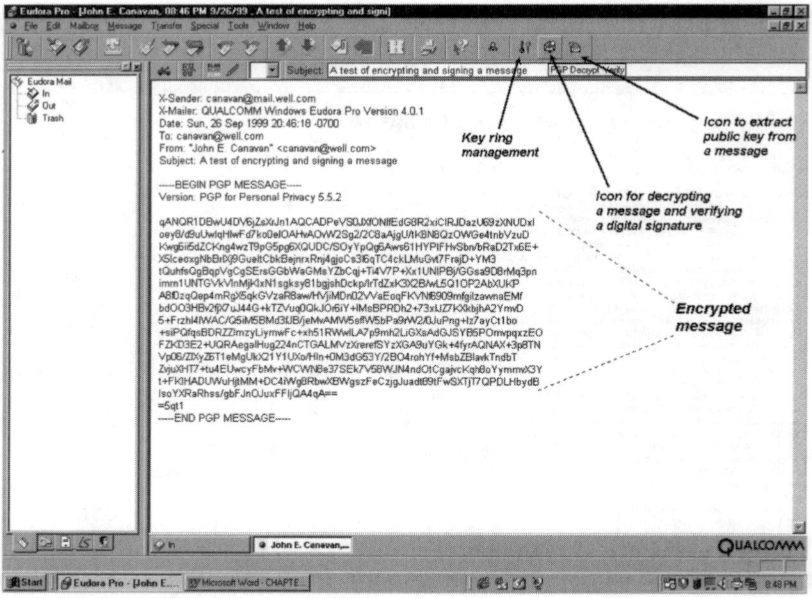

Figure 6.5 Encrypted and signed message.

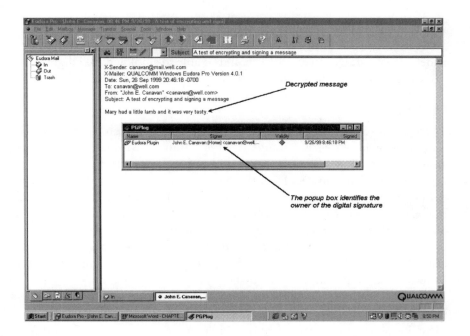

Figure 6.6 The results of the decrypt and digital signature verification process.

database, all you need to do is click on the decrypt verify button (indicated in Figure 6.5). This will decrypt the message and authenticate the sender by verifying the digital signature. If you do not have the public key of the sender, you can retrieve it from a key ring.

Figure 6.6 illustrates the results of the decrypt and digital signature verification process. In Figure 6.6, I have encrypted and signed a message and e-mailed it to myself. The PGP program is automatically able to verify that I signed the message. If my public key or the public key of an originator was not loaded in my database, then the signer would be listed as "unknown."

As stated previously, PGP can work with many e-mail programs. I could have just as easily used Exchange or Outlook to demonstrate PGP.

Privacy-Enhanced Mail (PEM)

PEM is a proposed standard that defines the use of public key encryption to secure e-mail for transmission on the Internet. The standard also provides for authentication. PEM uses a hierarchical organization for authentication and the distribution of keys. For a key to be valid it must be signed by a CA. The hierarchy needed for authentication does not yet exist. This lack of the hierarchy infrastructure is probably one of the main reasons PEM has not been widely deployed. However, PEM should be able to employ X.509 digital certificates for the purpose of authenticating the identity of the sender.

PGP Versus PEM

There are several major differences between PGP and PEM. First, PGP is a product, while PEM is a standard. In addition, PEM does not allow for anonymous messages. When a message is signed with PEM, the signature can be reviewed by anyone. Even those who cannot decrypt the message can determine the signer of the message. The PEM standard relies on a formal hierarchical public key system, which has yet to be implemented. PGP relies on a web of trust, a more informal process that utilizes key rings maintained by various organizations. For this reason, PGP is not well suited for commercial use. In fact, you may find that many corporate IT departments do not allow it to be loaded on company owned systems.

Secure MIME (S/MIME)

MIME is an extension of the original Internet e-mail protocol standard that specifies how messages must be formatted, so they can be exchanged between different e-mail systems. S/MIME is a standard proposed by RSA that describes a secure method of sending e-mail that uses the RSA encryption system. S/MIME is supported by Microsoft and Netscape in the latest versions of their Web browsers and has been endorsed by other vendors that make messaging products. RSA has proposed S/MIME as a standard to the Internet Engineering Task Force (IETF). An alternative to S/MIME is PGP/MIME, which has also been proposed as a standard.

In the example above, we reviewed how we could use Eudora and PGP for secure e-mail. PGP uses public key cryptography and an informal organization of key rings to provide message confidentiality, integrity, and sender authentication. S/MIME employs digital certificates with digital signatures for sender authentication. It also uses hashing to ensure message integrity and a combination of secret key (symmetric) and public key (asymmetric) encryption to ensure confidentiality.

We can illustrate how S/MIME functions by using Microsoft's Outlook Express. MS Outlook is designed to support S/MIME. The first step is to install a personal digital certificate in Outlook Express. A digital certificate is often called a digital ID. The two terms are synonymous. Installing the digital certificate is easily done by going to the "options" menu and clicking on the "security" tab. There you will find the option "get digital ID." The option is circled in Figure 6.7. From there Outlook Express will walk you through the process and even link you to the CAs that offer digital certificates. There are several from which to choose. Two of the more widely recognized CAs are Verisign (Figure 6.8) and Thawte (Figure 6.9). However, these are by no means the only choices.

From these sites, you can order a personal digital certificate for a nominal fee. CAs usually offer different levels or classes of certificates. The more work the CA puts into verifying the recipient's identity, the higher the class and therefore the higher the cost. In addition, the higher class certificates should provide a greater level of confidence in the identity of the individual to whom the certificate is was issued.

Figure 6.10 illustrates Outlook Express, which already has a digital certificate installed. Clicking on the "security" tab and "advanced settings," you can view the settings. The encryption algorithm listed is 3DES.

Figure 6.11 illustrates the available encryption algorithms. They are 3DES, DES, RC2 with 128-bit encryption, and RC2 with 40-bit encryption. Obviously, DES and RC2 are not the most secure algorithms, but they are better than having nothing at all.

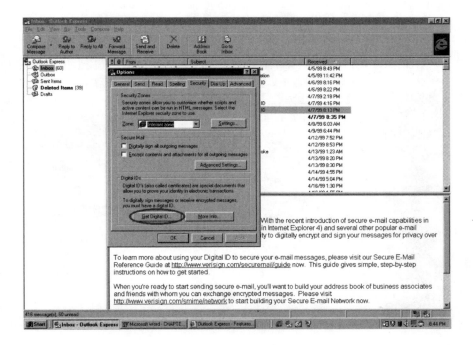

Figure 6.7 Outlook Express—Get Digital ID.

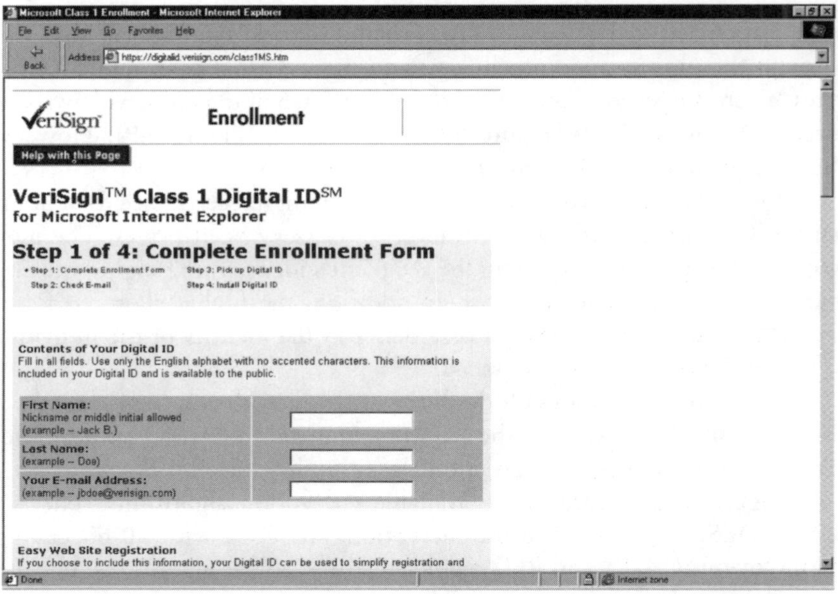

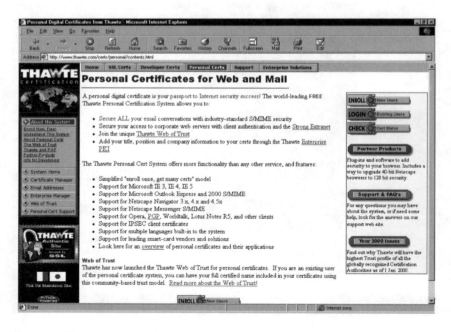

Figure 6.8 Verisign enrollment site. (Reprinted with permission from VeriSign, Inc.)

Figure 6.9 Thawte Web site. (*Source:* Thawte Corporation. Reprinted with permission.)

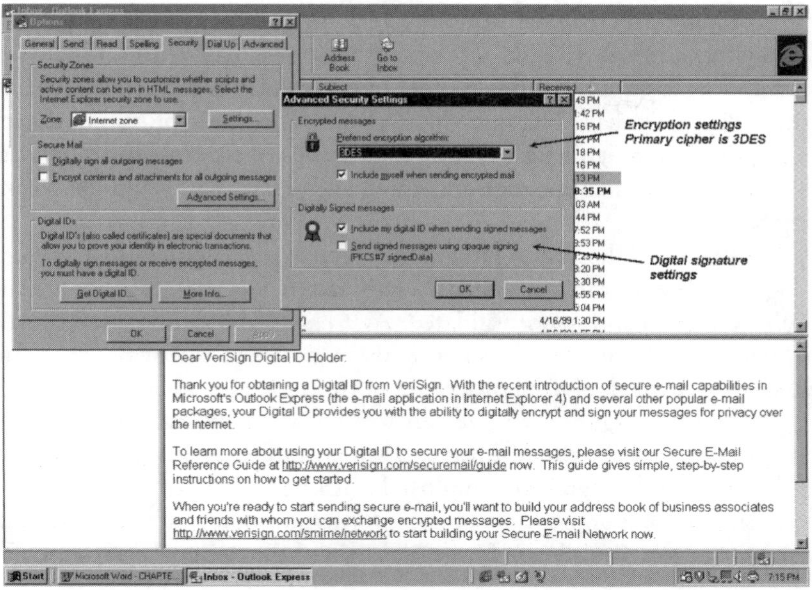

Figure 6.10 Outlook Express—Advanced security settings.

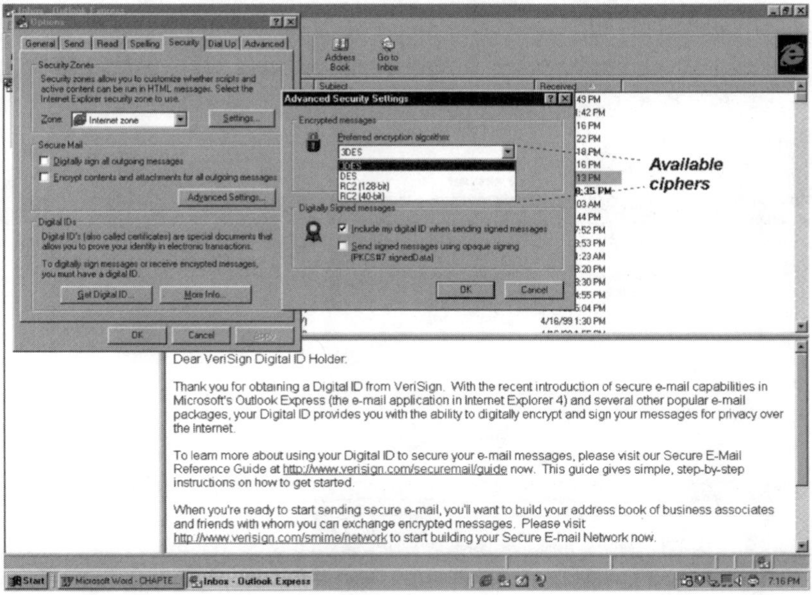

Figure 6.11 Outlook Express—available ciphers.

In Figure 6.11 you can see that Outlook gives you the option to send your digital certificate (digital ID) whenever you sign an e-mail. Figure 6.12 illustrates the Outlook Express toolbar options that are used to encrypt and digitally sign an e-mail. The right-hand option is for encrypting and the left-hand option is for signing a message. Figure 6.13 illustrates how to view the properties of an e-mail message encrypted and signed with Outlook Express using S/MIME.

Figure 6.14 illustrates viewing the general properties of a message. In Figure 6.14, we can see that the certificate is a class 1 certificate issued to John Canavan and is not validated. As a result, this is a low-level certificate, which does not provide much authentication of the owner's identity. Figure 6.15 shows the Detail properties of the digital certificate.

Looking at Figure 6.15, we can see that the certificate was issued by VeriSign and view the thumbprint and serial number for the certificate. We can also see that the algorithm employed is RSA 512-bit.

Figure 6.16 is an example of the information that can be viewed under the Advanced tab. In this case I have highlighted the Public Key option. This

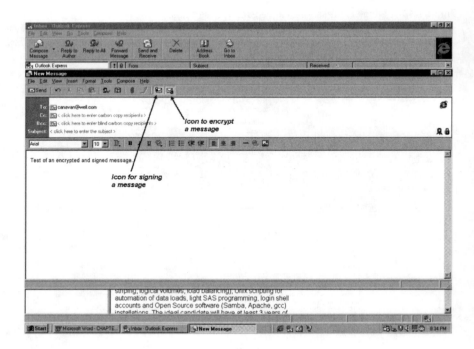

Figure 6.12 Outlook Express—icons to encrypt and sign.

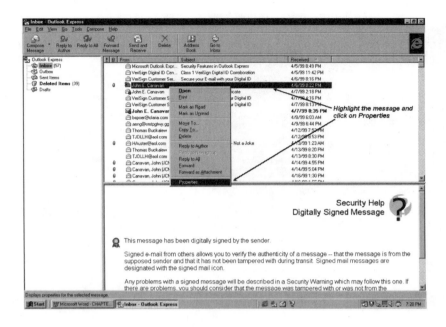

Figure 6.13 Outlook Express—message properties.

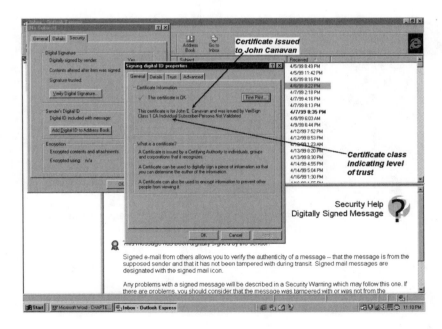

Figure 6.14 Outlook Express—certificate properties.

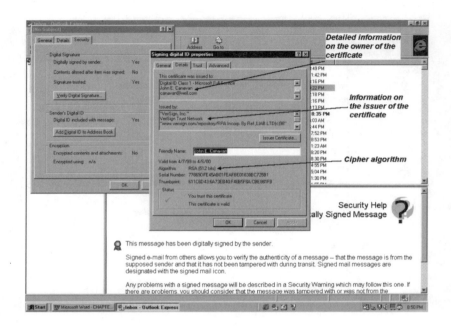

Figure 6.15 Outlook Express—certificate properties.

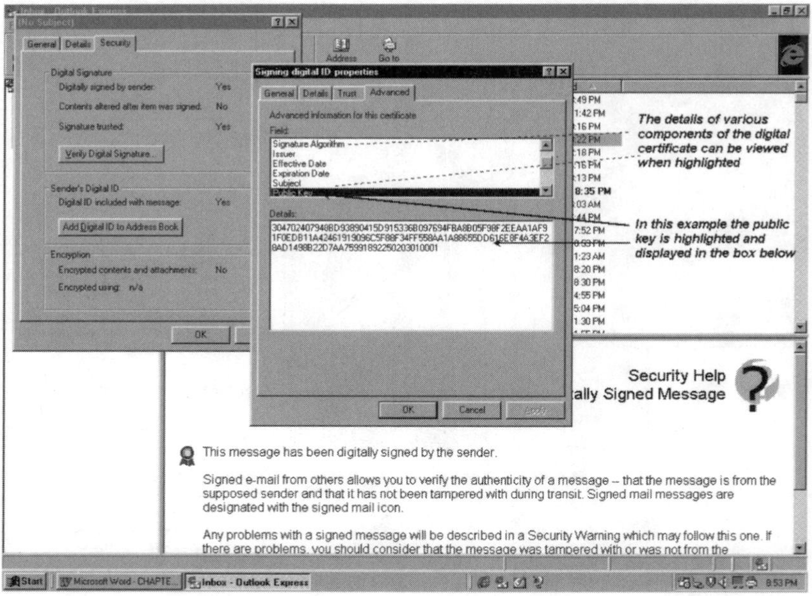

Figure 6.16 Outlook Express—certificate properties.

option displays my public key. As you recall, my public key can be used to encrypt messages, which only I can decrypt by using my private key.

MIME Object Security Services (MOSS)

MOSS is another secure e-mail option. MOSS is short for MIME Object Security Services. MOSS is derived from PEM and is similar to S/MIME in that it is a proposed Internet standard for providing security to MIME. MOSS depends on the existence of public/private key pairs to support its security services. Users must exchange public keys with those other users with whom they wish to exchange MOSS e-mail. Like most of the other protocols, MOSS relies upon digital signatures and encryption to provide authentication of the sender and message integrity and confidentiality.

MSP

MSP, which is used by the military in the Defense Message System, has signed receipt capability that provides nonrepudiation with proof of delivery. Unless you're in the military you most likely will not be exposed to this protocol.

Web-Based E-Mail Services

Many people use free Web-based e-mail services from companies such as Yahoo, Microsoft, or AOL. For example, Microsoft's Hotmail service has approximately 40 million subscribers. In general, Web-based e-mail services should be considered very unsecure. There have been numerous security breaches reported with these e-mail services.

In 1999, several vulnerabilities were discovered with Microsoft's Hotmail alone. One reported problem allowed potential hackers full access to e-mails stored on Hotmail. That same year, a similar vulnerability was reported with Network Solutions' free Web-based e-mail service. Another reported vulnerability involved the way Hotmail handled Javascript code. This vulnerability enabled hackers to present a bogus password entry screen. By doing so hackers could steal the passwords to accounts, thereby gaining full access to the accounts. While some Web-based e-mail service providers, such as Hushmail (Figure 6.17) and PrivacyX (Figure 6.18), offer the ability to transmit encrypted e-mail, you are still relying on the service provider to have adequate security controls.

As a rule, a corporation should not permit its employees to use free Web-based e-mail services for company business. In fact, they should restrict

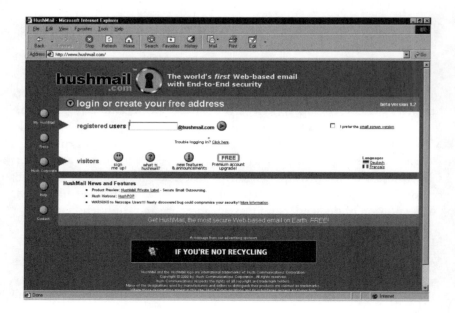

Figure 6.17 Hushmail.com. (*Source:* Hush Communications Corporation. Reprinted with permission.)

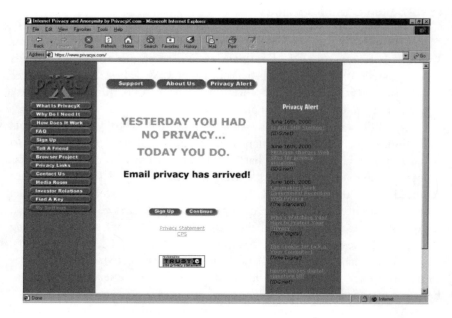

Figure 6.18 Privacyx. (*Source:* Privacyx.com Solutions Inc. Reprinted with permission.)

or monitor users who send or forward e-mail to these services. E-mail to these services should be filtered to ensure that sensitive or proprietary information is not being transmitted to what is potentially an open environment.

Security of Stored Messages

Generally, most discussions regarding e-mail security cover the security during the transmission of the e-mail and the authentication process. As we have seen, encryption is useful for ensuring confidentiality and integrity during transmission of a message and for authenticating the sender's identity. However, many people overlook the risks associated with stored e-mail. We have already discussed examples of Web-based e-mail services that have been compromised, with associated e-mail accounts exposed. However, even company e-mail is at risk to disclosure.

E-mail is certainly at risk to disclosure if it is stored on a centralized service. E-mail stored locally is somewhat more secure, but there may still be copies of messages stored on central servers. On more than one occasion, an e-mail message has come back to haunt its sender in a court of law. One famous case is an e-mail message sent by Bill Gates that included embarrassing information about Microsoft's business practices. This e-mail surfaced in the antitrust case brought against Microsoft. Even messages that have been deleted have been recovered to the consternation of the person who believed that he or she had deleted the message.

Some encryption packages, such as PGP, allow users to store files in an encrypted format. To decrypt the files requires entering in a password that the user assigns. However, even if e-mail is stored in an encrypted format, you can still be legally compelled to reveal the contents.

A company called Global Markets purports to offer a solution to this problem. Global Markets (www.1on1mail.com) has an e-mail service that reportedly not only encrypts e-mail but that has a self-destruct feature as well. This is another free Web-based e-mail service. The software deletes e-mail two hours after receipt and overwrites the file space on the disk, so that it cannot be recovered by undeleting the file. Another company that offers a similar service is Disappearing, Inc. (Figure 6.19).

However, to function, these services usually require that both the sender and recipient install and use their client software. As with any Web-based e-mail service, you are trusting that the service provider can ensure the security of its e-mail servers. In addition, either the sender or the recipient can print a copy of the e-mail, which can defeat the whole scheme. Finally,

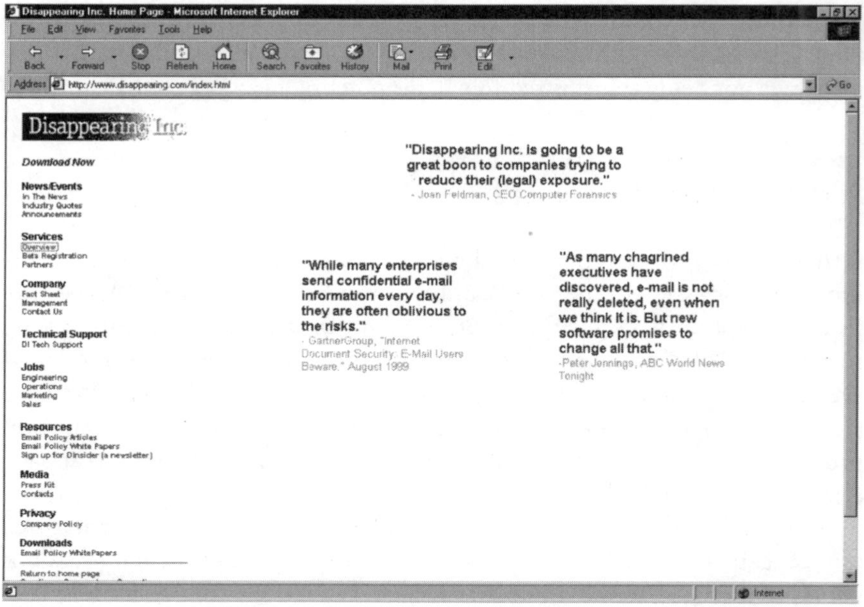

Figure 6.19 Disappearing, Inc. (*Source:* Disappearing, Inc. Reprinted with permission.)

if your e-mail is so critical and sensitive that it requires an automatic self-destruct feature, then you shouldn't be using a free Web-based e-mail service in any case.

Identity: Spoofing and Hiding

Hackers masquerading or spoofing another individual's e-mail identity represents an increasing practice. The surest way to do this is to obtain the password to a legitimate user's e-mail account. If someone gets access to your e-mail account they can send messages that appear to originate from you. A simpler approach would be to spoof the e-mail header, so that the message appears to originate from someone else's e-mail account.

This spoofing approach, which is often used in a type of denial-of-service attack, is an example of using e-mail as a weapon. Masquerading as someone else, a hacker can send a derogatory or inflammatory e-mail to a group distribution or a mailing list. When the subscribers to the mailing list reply to the e-mail, it is the innocent victim that gets flamed, not the hacker.

If someone simply wants to hide his or her identity, he or she can use one of a dozen remailer sites on the Internet. A remailer is an Internet site to which you can send e-mail for forwarding to an intended destination, while concealing your own e-mail address. PrivacyX (Figure 6.18) provides anonymous e-mail capabilities. One of the best known sites is anonymizer.com, also known as the Anonymizer (Figure 6.20).

Both PrivacyX and the Anonymizer also offer anonymous browsing capabilities. There are several sites that provide either anonymous e-mail, browsing, or both, although the effectiveness of each site's ability to actually shield the user is mixed. Basically, they attempt to strip off any identifying characteristic from a user's session that could be used to trace back to the originator. Characteristics such as IP address, alias, or originating network are stripped off and replaced with generic information.

There may be times when an individual has a legitimate reason to conceal his or her identity when sending e-mail. These remailers can be used by whistle blowers who wish to remain anonymous for fear of reprisal. A remailer can be used by anyone who wishes to express an opinion on a subject but who is afraid of the consequences that certain opinions can bring. See Figure 6.21.

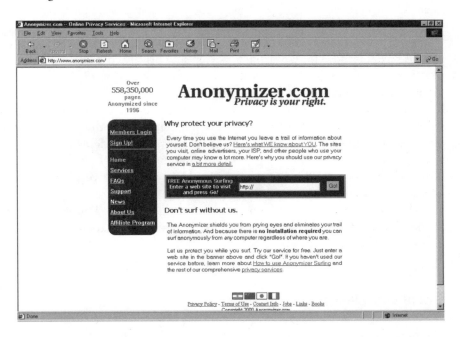

Figure 6.20 Anonymizer.com. (*Source:* Anonymizer, Inc. Reprinted with permission.)

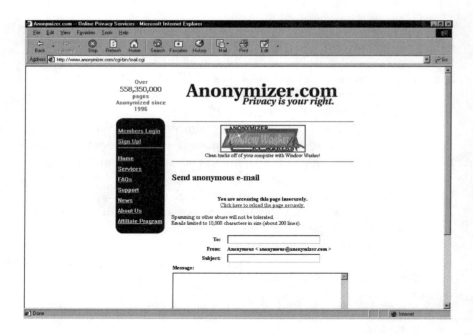

Figure 6.21 Anonymizer.com. (*Source:* Anonymizer, Inc. Reprinted with permission.)

A recent trend is for government agency and private corporations to use the courts to force ISPs, on-line bulletin boards, and chat rooms to divulge the identities of individuals posting e-mails and messages. There have even been cases where service providers freely divulged information about subscribers without a court order. For example, in 1999, the U.S. Navy requested information from AOL on the identity of a serviceman who had posted a message stating he was gay. In an abominable breach of trust, AOL provided the Navy with the serviceman's identity. Armed with the man's identity, the Navy initiated action against him.

Remailer services can often be used for benign reasons. Unfortunately, an individual who wishes to anonymously threaten or harass another individual can also use them.

E-Mail as a Weapon

One way that e-mail can be used as a weapon in an attack is by spamming someone. SPAM is unwanted bulk e-mail. A high volume of SPAM can be used as a very effective denial-of-service attack. By inundating a targeted system with thousands of e-mail messages, SPAM can eat available network bandwidth, overload CPUs, cause log files to grow very large, and consume all available disk space on a system. Ultimately it can cause systems to crash.

As discussed previously, SPAM can be used as a means to launch an indirect attack on a third party. SPAM messages can contain a falsified return address, which may be the legitimate address of some innocent unsuspecting person. This can result in an innocent person whose address was used as the return address to be spammed by all the individuals that were targeted in the original SPAM.

E-mail filtering can prevent much of the unwanted e-mail from getting through. Unfortunately, it frequently filters out legitimate e-mail.

E-mail is also used to deliver virus payloads. Some viruses such as the Melissa virus have gained a great deal of notoriety. It is interesting to note that for all the reports of the cost of the Melissa virus, it was a relatively benign strain of virus. The Melissa virus was spread as an e-mail attachment. When executed, it searched the address book of the infected system and sent out copies of itself to the first 50 e-mail addresses it found in the address book. While it is true that it infected untold thousands of systems, clogged networks and servers, and cost millions of dollars to clean up, it really did not actively do damage. Can you image the damage it could have caused if the virus had also been designed to delete files? The cost would have been staggering.

E-mail payloads can also be designed to steal information, such as passwords, from unsuspecting victims. One example of such a virus hit AOL users in 1999. When executed, the virus was designed to steal AOL passwords and e-mail them back to the originator of the virus. An even more dangerous virus was the "Love Bug," which hit millions of systems worldwide in May 2000. This virus was similar to the Melissa in that it was spread as an attachment to e-mail with the subject "I Love You." Like the Melissa virus, the Love Bug virus self-propagated by e-mailing copies of itself to e-mail addresses listed in the infected PC's e-mail address book. The virus code also contained a Trojan horse program that sent the cached Windows passwords of the unsuspecting recipients who opened the virus-laden attachment to an e-mail account in the Philippines. The Trojan horse program also had the ability to steal passwords to dial up Internet services from end users' PCs.

A new dangerous development is e-mail viruses that can spread without the recipient opening an attachment file. As a result of a vulnerability with IE5 and Microsoft Office 2000, HTML-enabled e-mail systems can be susceptible to virus attacks, even if the e-mail recipient does not open an attachment. You don't even have to use IE5 for e-mail. Simply having the software installed on a system with the default security settings can make the system vulnerable. The problem is caused by a programming bug in the IE5 ActiveX controls.

One example of this type of virus is Kak. Simply using Microsoft's Outlook Express to preview an e-mail infected with the Kak virus infects the recipient's system. It is not necessary to open an attachment to infect the recipient's systems. According to MSNBC, 50,000 clients of Shoppingplanet.com received an e-mail newsletter infected with the Kak virus. Fortunately, the virus is relatively benign. It does not delete files. It simply propagates. However, there are more malicious versions of this type of virus going around.

There are short-term measures that can be employed when there is an widespread outbreak similar to the Melissa or I Love You viruses. Shortly after the Melissa virus incident, I remember reading an account of how the outbreak had affected one particular network administrator. This particular administrator recounted the story of how his corporate e-mail server was infected by the Melissa virus. Like millions of individuals whose machines were infected by the Melissa virus, he received an e-mail from a coworker with an attachment. He opened the e-mail and clicked on the attachment. As soon as he had done so he knew he had been hit by an e-mail virus. He could see e-mails going out from his system to other individuals in the company. He realized quickly that the virus was spreading exponentially within the company, because he was receiving automatic acknowledgments that the e-mails sent out by his system had been read. No doubt those recipients clicked on the attachment and were infected, further spreading the virus within the organization. The administrator frantically attempted to contact individuals to tell them not to open the e-mails. He sent out urgent e-mails telling everyone to delete the particular e-mail with its attachment. What he should have done was run into the computer room and shut down the e-mail server. An even quicker response would have been to unplug it from the network. Without the server in operation the virus could not be spread.

Shutting down the e-mail server is just one example of the short-term solutions that can be employed during the outbreak of a particularly virulent e-mail virus. Other options include shutting down the company's e-mail gateway to the Internet. This will not help if a virus has already spread to the corporate network, but it is an option if the network has not yet been infected. Once you've identified the size of the e-mail spreading the virus, you can place a size limitation on all e-mails. By specifying a maximum e-mail size smaller than the infected e-mail, you effectively block the virus from spreading. You can also block any e-mails with attachments or simply block the attachments and allow the e-mail message through; you can block all attachments or only block those with a specified file type, such a *.vbs, so that they are automatically removed for e-mail messages. Another option is to block all e-mails based on the subject. If the e-mail spreading the virus has a particular subject, as the I Love You virus did, you can effectively block the spread. Your options largely depend on the type of e-mail server, routers, and firewall employed and their capabilities.

Another example of an e-mail virus that was more of an embarrassment than a threat was one that made the rounds in 1999. The e-mail arrives with the subject "Check this" or "Check this out." The virus created a link to an adult Web site and also searched the address book of the infected system. It would then e-mail copies of itself to the addresses in the address book. When the recipient received your e-mail they would not only be infected, but they would think you were telling them to check out a porn site. This kind of virus could really do wonders for your career if it was mailed out to your boss and all your coworkers.

As a general rule, whenever possible you should scan for viruses at the e-mail server level. Relying on scanning at the individual workstation is not only undependable, but it can be much more difficult to administer. This is not to say that you should not perform workstation-level scanning. It's just better to have multiple layers of detection. If is also very important that you continually update your virus scanner. New viruses are detected constantly. As a result, manufacturers of virus scanners issue regular updates to counter new viruses. Unfortunately, however, virus scanners are always behind the viruses in terms of being current.

If you use an Internet e-mail service you cannot control whether it scans for viruses at the server level. Even some of the services that do virus scanning only do a limited job. For example, Microsoft's Hotmail has been criticized in the past for using a version of a virus scanner that misses some virus. Once again, you are relying on the thoroughness of your service provider. You have to ask yourself whether you think your service provider does a good job at providing security, confidentiality, and protection from viruses.

Policies

Every organization that employs e-mail needs to develop and publish a company policy covering the use of company owned e-mail. Chapter 14 covers this in detail, but for the purposes of our discussion here, I want to touch on a few points.

First, a policy needs to define what should and should not be e-mailed. The policy should also stipulate the precautions that need to be taken depending on the nature of the information being e-mailed. For example, if the information is of a confidential or proprietary nature then encryption should be required. The policy should go so far as to stipulate the type of encryption and the level of encryption. Another example might be to stipulate that certain information is not to be sent to outside mailboxes or to services such as Hotmail or Yahoo.

Any policy should also deal with the storage and retention of e-mail. One reason for this is to ensure that servers do not become cluttered with useless e-mails that are no longer needed. Another reason to develop such a policy is to ensure that information that must be retained is retained. It is also needed to ensure that information of a confidential or proprietary nature is not left sitting around on servers or backups. Information tends to migrate. Information that is stored on a secure server today may find its way to a not so secure server in 12 months.

Deleting old e-mail can also save an organization from liability for actions taken by its employees. Organizations often find themselves in court for the actions of employees even though the organization neither knew about nor condoned the actions. There have been cases where the evidence of the activities was stored on the company's e-mail servers. A company can develop a storage and retention policy that mitigates such risks.

Doing so, however, can be a double-edged sword. An organization may lose information that it eventually needs and should take care in determining what information to destroy. Understand that I am not recommending that organizations destroy e-mail simply to hide activity for which they might be liable. A company should definitely not destroy information that the organization knows is evidence of illegal activity. The destruction of evidence is a criminal act.

In addition, any storage and retention policy that stipulates the purging or destruction of e-mail should also include a retention period. The retention period should include a schedule for the destruction of e-mail, and that schedule should be followed. If an organization were to find its e-mail records subpoenaed, it could look very suspicious if the destruction of e-mail appeared to be nonroutine. Even if there is no sinister motive for the destruction of the e-mail, the timing of the act could make the organization look guilty. However, if a policy exists that stipulates the routine destruction of e-mail and that routine is adhered to, then the action is less likely to appear suspicious.

In addition, every e-mail policy should address the issue of e-mail monitoring and disclosure. The policy must first address whether it will be the organization's practice to monitor e-mail. If the organization chooses to monitor e-mail then that must be communicated to the employees of the company and possibly the customers of the company. If an organization does choose to monitor e-mail then strict guidelines should be developed covering who has authorization to perform the monitoring. In addition, it should be communicated to all employees that the monitoring of e-mail can result in the possible disclosure of the information intercepted. In others words, companies need to tell people that they should not put information on the company e-mail system that they would not want to be made public.

E-Mail Privacy

Many individuals are outraged at the thought that e-mail may be monitored. They feel that e-mail is a confidential communication that is entitled to the privacy afforded to other forms of communication. However, as long as organizations can be held liable for the actions of their employees, companies will continue to monitor e-mail.

Until recently, most organizations that did monitor e-mail would only perform random spot checks or would act when there was reason to believe intervention was required. Now there are software packages available that allow organizations to screen all e-mail. These software packages allow an organization to develop rules that are used to identify e-mail that should be inspected. These tools provide organizations with much more flexibility in what they screen for and allow them to take a proactive approach to monitoring the content of e-mail.

In 1999, APBNews.com reported that approximately 20% of *Fortune 1,000* companies used monitoring software and that the International Data Corporation reported that approximately 80% of large corporations are expected to deploy such systems by 2001.

The companies that install these monitoring systems are not just being nosy. Companies must protect themselves from the inappropriate or illegal activities of their employees. They also have a duty to protect their employees, and monitoring e-mail is one way they can do so. In addition, many companies are concerned about the theft of intellectual property and proprietary company information. Product designs and customer lists can easily be slipped outside of a company using e-mail. Finally, an organization has the right to ensure that company assets are being used for company business.

E-mail is no different from the company telephone system. Companies monitor phone calls to ensure employees are not running up charges for personal long-distance calls. In the same way, it can cost an organization real dollars if 25% of the e-mail being exchanged is not business-related. However, if this type of monitoring is abused or used for the wrong purpose, the results can be devastating.

I expect that the morality and legality of this issue will be debated for some time. Recently, a bill was passed in the state of California that required those doing business with the state to notify employees in writing prior to any monitoring activity taking place. The bill was eventually vetoed by the governor, so its future is uncertain.

I think it is reasonable to disclose to employees the company's plans to monitor e-mail. However, it should only be necessary to provide the disclosure once. A company should hold open the right to monitor e-mail whenever necessary. It should not be necessary to provide notice prior to each instance of monitoring.

If you are really troubled by the monitoring of e-mail then private companies are not the only entities you need to concerned about. Recent initiatives by the U.S. government, such as the Fidnet proposal, would allow government agencies to conduct ongoing surveillance of Internet traffic such as e-mail. The purpose of these initiatives is said to be fighting crime and terrorism. However, critics and privacy advocates believe that it is big government over extending its reach and prying into citizens' private lives.

For years there have been reports that NSA has a secret project code named Echelon that has been monitoring all Internet e-mail. The monitoring supposedly employs keyword searches to identify suspect e-mails. Echelon is reported to be a global network of computers that automatically searches through millions of intercepts of fax, telex, and e-mail for preprogrammed keywords. Supposedly if an e-mail contains certain words such as "bomb," "revolution," or "embassy," it will be flagged for examination.

The U.S. government is not alone. Certainly China and Russia monitor e-mail, at least within their domestic borders. In addition, other countries such as Great Britain and France practice surveillance to some degree. Great Britain is reported to be a partner in the Echelon project. In addition, Great Britain has enacted the Interception of Communications Act to which a modification has been proposed that would legally sanction the British government's interception of e-mail and all other Internet traffic.

Even developing nations are monitoring e-mail, perhaps even more so than in the industrialized nations, because many developing nations do not have the same laws that industrialized nations have protecting civil liberties.

For example, there was a recent incident in Sri Lanka where the minister of science and technology read out loud at a cabinet meeting an e-mail that had been sent to the former prime minister of Sri Lanka. The minister had been able to intercept the e-mail from a Sri Lankan ISP. There have also been accusations that the Sri Lankan ruling government is intercepting e-mail from corporations and businesspeople and selling the information to companies with close ties to the ruling party.

E-mail users working for a U.S. company doing business overseas should keep such examples in mind. If you do business with the local government or are in delicate negotiations with a local entity overseas and you are exchanging e-mail with a corporate office reporting on the status or tactics of the negotiations, you would be well-advised to secure your e-mail.

Auto-Responses

My final observation regarding e-mail is actually a personal pet peeve: Be careful in your use of out-of-office auto-responses. If you must use one, make sure that it is only in response to internal users. In other words, the out-of-office auto-response should only go to other people within your organization. It should not go out in response to e-mail received from the Internet.

From time to time, I have subscribed to different security-related e-mail mailing lists. If you subscribe to any of these lists you will receive every e-mail sent to the list and their corresponding responses. Thousands of individuals subscribe to these mailing lists. Some are white-hat people, and some are black-hat. On more than one occasion, I have seen auto-responses to the mailing list announcing that a particular individual was out of the office until some specified date. Usually these out-of-office auto-responses are for a system administrator or security administrator, listing their name, address, and telephone number. Everyone who subscribes to the mailing list—thousands of individuals—gets the out-of-office message. Besides being annoying, the auto-response could provide useful information for any hacker who wanted to find a system that might not be monitored at the moment or who wanted to masquerade as a company system administrator. Accordingly, I recommend that you restrict out-of-office auto-responses to the local network.

7

Operating System Security

Operating System Guidelines

Network security begins at the individual system level. As the saying goes, a chain is only as strong as its weakest link, and a network is nothing more than a chain of systems. As a result, for a network to have a high level of security, all of the systems on the network must be properly administered and monitored.

Very few organizations adequately administer and monitor systems that reside on the internal network. This defense-in-depth approach requires more of a commitment to security than most organizations are willing to make. Key to a defense in depth is the deployment of a multitiered strategy to network and system security. Instead, most organizations choose to employ a perimeter defense. This approach relies on hardened border systems, usually firewalls and routers, that are designed to monitor and control traffic between an internal trusted network and an external untrusted network. The assumption is that the perimeter or border systems will secure the internal systems. There are a number of problems with the perimeter defense. First, if an organization's border systems are ever compromised and penetrated, the entire internal network could be open to attack. Hardening the internal systems can help to decrease the amount of damage from the breach of a perimeter system. At the very least, adequate monitoring of the internal systems may at least detect a breach from the outside.

In addition, every organization that uses computers faces the threat of hacking from individuals within the organization. Employees with malicious intent who want to obtain information such as employee salaries or view other employees' files are also a threat to an organization's computers and networks.

Critical systems should be configured to monitor logins, failed logins, and all network activity. Most every computer and NOS has utilities for monitoring this kind of activity. UNIX in particular can be configured to record all sorts of activity that can be reviewed for security purposes. For example, almost every version of UNIX allows you to monitor logins through the wtmp file and records failed login attempts.

One simple security measure an organization can employ for UNIX systems is to review the failed login log file on a daily basis. This log displays every failed attempt to log into the system. This can alert a company to the first indications of someone probing its system. Depending on the version of UNIX, an organization may even be able to determine whether the attempted login was over the network, and it can even display the IP address from which the connection originated.

Some system administrators question the wisdom of using the failed-login log file feature. They believe that the log file may inadvertently record the password for an account, if the account name and password are entered out of sequence. While in theory this is a possibility, in practice I have never known it to be an issue.

When reviewing the failed login log file, if there are multiple entries for a single account, it may be an indication that something is wrong and should be investigated. If there are unfamiliar IP addresses attempting to connect to the system, then this should also be investigated. Both of these activities could be indications that someone is probing a system.

Another useful UNIX log is the sulog. Most versions of UNIX record failed attempts to spawn another process and switch to another user with the "su" command. This is recorded in the sulog log file. Entries in this log file may be the result of someone probing a system and attempting to gain privileged access. Any entry in this log should be traced to determine if it is legitimate or not. There are accounts that will have legitimate reasons for using the su command. For example, the operator's or administrator's accounts may frequently perform su to root. If, however, the log shows someone attempting to su to root who should not be attempting such a function, an organization should investigate the occurrence.

Another log that can be useful is the wtmp log. This file records information for every account that logs in and out of a system. It gives the time and duration of the login. For most versions of UNIX, an organization can also determine whether the connection was from a tty, telnet, or rlogin connection or was an ftp connection. In addition, it can distinguish telnet and rlogin connections from ftp connections by the device type. The wtmp file is stored in a binary format. As a result, it is necessary to use the "last" command to display its contents. A simple review of this file, on a daily basis, can turn up anomalous behavior—for instance, an ftp connection from an account that shouldn't be using ftp or accounts logging in at odd hours.

Since these logs reside on the system's local disk drive, it is possible for someone to alter the files. It is recommended that hardcopy printouts of the logs be generated daily to be reviewed and stored. The log files should also be cleared daily or weekly. There are a couple of reasons for doing this. First, it reduces the risk of the files being altered. Second, in the event the system is ever compromised it may be necessary to refer to the hardcopy printouts to help in determining exactly when the system was first compromised. The process of printing and clearing the files can be automated relatively easily.

Windows NT Server also offers the capability to monitor various events utilizing the Event Viewer. Windows NT Server records events that affect system components, security, and applications. The system log records events that affect drivers, printers, hardware and other components. The application log records events that affect the software and files. The security log records events such as failed logins and changes to user rights or audit policies. An organization can view all events at once or filter only for one component.

The Windows NT auditing feature records which resources were accessed, who accessed them, and what action was attempted. The Event Viewer also shows whether the attempt was successful. Figure 7.1 illustrates the Event Viewer with a filtered view of security events. In Figure 7.1, the security events displayed are failed logins. An organization can obtain detailed information about a particular event in the security log by double-clicking on that event.

Figure 7.2 shows the detailed information for the selected event. In Figure 7.2, we can see that someone attempted to login to the system with the username DEBBIE. The login failed either because the username did not exist or due to an incorrect password.

All the measures described above comprise a first step to securing and monitoring a system. These rudimentary steps can help to identify when a system is being probed. Other measures should also be taken to safeguard and firewall systems. There are several tools available that enhance an administrator's ability to monitor his or her system. Some of the available tools are discussed at the end of this chapter, and Chapter 15 describes others.

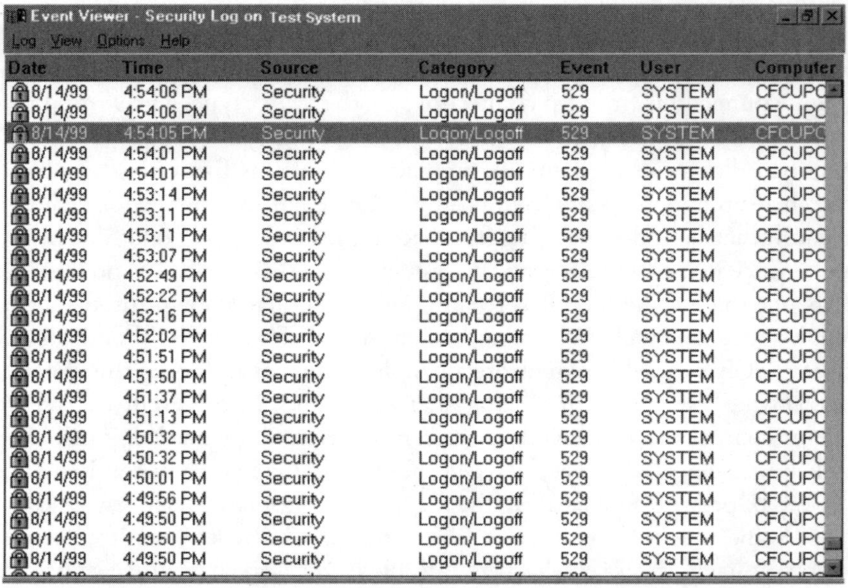

Figure 7.1 Windows NT Event Viewer.

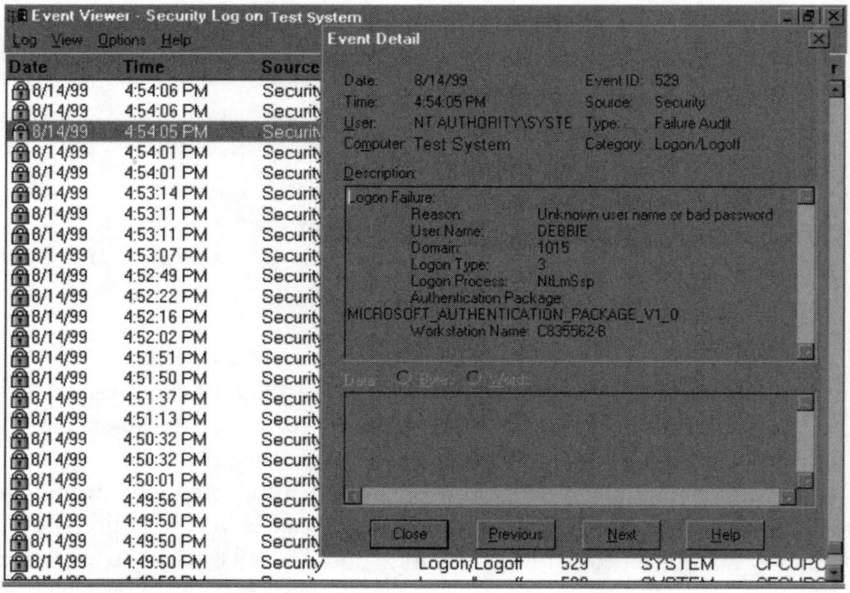

Figure 7.2 Windows NT Event Viewer.

Organizations need to determine what measures are necessary for their system, based upon their environment. These measures are no substitute for a firewall, but having a firewall is no excuse not to monitor a system. If a system or systems are in an environment where the network is potentially hostile, then additional measures are most certainly in order. Even if a system sits on a secure or trusted network or behind a firewall, it is necessary to secure and monitor the system. Network security begins at the individual system level. An organization has no idea whether the next system administrator down the line is doing his or her job properly. In fact, employees could be hanging dial-up connections off of the system without proper security measures. Remember, a network is only as secure as the individual systems on that network.

Passwords

The first measure of a system's security is how effective it is in authenticating and identifying its users. There are three basic schemes for identification and authentication: something you know, something you have, or something you are. The most commonly employed scheme is "something you know," and the most widely implemented variation of this scheme is the use of passwords.

Passwords are used by most every system or network as the first and usually only means of identification and authentication. Even though passwords are the most widely deployed scheme of authentication, they are perhaps the weakest link in any system security scheme. However, there are a number of measures an organization can take to lessen the risks associated with the use of passwords: Obviously, passwords should never be shared between end users or employees. Accordingly, every organization should have a policy that clearly states the users' responsibility to maintain password secrecy and the consequences for failing to do so.

Meanwhile, however, people too often use passwords that are too short and/or too easy to guess or decipher, or they simply never change them. There are programs known as "crackers" that are easily obtained from the Internet that can be run on most systems to decipher the passwords in the password file.

Even if a password is encrypted for transmission between a client and a server, it can be captured and retransmitted at a later time as part of a "replay attack." Countermeasures for this include one-time passwords, tokens, or schemes such as Kerberos.

There are four general types of attacks on system passwords:

- Brute force;
- Dictionary-based;
- Password sniffing;
- Social engineering.

Brute Force

Brute-force attacks attempt to breach systems by trying every possible combination of letter and number till a match is found that provides access to the system. A brute-force attack is most effective if passwords are short in length and the passwords are only letters or only numbers, not a combination of both. The longer the password the more effort it takes to attempt every possible combination. Making a password a mix of letters, numbers, and special characters increases the difficulty exponentially.

Dictionary-Based

Dictionary-based attacks are much more effective then the brute-force approach. Many operating systems maintain a password file. This password file is a database of usernames and passwords. The passwords are almost always stored in the password file in an encrypted format. Dictionary-based attacks actually utilize programs that compare the encrypted passwords in the password file to encrypted words in a dictionary file. When a match is found, a password is found. Obviously, the dictionary-based method is most effective against passwords that are common or known words, names, or terms. Some systems try to get around this problem by not having a password file or not storing passwords. Windows NT for instance does not store passwords in a password file. Instead NT stores the hashed values of the passwords. However, password cracking programs exist for all computer and NOSs.

Password Sniffing

As stated in Chapter 2, network sniffing or packet sniffing is the process of monitoring a network to gather information that may be useful in an attack. One of the things that can be observed through network sniffing is passwords. With the proper tools, a hacker can monitor the network packets to obtain passwords or IP addresses.

Password sniffing is particularly a threat for users who log into a system over a network using telnet, rlogin, ftp, or a terminal emulator. For example, when a user logs into a UNIX system over a network using telnet, the password is transmitted to the system as cleartext. The system passes the cleartext password through the password encryption algorithm and compares it to the value stored in the password file. If they match, then the user is authenticated and allowed access to the system.

Generally, programs, such as telnet, rlogin, and terminal emulators do not encrypt passwords entered at login for transmission to the system. As a result, when a user enters his or her password, it is transmitted in the clear, meaning anyone monitoring the network with a sniffer can read the password.

There are several different network sniffer programs available. Some are commercial products, and some are freeware. Figure 7.3 is an example of Network Associates' Sniffer Pro software. Sniffer Pro is a commercial software product that is typically used to monitor and diagnose problems with network perform. In Figure 7.3, the system with the Sniffer Pro software is on a small test network with two other systems to demonstrate network sniffing. For demonstration purposes, a telnet session is initiated from one system to the another. Figure 7.3 illustrates how Sniffer Pro can capture the IP

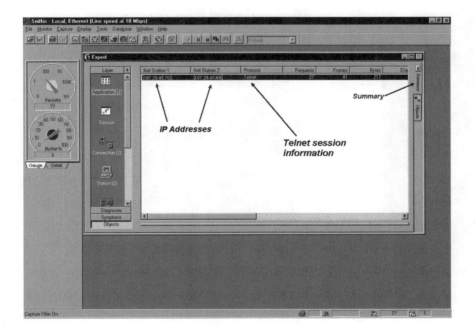

Figure 7.3 NAI's Sniffer Pro.

addresses of the two systems and the fact that the connection is a telnet session.

Figure 7.4 shows the detail information on the session. In Figure 7.4, the captured account username and password are listed in the "last user name" section. In this case, the account is "root," and the password is "secret-password." If I were a hacker, I could potentially capture this information and gain privileged access to the system.

Sniffer Pro, like most network sniffers, has the ability to store all captured information to a log file. As a result, a hacker could start up the network sniffer and leave it running for hours or days. He or she could then retrieve the log file and scan all captured network activity at leisure.

The risk associated with telnet and ftp is not just confined to UNIX. These utilities can also be used to connect to a Windows NT or 2000 server. However, they are most often used in the UNIX arena. The Windows graphical user interface, with its click and drag capabilities, makes utilities, such as telnet and ftp, largely superfluous. However, even Windows and Novell passwords can be vulnerable if they are captured by someone using a packet sniffer.

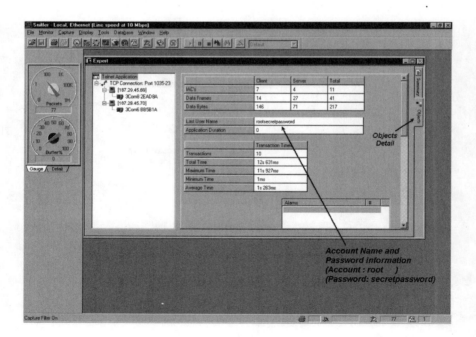

Figure 7.4 NAI's Sniffer Pro.

When a user logs into Windows NT the password is hashed at the workstation before being transmitted to a server. Windows NT employs MD4 as the hashing algorithm. When the Windows NT server receives the hashed value, the server compares it to the value stored in the hash file. A challenge-response protocol is used to verify the password entered at the client. If they match, the user is then authenticated and allowed access to the system or network.

A user logging into a Windows NT server typically sends his or her username and domain name across the network in cleartext. Someone on the network with a sniffer can potentially capture the cleartext and the challenge-response. If it can be captured then the challenge-response can potentially reveal the hashed value of the user's password. The hash value can then be subjected to a dictionary-based attack.

Windows NT does allow for optional authentication protocols, such as NT LAN Manager (NTLM). NTLM is the primary authentication protocol employed by NT. For Windows 2000, Microsoft has replaced NTLM with Kerberos as the primary security protocol for access to resources within or across Windows 2000 server domains. However, Kerberos can only be used between Windows 2000 systems. All other Windows clients must still use NTLM. In addition, Microsoft has been criticized for using proprietary data formats in its implementation of Kerberos.

With Novell, the process is as follows: When a user logs into Netware, the workstation receives a session key from the server. The workstation encrypts the password using a combination of session key and a user ID before transmitting it to the server. The server receives the encrypted password, decrypts the password, and authenticates the end user. Someone on the network with a packet sniffer could potentially capture the encrypted password in transit. It could then be subjected to a dictionary-based attack. The Windows NT and Novell Netware schemes that protect passwords in transit make it more difficult to obtain passwords—but not impossible.

Password Sniffing Countermeasures

There are several steps that an organization can take to reduce or eliminate the risks associated with network packet sniffers. One is to use network switches instead of network hubs. Switches can be used to segment a network and create virtual LANs (VLANs), which divide a switch into network segments that cannot see each other's packets. Network segmentation is discussed more in Chapter 8.

Another option is to employ a VPN, discussed in detail in Chapter 11. Another approach is to use a program like SSH, a UNIX program designed to provide strong authentication and secure communications over an unsecured network. SSH is designed to be used in place of other programs such as telnet, rlogin, rsh, and rcp. SSH communications can be encrypted using IDEA, DES, 3DES, or RC4. Encryption keys are exchanged using RSA key exchange. SSH can protect against IP spoofing, IP source routing, DNS spoofing, and interception of cleartext passwords and other data by intermediate hosts. SSH can be purchased from various sources or downloaded at no charge from a number of sites on the Web.

Another countermeasure to password sniffing is to use one-time passwords. There are several different one-time password schemes. The most widely implemented scheme employs smart cards or token cards.

One of the best known products is RSA's SecurID, which uses a time-based token card (see Figure 7.5). The card displays a number that is synchronized with a login server. To access a system employing SecurID, it is necessary to enter the synchronized number. The number changes constantly and is never the same twice.

Other smart card products employ a challenge/response scheme. When you attempt to login, the system issues a challenge. The user enters the challenge into a card that the user keeps; this card then displays the appropriate response. Subsequently, the user enters that response from the card into the system to gain access to the system. Both the challenge and response are never the same twice, so it does not matter if the response is sniffed and captured on the network. The challenge and response are only applicable at that moment and will never be used again.

Figure 7.5   SecurID.

Social Engineering

It is amazing how easy it is to get someone to divulge a password over the telephone. Hackers posing as system administrators calling end users or posing as end users calling the IT support line have been very successful in their attempts to gain passwords to systems. This type of problem is one of the most difficult to control, because it requires modifying people's behavior, and there is no technology that you can implement to prevent it. Most people are trusting by nature and are not on-guard for this type of maneuver. The only way to prevent this type of ploy from being successful is through training and education.

Password Guidelines

Passwords should be at least eight alphanumeric and special symbol characters in length and should not be known words or names that can be found in a dictionary. Users should be restricted from using all numbers or all letters in a password.

The maximum number of times any single character can be repeated in a password should be restricted to three. This is to prevent someone from using a password that is all one word or letter, such as aaaaaaaa or 22222222. If possible, users should be required to use at least six distinct characters in an eight-character password. Some systems allow you to assign a mask that dictates the password format.

Other things to avoid using as passwords include telephone numbers, license plates, and birthdates. Whenever possible include special symbols (*&@#%$) in passwords.

System controls should be configured to restrict users from using the same password more than once or at least set the system so that 36 weeks must pass before a user can reuse a password. If possible, the controls should also be configured to require that eight to ten new passwords be used before an individual can reuse an old password again.

Passwords should have a minimum and maximum life. The minimum life should be a few days to a week. The maximum life should be 45 days. All system and network accounts should be forced to change their passwords at least every 45 days. Passwords should have a minimum life to prevent someone from changing an account's password enough times in a single day to get around the restriction on using the same password more than once. The minimum will also prevent a hacker from changing an account's password, then changing it back to the original password, to avoid detection.

Passwords must never be the same as the account username. Nor should a password be something associated with the account username (i.e., username = system, password = manager). Years ago I worked on Digital Equipment Corporation (DEC) VAX/VMS systems. All VAX systems had two special account usernames, one was called "system" and the other was called "field." The "system" account was intended to be used by the system administrator, and the "field" account was intended to be used by DEC field service technicians. At more than one site at which I worked the "system" account had the password "manager" or "administrator," and the "field" account had the password "service." Back then it was not uncommon to find those usernames and passwords being used on many of the VAX systems installed.

Some systems can generate passwords that consist of a random combination of letters and numbers. System-generated passwords are usually not susceptible to dictionary attacks. However, speaking from personal experience, I do not recommend system-generated passwords. System-generated passwords are difficult to remember, which causes users to write them down, thereby creating a security hole rather than plugging one. If the password is not selected by the end user, it has no meaning and nothing to make it easily remembered. When end users cannot remember passwords, they write them down on those little yellow stickies and stick them on their computers or monitors—either that or they call the IT help desk every other day and ask for a new password.

Most systems store passwords in an encrypted format. Most versions of UNIX also support the use of shadow password files. Shadow password files add an extra level of security by keeping the encrypted passwords in a separate file from the "passwd" file. The shadow password file can only be accessed by "root," and not normal, system users.

It has been my experience that it is sometimes necessary to share a password for a privileged account with someone outside the organization. Usually, it is necessary when a vendor is installing a system or providing support. In these circumstances, I recommend that you change the password for the privileged account to something innocuous, so the vendor can log into the system to work, but then change the password again immediately when the vendor has finished its work. Individuals outside of the organization should never have passwords to privileged accounts.

Many systems, when first installed, have system account usernames with preset passwords or no passwords at all. If these account usernames are not needed they should be deleted. If the accounts are required, then reset the passwords.

In today's business environment end users can have many accounts on different systems and networks. Where I presently work most users have at least three different accounts and passwords that must be entered to function. Quite a few have more than five accounts and passwords. Some administrators recommend picking different passwords for different machines or network nodes. While this should theoretically be a more secure approach, in practice it has significant drawbacks and I don't recommend it. I have found that requiring a different password for each account creates vulnerabilities, because people can't remember all of their passwords. As a result, the end users write them down and store them in an easily accessible location. One alternative to this problem is to implement a single sign-on system. Chapter 8 discusses single sign-on systems in more detail.

Access Control

Once a system identifies and authenticates an account as having legitimate access to the system, the end user is allowed to log in. Once the user is logged into the system, the user is given authorization to access system resources, such as files. The authorization can be thought of as access privileges. The discretionary privileges can be defined by an access control list (ACL). An ACL is the mechanism that restricts or grants access to a system's resources. Each system resource or object has an ACL, which lists the users or entities that can access that resource. Each entry within the ACL defines the access rights for the entry to the resource. In other words, access rights will dictate such rights as whether the user or entity has read, write, or delete access to the resource. An ACL specifies the privilege level required to access a system resource. The ACL specifies the permission level that must be granted, with respect to a protected resource, to access the resource.

It is stating the obvious to say that an organization should use some method that controls employee access to its systems and networks. This can include some kind of menu system or some mechanism for monitoring and controlling access levels to data and applications. ACLs should be assigned for the network and individual systems. Even Windows-based client/server applications are designed with back-end methods of controlling access to the various functions.

Permissions

Most computers and NOSs employ the concept of "permissions" for controlling access. Permissions specify what operations different users can perform on specific files and directories. Every user is assigned a level of access to each directory and file. Every user and file are assigned to a group. Groups can be specified in the ACL. Rather than having separate entries for individuals of a common group, a single entry for the group in the ACL can specify the permissions for all the individuals. With most systems there are at least three or four levels of permission:

- *Read:* An end user assigned this access level, either to a file or a directory, has the ability to read and view the contents and properties.

- *Write:* An end user assigned this access level, either to a file or a directory, has the ability to write to or alter a file or create files in the directory and in some cases alter the access rights to a directory or files in the directory.

- *Execute:* This privilege, when granted, allows the end user to execute programs in a given directory.

- *Delete:* This access right allows the end user to delete a file, directory, or files in a directory.

With most computer and NOSs file access is divided into three levels that depend on the group to which the user belongs: owner, group, and public or world. (In addition, each "group" is assigned access levels to particular resources.) These levels are described as follows.

- *Owner:* This group refers to the owner of a file or resource. The owner is designated either by virtue of having created the resource or by being given, or taking ownership of, the resource. The owner of a particular resource usually has read, write, execute, and delete rights to the resource, but that is not always the case. It is not uncommon for an owner of a resource to accidentally remove all of his or her access rights to a resource. This can be done by removing all permissions from the file or by transferring ownership of the file to someone else. Usually, when this occurs the user cannot get the rights back without assistance from a system administrator.

- *Group:* This group refers to users that share a common bond, such as working in the same department. For example, all users in human resources would have a group bond. The users within the human resources group can be assigned read, write, execute, or delete access to a particular file. The ACL for the particular resource could specify that all individuals in the human resources group are assigned read, write, execute, and delete permission. Other groups could be excluded from having any permissions or could be given limited access, perhaps read only.

- *World or public:* This group refers to the access level that everyone has to a resource. With Windows this group is designated as *Everybody.* The world can be assigned read, write, execute, or delete access to a particular resource, such as a file or directory, but it is usually restricted to read access for security reasons. Frequently, resources on a network such as printers or a shared directory available to all users will have limited access levels assigned to the world or public group. Printers in particular require some level of access to send print jobs to the resource. You just need to ensure that the access levels are only those needed to function. You should be careful about giving the world or public group "delete" level access to any resource. For example, if you give the world delete access to a network printer, then anyone can delete that resource either accidentally or maliciously.

Some operating systems use more than four levels of access permissions. Novell, for instance, uses eight different levels. Table 7.1 lists Novell Netware's access privileges.

Table 7.1
Novell Netware's Access Privileges

Privilege	Function
Access control	Allows the user to add and delete trustees and change rights to files and directories
Create	Gives the user the right to create subdirectories and files
Erase	Allows the user to delete directories and files
File scan	Allows the user to view file and directory names in the file system structure
Modify	Allows the user to change file attributes and to rename directories and files
Read	Allows the user to open and read files and execute applications
Supervisor	The equivalent of root access in UNIX or Administrator in NT, gives user all rights
Write	Allows the user to write to a directory or modify a file

In contrast, UNIX uses only three permissions. They are read, write, and execute. Figure 7.6 illustrates the assigned file permissions with a UNIX file system; the access rights are displayed in the column on the far left-hand side, while the file name is in the column on the far right-hand side.

In Figure 7.6, the permissions in the left-hand column consists of 10 letters or dashes(-). The first character in the column indicates the file type. If the line begins with a "d" then it is a directory, while an "l" indicates a link. If the line begins with a "-" then it is a standard file. The next nine characters indicate the access rights for the three categories or groups of owner, group, and other. "Other" is the UNIX equivalent of world or public. The first three characters indicate the access rights for the category owner. In Figure 7.6 the first line shows that the file TCP_WRAP.TAR has the access rights of "rw-rw-rw-." Those nine characters are the access rights assigned to the three categories of owner, group, and other. All three groups have read (r) and write (w) access, but not execute. Figure 7.7 illustrates an example of privilege rights where the group owner has read and write access; group has read and execute access; and other only has read access.

Microsoft's Windows NT also employs ACL and the concept of groups. Figure 7.8 illustrates the User Manager utility in NT. Various accounts, such as Administrator, Guest (that should be deleted), John, and other default accounts are listed in the top half of the screen. In the bottom half of the screen, the various groups are listed. They include Administrators

```
Telnet - solaris                                              _ □ ✕
Connect  Edit  Terminal  Help
$ ls -l | more
total 1447
-rw-rw-rw-    1 root     other    344064 Apr 16 04:30 TCP_WRAP.TAR
lrwxrwxrwx    1 root     root          9 Apr 16 01:22 bin -> ./usr/bin
drwxr-xr-x    3 root     nobody      512 Apr 16 02:02 cdrom
drwxrwxr-x   17 root     sys        3072 Apr 16 01:59 dev
drwxrwxr-x    4 root     sys         512 Apr 16 01:54 devices
drwxrwxr-x   23 root     sys        3072 Apr 16 04:26 etc
drwxrwxr-x    5 root     sys         512 Apr 16 01:18 export
dr-xr-xr-x    2 root     root          2 Apr 16 07:08 home
drwxr-xr-x   10 root     sys         512 Apr 16 01:43 kernel
lrwxrwxrwx    1 root     root          9 Apr 16 01:22 lib -> ./usr/lib
drwx------    2 root     root       8192 Apr 16 01:17 lost+found
drwxrwxr-x    2 root     sys         512 Apr 16 01:22 mnt
dr-xr-xr-x    2 root     root          2 Apr 16 07:08 net
drwxrwxr-x    4 root     sys         512 Apr 16 01:26 opt
drwxr-xr-x    3 root     sys         512 Apr 16 01:24 platform
dr-xr-xr-x    2 root     root       3776 Apr 16 07:08 proc
drwxrwxr-x    2 root     sys         512 Apr 16 01:43 sbin
-rw-rw-rw-    1 root     other    344064 Apr 16 06:02 tcp_wrap.tar
drwxrwxrwt    3 sys      sys         152 Apr 16 03:17 tmp
drwxrwxr-x   24 root     sys         512 Apr 16 01:50 usr
drwxrwxr-x   19 root     sys         512 Apr 16 02:01 var
--More--
```

Figure 7.6 UNIX file permissions.

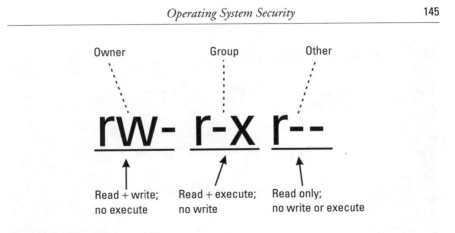

Owner   Group   Other

rw- r-x r--

Read + write; Read + execute; Read only;
no execute   no write   no write or execute

Figure 7.7 Group access privileges.

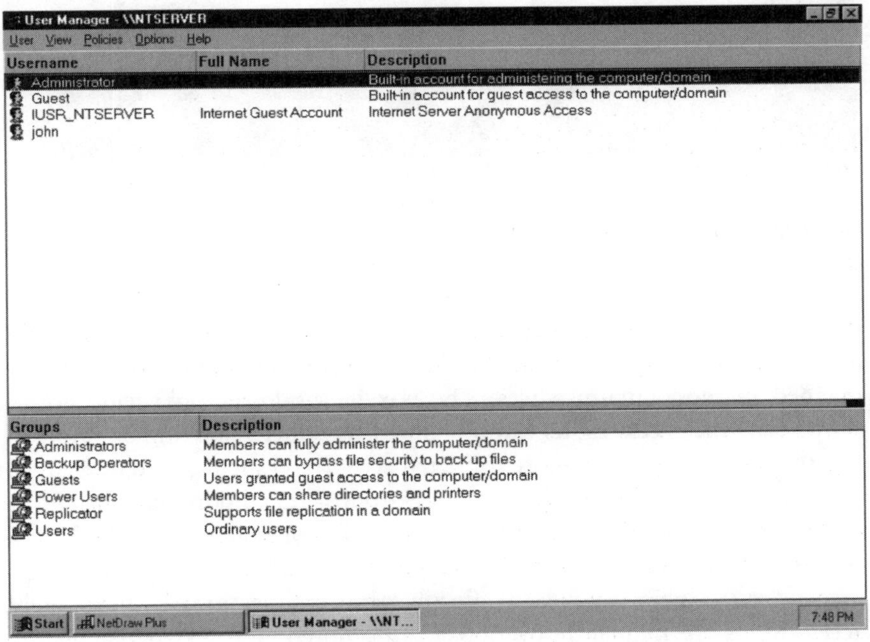

```
User Manager - \\NTSERVER                                          _ 8 X

User  View  Policies  Options  Help

Username          Full Name              Description
Administrator                            Built-in account for administering the computer/domain
Guest                                    Built-in account for guest access to the computer/domain
IUSR_NTSERVER     Internet Guest Account Internet Server Anonymous Access
john




Groups            Description
Administrators    Members can fully administer the computer/domain
Backup Operators  Members can bypass file security to back up files
Guests            Users granted guest access to the computer/domain
Power Users       Members can share directories and printers
Replicator        Supports file replication in a domain
Users             Ordinary users


Start   NetDraw Plus      User Manager - \\NT...                      7:48 PM
```

Figure 7.8 Windows NT server user manager.

and Power Users. It could also include groups such as human resources and accounting.

Figure 7.9 illustrates the access rights that are assigned to the network resource VOL1. In this case, VOL1 is a disk drive. As we can see in the box

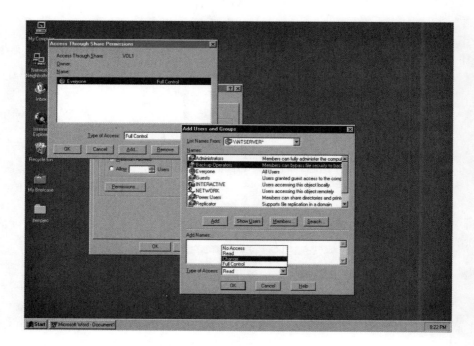

Figure 7.9 Windows NT access controls.

in the upper left-hand corner of Figure 7.9, access rights are very liberally defined in the group. (Everyone has full control.) This would not be recommended in most circumstances. The box in the lower right-hand corner shows how the access rights can be refined by either removing everyone all together or by assigning a more restricted access level such as read or change.

Access control, permissions, and groups are important concepts to understand because they are important tools for controlling end users' access to system resources. When used in conjunction with effective group assignment, access rights can be an effective security measure. Unfortunately, access rights are frequently overlooked or ignored, and group assignments usually entail nothing more than assigning all users to a single group. As a result, the access rights to critical system files frequently leave the system vulnerable to being compromised.

General Recommendations

Suppress system welcome banners or messages that provide information at the login prompt. Systems often have welcome messages that provide information on the operating system, the version, and the organization to which the system belongs. Figure 7.10 is an example of the type of information that is often displayed at login.

In Figure 7.10, a potential hacker would be provided with a wealth of information regarding the system without even having to login. The first line displays information about the operating system. Looking at the banner line, the first thing the hacker will see is HP-UX. This is Hewlett-Packard's version of UNIX, so the hacker will know the operating system is UNIX and that the make is HP. The next entry on the line is "opticarc," which the hacker will know is the name assigned to the system. The next entry is the "B.10.20." This is the version of the HP-UX operating system that the system is running. Knowing the version of the operating system allows the hacker to use vulnerabilities known to exist for a specific version of an operating system. Knowing the operating system and the version takes some of the guesswork out of the hacking process. The last entries tell the hacker that it is an HP 9000 E series model 816 and that it is using ttyp1 for the port device.

One of the jobs of a system administrator is to make it as difficult as possible for someone to hack the network and systems for which he or she is responsible. Providing information prior to a login, like we see in the

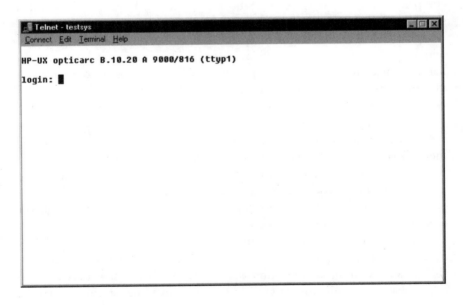

Figure 7.10 An example of a banner message.

example above, actually makes it easier for a hacker to compromise the system. There is no reason to provide that information at login. The only individuals who are really going to take note of it are the ones you least want to see it.

You should also avoid using banners that say "Welcome to" with some line identifying the company or a system belonging to the company. I've seen systems that have had a welcome banner that said something to the effect of "Welcome to Acme Bank's computer system." You should avoid this for two reasons. First, the "welcome" statement has been interpreted in some courts of law as an invitation to use a system. As such, a hacker can argue that he or she assumed that he or she was welcome to access the company's systems. To facilitate potential prosecution of future hackers, it is recommended that welcome banners not be used.

Second, it is better not to provide any information in a login banner that identifies the company to which the system or network belongs. My thinking is the less information you provide to a hacker the better. Stating the name of the organization can provide a hacker with some indication about the nature of the information stored on the system.

However, many authorities recommend using a system login message that states that access to systems and networks are restricted to authorized personnel only. To include this type of message, it is necessary to disclose the company's name to state exactly who has legitimate access. The statement should say something to the effect that the system or network is intended solely for the legitimate use of company XYZ and that anyone using the system without authorization will be prosecuted. The wording can vary and the name of the company can be changed, but the basic purpose is to put hackers on notice that they will be prosecuted if caught. In some jurisdictions this type of disclosure is required if you wish to prosecute a hacker.

These types of banners or system messages can be displayed at login before users enter their username and password or after they have entered them. If you choose to have a banner display before the username and password are entered, provide as little information as possible. If you choose to use a system login disclosure message that provides the name of the company, then have the message display after the end user has entered in the username and password and has been given access to the system.

Another recommended measure to implement is to limit the number of times a user can attempt to login to three attempts. Many systems have the ability to lockout an account after a specified number of failed attempts to login. It should require the intervention of a system administrator to reset the account once it has been locked out. While this can create more work for the IT help desk staff, it can help to identify potential problems. At the very least it will identify individuals within the organization who require additional training because they are having problems with their passwords.

Many systems display a last login message. Many systems also display last attempted login or last failed login message. While this may be useful information, don't expect anyone to really notice it. Most people, including myself, don't pay any attention to these messages, so don't put much faith in them as a tool to identify problems.

Generally, it is a good idea to keep operating systems up-to-date with the latest releases of the operating system (within reason) and to load recent service packs or patches to fix identified bugs. While it is possible that a new version of an operating system or a software patch could contain a new vulnerability, it will take time for the vulnerability to be discovered. The risk is greater running an old version of an operating system, because the vulnerabilities that can be exploited are usually well-known.

On any system or server you should only run those services that are needed to function. Turn off everything else not needed. For example, if you're not going to be using ftp or DNS, do not configure the system to run them. This is particularly important for UNIX systems, but it applies to all other operating systems as well.

If possible, you should institute periodic reviews of user accounts. The review should delete accounts that are no longer needed. If an end user is no longer with the organization or no longer subscribes to the service, his or her account should be deleted. The review should also identify inactive accounts. Hackers target inactive accounts. They are the best way to create multiple entry points into a system.

This review process is easier said than done. It may not be practical if you are working in an environment with thousands or tens of thousands of accounts. However, there are security packages on the market that make this kind of process much easier.

Modems

Modems connected to systems on the network are perhaps the single greatest source of security vulnerability in most organizations' network infrastructure. Many organizations implement comprehensive security measures to protect the company's network only to have the measures undone by a modem connected to a system that was connected to the network.

The rule should be, if the system is on the network then there is no modem attached. Only stand-alone systems should be set up with modems. Putting a modem on a system connected to a network that resides inside a firewall is like putting a deadbolt on the front door, while leaving the back door wide open. A system connected to the corporate network should never be allowed to dial into another network such as the Internet without security precautions. It creates an unprotected gateway between the corporate network and the Internet through which it is possible for a hacker to gain access. It is also a method through which someone can perform an unauthorized transfer of files, both in and out. If you want to be able to monitor the flow of information, then all traffic should be required to go through a firewall.

If it is absolutely necessary to install modems on systems connected to the corporate network, then closely monitor all activity on those modems. It is possible to configure most operating systems to log activity for the modem ports. The report log for the modem ports should be reviewed daily to ensure that any connections to the port is for legitimate reasons.

Organizations with remote users that have to provide dial-in access should consider using security modems with dial-back capability or a secure ID scheme. At the very least, they should not leave the modem connected all the time. They should only connect it when it is actually being used and unplug it when the work is completed. Business requirements will really dictate what an organization can and cannot do. A company with end users that require remote access do not have the option of leaving modems unplugged. Small shops with only a few modems should find it fairly simple to monitor and secure their modems. On the other hand, for operations with very large networks or ISPs, monitoring modems is much more problematic. There are programs or systems available that actually detect modems on the network. These systems vary in their effectiveness and can be dependent on the type of network and how it is configured.

To a limited extent, companies can control modem connections if they employ a digital PBX telephone system. Modem connections simply will not work through a digital PBX, and refraining from installing any analog circuits eliminates much of the risk. However, most organizations have analog circuits installed for fax machines, which can be used by a modem. In addition, cellular technology can allow a user to completely bypass the company PBX.

The vulnerabilities associated with modems connected to a corporate network illustrate why it is so important to harden every system on the network. Firewalls are too easily circumvented to be the sole source of security for the internal network.

Information Availability

One of the key components of information security is "availability." This refers to the ability to access the information on a network or system when it is needed. Not only must the data be accessible, but it must also be timely and accurate. One of the best ways to ensure availability is through data redundancy. Data redundancy can be achieved in different ways. Each method provides a varying degree of redundancy and backup. In addition, each method has different requirements in terms of recovery time should it be necessary to resort to backups. Different methods of providing data redundancy include disk mirroring, redundant array of independent (or inexpensive) disks (RAID), data streaming, hot backup, and total redundancy—described as follows.

- *Disk mirroring:* Disk mirroring is a rather generic term for the process of duplicating data from one hard disk to another hard disk. Mirrored drives operate in tandem, constantly storing and updating the same files on each hard disk. Should one disk fail, the file server issues an alert and continues operating on the other disk. The normal procedure in the case of a mirrored disk failure is to bring the server down at the earliest opportunity and replace the damaged disk. The system will automatically copy the redundant data on the file server to the new disk. The mirrored disks can be configured with a shared controller or with separate controllers. Obviously, the configuration with separate controllers provides more redundancy. For organizations whose systems operate on a 24×7 schedule, disk mirroring also enhances the ability to perform backups. With most operating systems, open files can not be backed up, because they are open and being updated by another process. As a result, if you backup a system on which files are being updated, you will get an incomplete backup. Disk mirroring provides two sets of identical files on separate disks. As a result, when it performs a backup, an organization has the ability to "break" the mirror to back up one full set of disks. This, in effect, stops the mirror process for the mirror disks. The live files on the "mirrored" disk will continue to be updated by transactions and processes. The files on the "mirror" disk will be static, because the mirror process has been broken. As a result, it is possible to get a complete backup of the mirror drives. When the backup process is complete, you simply reinitiate the mirror process, and it will update the mirror disks with the changes that have occurred on the mirrored disks while the backup was taking place.

- *RAID:* RAID is a category of disk drives that employs two or more drives in combination for fault tolerance and performance. RAID disk drives are used frequently on servers. There are a number of different RAID levels with the most common being 0, 3, and 5:

  - Level 0 performs data striping, or spreading out blocks of each file across multiple disks. While this can improve performance it does not provide redundancy or fault tolerance.
  - Level 1 is disk mirroring as described above.
  - Level 3 is basically the same as level 0 but with redundancy.
  - Level 5 performs data striping at the byte level with error correction, which provides enhanced performance and reliable fault tolerance.

- *Streaming:* Before RAID and disk mirroring became generally available, certain operating systems offered the feature of streaming. Disk drives were less reliable years back, or at least they seemed to be less reliable. By comparison, today's disk drives are much more reliable and have a longer mean time between failures. Years ago it was not uncommon to have a disk drive fail without warning. In this environment streaming was employed. Streaming is the process of writing transactions to another media at the same time the transactions update the data files. One common implementation is to write the transactions to tape. As transactions take place and update database files on the disk drive, they are simultaneously written to tape.

  If a disk drive crashed in the middle of the day, you could restore from the previous night's backup and then just update the files with the day's transactions that had been streamed to tape. Streaming gave system administrators a process that recovered all data, even if a disk drive crashed during processing. However, the streaming process creates a lot of overhead in terms of CPU and I/O on a system. This additional burden could really affect system performance.

- *Hot backup:* Hot backup is a technique used to provide for the ongoing operation of a LAN should a file server fail. In this technique, two file servers operate in tandem. Data is duplicated on the hard disks of the two servers. In effect, this is like disk mirroring but across two servers instead of one server. If one server fails, the other server automatically assumes all LAN operations without any outage being apparent to the user of the LAN. The servers can be immediately adjacent to one another or may be thousands of miles apart.

It is not uncommon for organizations to maintain entirely redundant data centers. For example, many large financial institutions maintain duplicate data centers. Several large financial institutions in California maintain one center in northern California and another in southern California, with both centers being connected together by very high-capacity, high-speed circuits. This is only prudent considering California's propensity for earthquakes. In some instances this redundancy is reflected in the financial institution's ATM network. Two ATMs sitting side by side may be connected to different data centers.

Useful Tools

There is a wealth of useful tools available that assist in tightening operating system security and enhancing the general operation of most systems. Many of these tools are available free of charge and can be downloaded from the Internet. Unfortunately, most all of them are for UNIX-based systems. This is largely due to UNIX's history as an open operating system used extensively in the academic community. A list of some of the tools available on the Internet follows:

- *Computer Oracle and Password System (COPS):* COPS was written by Dan Farmer at Purdue University. COPS is a collection of tools that can be used to check for common configuration problems on UNIX systems. COPS checks for items such as weak passwords, anonymous ftp, or just tftp, and inappropriate permissions. COPS details its findings in reports that an administrator can use to strengthen a system's security. COPS is available at a number of sites, including the Department of Energy's CIAC Web site at http://ciac.llnl.gov/ciac/SecurityTools.html. In fact, there are all sorts of useful tools at the CIAC site. The source code for all of the tools is available, and they are all free of charge.

- *Security Administrator's Tool for Analyzing Networks (SATAN):* The SATAN tool is designed to help system administrators recognize several common networking-related security problems. SATAN identifies and generates a report on problems along with information that explains each problem, the possible consequences of the problem, and how to fix it. The major difference between COPS and SATAN is that SATAN concentrates on specific network configuration issues, while COPS is more concerned with host specific issues. SATAN can be downloaded from various sites, including CIAC.

- *Security Administrator's Integrated Network Tool (SAINT):* An updated and enhanced version of SATAN that is designed to assess the security of computer networks, SAINT can be downloaded at www.wwdsi.com/saint.

- *TITAN:* Created by Brad Powell of Sun Microsystems, TITAN is similar to COPS in that it is a collection of scripts that are designed to strengthen a system's security. The major difference between COPS and TITAN is that TITAN works at a lower level in the operating system fixing configuration errors, while COPS checks for problems such as file permissions and weak passwords. TITAN will not only report on findings, it will actually correct problems. Like COPS and SATAN, TITAN checks for different aspects of security. These programs are not mutually exclusive; running one of the programs does not dilute the benefit of running the other.

- *TIGER:* Similar to COPS in that it is a set of scripts that check a system's configuration. However, it is considered easier to configure and use than COPS. TIGER was originally developed at Texas A&M for checking UNIX system security. TIGER is available at various sites, including Purdue University's COAST site and CIAC.

- *TCPWrapper:* A UNIX network security monitoring program that filters access based upon IP addresses to the various inetd-invoked services. This program allows for the monitoring and control of connections via tftp, exec, ftp, rsh, telnet, rlogin, and finger. Access can be controlled at both the user and service level. It can be very effective in providing an additional level of security to the systems on a network. TCPWrapper is available at a number of sites, including the CIAC site. I highly recommend this program for securing UNIX systems.

- *Tripwire:* A file integrity-monitoring program developed in 1992 at Purdue University. The utility compares a specific set of files against information stored in a database from previous runs of the program. The database maintains a checksum representation or fingerprint of the contents of each directory and file. The database also contains information that allows an organization to verify the access permissions, ownership, groups, and other information that would be pertinent to the integrity of the file system. Any differences that the Tripwire program finds between the current run and the previous runs are flagged and logged. Tripwire can be run against system files to identify any changes in critical system files. If Tripwire is run on a regular basis, a system administrator can be relatively certain that the integrity of system files is maintained and remains free from unauthorized modifications. There is an open source version of Tripwire, which can be found at various Web sites including CIAC's. There is also a commercial version that can be purchased at www.tripwire.com.

Again, I must caution the reader about downloading files from the Internet. Even if you are downloading files from a known and trusted Web site such as CIAC or the CERT Coordination Center, *verify the source code*. For example, in spring 1999 there were security advisory bulletins circulated warning of a copy of TCPWrapper that contained a Trojan horse. If an unsuspecting system administrator installed the altered version of TCPWrapper on his or her system, the system would be vulnerable to attack. The tainted version of TCPWrapper contained a back door that would allow a hacker access to any system on which the program was installed.

8

LAN Security

LAN Guidelines

It is often difficult to distinguish where the individual server ends and the network begins. Some NOSs can be configured so that the end user logs into a domain to access network resources. For other NOSs the user logs into a server. In the case of the latter, the server is the network. As a result, much of what was discussed in Chapter 7 regarding system security can also pertain to LAN/WAN security. Certainly the discussion covering guidelines for passwords can be applied directly to network authentication. Conversely, much of what will be covered in this chapter can also be applied to system security.

Controlling End User Access

Creating an account and assigning a password are only small parts of giving someone access to the network. A network administrator also has to determine other account parameters such as when an end user can access the network, what groups the user is associated with, what files he or she can access, and limitations on network and server resources.

Concurrent Logins

Consideration should be given to restricting concurrent logins for end users. In other words, users should not be allowed concurrent sign-on privileges. Once an end user has logged into a network they should not be able to login somewhere else without first logging out from where they originally logged in. The only exception to this rule should be the LAN administrator and his or her backup. While I recognize that this could cause operational problems for some users, there are several reasons for limiting concurrent sign-ons. First, it saves network resources, such as memory and licenses. It can also prevent the unauthorized use of an account, so long as the user is logged in. It also prevents the user from forgetting to log out. When you allow concurrent sign-ons, the end users often lose track of where they are logged in and forget to sign off everywhere. Users can leave themselves logged into the network on a workstation without even realizing it. They open a window of vulnerability to the network and themselves when they leave accounts signed on.

One solution to this problem is to implement a process that automatically logs off inactive users. There are also systems that freeze a workstation or lock a keyboard on an inactive session, after a specified period of time. To release the keyboard lock the user must enter a password.

Certain operating systems provide some limited capabilities to lock inactive systems. For example, MS Windows screen savers can be configured so that they require a password. This isn't the most secure solution, but it can be better than nothing at all. The main drawback to this solution is that there is no ability for a system administrator to override the password protection. Third-party packages usually offer better solutions. There are systems available for most every network or computer operating system. The systems for client/server workstations usually operate very differently than those that are designed for terminal sessions.

With a workstation the process runs in memory. When there is no activity for a specified period of time, the process may run a time-out program that requires the password of an authorized user to reactivate the workstation. When using a terminal session for an operating system such as Unix or VMS, the time-out process is usually part of a menu system, or it may operate at the application level. As a result, if you are not in the particular menu system or application, but functioning at the operating system level, the time-out process will not work. There are programs available that run in Unix, VMS, and other midrange operating systems that search for idle user processes at the operating system level and "kill" them. The programs are designed to terminate processes that have been idle for a specified period of time. However, organizations run the risk of upsetting end users when they employ one of these programs.

Available Disk Space

It is important to limit the amount of disk space allocated to each end user. Giving users unlimited disk space may end up requiring the purchase of additional disk capacity. I have seen situations where users crashed servers because their accounts did not restrict the amount of disk space the user was allowed. In one instance, a user was running a report that spooled a massive file to disk. The result was that all the available space was consumed, and the server crashed. Users should also be encouraged to clean up their directories on a regular basis.

I recognize that the comparative cost for disk drives continues to drop to where the cost per megabyte is nominal, but disk drives still need to be backed up. That process entails time and personnel, which can increase your operating costs. Why go through the added expensive of backing up files needlessly when they can just as easily be deleted?

Restrictions to Location or Workstation

Consideration should be given to restricting, to a specific workstation, end users who are authorized to enter sensitive transactions or who perform particularly sensitive and/or confidential work. It is preferable to locate the station in a restricted area. Obviously, access to the server itself should be restricted to the LAN administrator and his/her backup.

Time/Day Restrictions

Consideration should be given to restricting end user access to business hours only, especially for those employees who are authorized to access and use sensitive and/or confidential data. If an employee does not normally work in the evenings and on the weekends, then the ability to access the network should be restricted for that time period. Most every operating system and NOS has the capability to restrict an account's access to specific time periods.

Access to Directories and Trustee Rights

Users should only be given access rights to directories they need to function. If a user needs temporary access to a directory, the access rights should be removed when they are no longer needed. Users should only be given the trustee rights they need to do their job. Once a right is no longer required, remove it right away. Trustee rights should be audited periodically.

File Attributes

File-access attributes, such as read, write, execute, and delete, should be granted based on need. In addition, files containing confidential or sensitive information should be restricted to a minimum number of users. File attributes for executables should be restricted. End users should only have read access to those files that are needed to function. Particular attention should be paid to operating system executables. If file attributes for executable files are not restricted, the executable files can be modified. With loosely defined file attributes, important executable files can be changed or replaced with Trojan horse programs.

Other Privileges

Network commands and executables should be restricted to administrators, auditors, and security personnel. With certain operating systems, such as Windows NT, consider renaming the administrator account to something else. That way a potential hacker won't know the name of the privileged account.

One of the things that every system administrator fears most is a hacker gaining privileged administrative access to a system over the network. Privileged accounts such as administrator for NT or root for Unix should not be allowed to login over the network. Network access to the administrative account can be restricted in different ways for different operating systems. Some operating systems offer tremendous flexibility to control the access of privileged accounts.

For example, AIX, IBM's version of UNIX, offers some of the best flexibility I've ever seen built into an operating system. AIX's design makes it very easy for even the novice administrator to prevent a hacker from gaining access to the UNIX "root" account. This is done through the AIX System Management Interface Tool (SMIT) utility. SMIT allows users to perform system administration and management commands without having to know the command line syntax. Using the SMIT interface, which is a hierarchy of menus, information is entered into several options. The dialog then executes a shell script to perform the system management function. With SMIT, organizations can assign attributes that control the environment for a particular account when it logs into the system. For example, SMIT users can restrict the ability of an account to rlogin or su. They can also prevent someone from gaining access over the network to particular accounts, such as root, by restricting the ability to log into the root account to specific devices. Using the SMIT utility it is possible to restrict the root account to specific tty devices. A tty device requires an actual physical connection to a serial port on the system. The steps to restrict the root account are described as follows:

1. Go into SMIT by typing in the command "SMIT."

2. Select the "security & users" option.

3. Then select the "users" option.

4. Next select the "change/show characteristics of a user."

5. You will then have to provide an account name. Enter the account name "root."

6. A menu listing will subsequently display the attributes of the root account. Arrow down the list until you reach the attribute valid ttys. In the field to the right you would enter the valid ttys for the root account. For example, "/dev/tty0,/dev/tty1" could be entered in the field. That would require anyone who wanted to log into the root account to use either tty0 or tty1.

7. Once you have entered in the tty devices to which you wish to restrict the root logins, you press F10 to exit.

I go through this exercise of listing the commands not in an effort to teach you AIX, but to demonstrate how simple it can be to accomplish the task. By restricting the root account in this way, even if someone had access to root's password, he or she would be unable to login to the root account if he or she didn't have physical access to the specific tty devices. A person certainly couldn't login over a network connection. Restricting the root account to specific tty devices also prevents someone from using the "su" command to switch to the root account. One of the things that is so nice about this configuration is that if you do try to login to the root account over the network, you don't get any descriptive error message explaining why you can't. It simply appears as if you entered an incorrect password.

With Windows NT you don't have quite as much flexibility, but the process of restricting network access to the administrative account is easier. Figure 8.1 shows the Windows NT User Rights Policy screen that can be found under the User Manager menu. This screen allows you to control whether an account can access a system over the network.

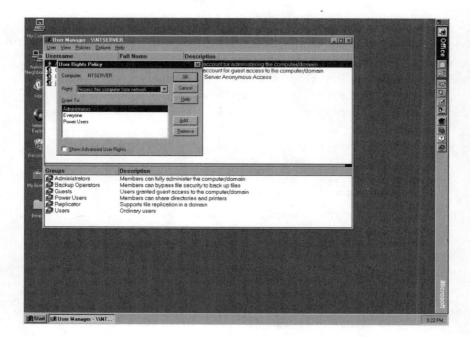

Figure 8.1   Windows NT administrator account.

Figure 8.1 displays the User Rights Policy pop-up window, which shows that "access this computer from network" is displayed in the "right" box and that the administrative account is highlighted. To restrict the ability to log into the administrative account over the network, you simply highlight the administrative account and click on the "remove" button. Figure 8.2 shows the screen after clicking the remove button. As you can see, the adminis- trative account no longer has the policy right to access the system over the network.

Now there is a tradeoff here between convenience and security. For instance, with UNIX, restricting root login to specific tty devices means that you have to have serial connections to those devices. This can also be an inconvenience if you are not at one of those specified devices and you need to get root access to your system. With Windows NT, prohibiting the adminis- trator account from accessing the system over the network means that you will have to have physical access to the server to administer the system. How- ever, the fact that no one else can get privileged access to the system, without having physical access to those specific devices or that specific system, is a security measure worth the inconvenience.

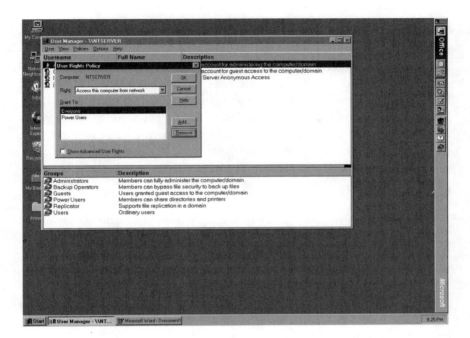

Figure 8.2 Windows NT administrator account.

With some operating systems or business environments, prohibiting network access to the administrative account is not a practical option. Restricting access in this way is not possible if systems are spread out over a wide geographic area and are remotely administered from a central location. However, there is a high level of security provided by restricting the ability to remotely administer a system or server over the network. It means that even those who know the administrator, supervisor, or root password, cannot login unless they have physical access to the system.

Remove Inactive Accounts

Organizations should review network user accounts on a regular bases and delete any accounts that are no longer required. Accounts for users or employees no longer with the organization should be deleted. Firms should also delete inactive accounts, removing or disabling username accounts that have not been accessed in the last three to six months. Hackers frequently try to exploit inactive accounts for the initial break into a system or as a means to gain access to a network again. They know they can alter an inactive account, by changing the password, for example, without fear of the change being detected by the user of the account.

In addition, guest accounts should be removed and anonymous FTP should be disabled. With NT or Netware, organizations should be careful about the access privileges they give to a guest account set up on their LAN. When the server is first brought up, delete the guest account from the group everyone and make specific trustee assignments to the guest account. The guest account should not have the same privileges as normal accounts.

Single Sign-On

Presently, every morning I enter in multiple usernames and passwords to gain access to the various networks, systems, and applications that I need in order to perform my job. I have a password for the NT domain, a password for the Novell server, different passwords for different UNIX systems, a password for my e-mail, and passwords for various applications.

Chapter 7 discusses guidelines for creating passwords. Those guidelines also apply to the password creation for network passwords. However, having so many passwords can be confusing to end users and, as we have discussed, can actually create vulnerabilities, because the only way the end user can remember the passwords is to write them down. One alternative to using multiple passwords is the use of a single sign-on (SSO).

With an SSO system users are only required to authenticate themselves once. Once users have authenticated themselves the SSO system handles the management and access to other network resources, such as servers, files, and applications.

The SSO can be achieved using several different approaches. We have already discussed one such system in some detail: Kerberos. With Kerberos users authenticate themselves once, and access to all network resources is controlled by the Kerberos server, which issues tickets or tokens. Another approach to SSO that we have already discussed is to employ a public key infrastructure that employs digital certificates to authenticate end users and determine network access. Other approaches include metadirectories or distributed computing environments (DCEs).

The foundation for metadirectories is rooted in the lightweight directory access protocol (LDAP). LDAP is a "lightweight" or thin version of the X.500 directory access protocol. Metadirectories can be used to synchronize passwords and user attributes among different NOS directories. DCE is an Open Systems Foundation (OSF) OSI-based specification that addresses distributed system security in a multivendor environment. It is similar to

Kerberos and designed to make it easier to authenticate users between different vendors' systems. Metadirectories, LDAP, and DCE are discussed in detail later in this chapter.

Some SSO systems use password caching, screen scraping, or scripting interfaces, as opposed to token-based systems such as Kerberos. The password-caching approach stores the password and passes it from one application interface to the next. The screen-scraping approach uses characters that would otherwise be displayed on a terminal screen. Screen-scraping programs enter in the characters that the end user would type in at the terminal. They, in effect, simulate the typing action of the end user. Scripting interfaces function much in the same manner as screen scraping.

An SSO system can allow users to centralize access and administration for end users, systems, and applications. This is certainly more efficient than having to add a new user into each individual system and/or application. A SSO also simplifies the authentication process for the end user. End users only have to authenticate themselves once to access all of the resources available to them. The authentication process can employ any combination of the three basic schemes: something you know, something you have, or something your are.

However, a SSO can have drawbacks. If the authentication is compromised (i.e., a password is stolen), then all resources available to the end user are vulnerable. In addition, you need to be cognizant of whether there are backups to the SSO in the event the system is down. If you recall, with Kerberos, if the Kerberos server is down then network resources are unavailable.

There are several SSO systems on the market from which you can choose. There are systems available for IBM, Novell, Axent, and Computer Associates just to name a few. There are many others out there and they all employ different approaches and emphasize different aspects of SSO. Some emphasize central administration; others emphasize security, while still others emphasize simplifying the process for the end user. If you are interested in a SSO system, I suggest you do a lot of research before implementing one.

Policy-Based Network Management

One tool to consider if you wish to employ single sign-on capabilities is a policy-based management approach. The policy-based network management approach is becoming increasing popular for organizations with medium to large networks. This is especially true with the recent release of Windows 2000 with its Active Directory Services (ADS).

Many organizations are finding it increasingly difficult to manage networks that incorporate hundreds if not thousands of nodes distributed over a large geographic area. Policy-based network management is the process of bringing together the properties of various network resources under a central administrative control. There are several goals of a policy-based management system. The first is to simplify the network management process. Another is to ensure the security and integrity of the network through centralized management of the distributed network resources. Policy-based management is also concerned with the availability of network resources. Policy-based management ensures that critical network traffic receives the necessary resources. This is achieved by the use of policies that prioritize network traffic, so that a critical business application doesn't have to compete for network bandwidth with an employee surfing the Internet for stock quotes. Policy-based management is often implemented for quality-of-service objectives.

From a security perspective, policy-based management can provide the ability to consolidate policy information for network resources. This includes ACLs, ownership, and availability. One of the key elements of policy-based management is the concept of directory services.

A directory can be thought of as a comprehensive listing of objects. In its most basic form, a directory is a repository of information about objects, such as user accounts, places, and things. A typical network implementation contains object resources, like printers, applications, databases, user accounts, and servers. For a network, a directory is essentially a database that stores information on all the network resources, which includes network devices, users, groups, volumes, and passwords. The basic function of directory services is the ability to locate, name, and communicate with all of those network resources. Directories are really just repositories of information combined with access methods and related services. Every NOS implements some form of directory services. NOSs have always had some form of directory system for accessing and managing resources. If they didn't, network resources would be inaccessible. However, the different NOSs have stored directory information in a variety of proprietary formats. This has been a major obstacle to the various NOSs being able to share directory service information.

In the late 1980s, the X.500 Directory Access Protocol (DAP) standard was developed in an effort to create and integrate a universal directory service. The OSI-based protocol specification provided client applications with a way to access and exchange the directory information. It was an effort to tie together the disparate and proprietary directory services. The DCE specification was an outgrowth of X.500. Unfortunately, since both X.500 and DCE were both OSI-based they never really experienced wide acceptance. Like OSI, they were cumbersome and monolithic in there approach. They were examples of a bad implementation of a good idea.

A more recent development is the LDAP, a slimmed-down version of the X.500 DAP. LDAP focuses on only the protocols that client applications use to access the directory and does not include all of the overhead associated with X.500. LDAP represents the least common denominator of directory services information. LDAP is supported in numerous client applications and offers a common way to look up information from an X.500 directory or any directory that supports the LDAP standard.

There are some security issues with early versions of LDAP in that they employed a cleartext password authentication mechanism. The risks associated with a cleartext password are obvious. LDAP version 3 includes an extension for Transport Layer Security (TLS), which specifies a security scheme utilizing SSL technology. This mitigates the risk associated with the transmission of a cleartext password.

There are a number of directory services networking products on the market. Some are X.500- and/or LDAP-compliant, and some are not. Some are fading technology, and some are rising stars. For example, there is Banyan's StreetTalk, Sun's NIS (Network Information Service), and IBM's implementation of DCE. These fall under the category of fading products, which use older technology.

Other products include Novell Directory Services (NDS), Netscape's Directory Server, and Microsoft's Active Directory. All three of these products support the LDAP specification. Netscape is presently only a marginal player in the directory services war. As such it may be too late for it to build momentum for its product. NDS, which is the most mature and probably the most robust of the three, provides a repository for information about users, passwords, groups, servers, volumes, and applications. In many ways, Novell is pinning its future as a company on NDS, which is being adopted by many vendors and is the most widely implemented network directory service. There are versions of NDS for Netware, Sun Solaris and other varieties of Unix and Linux, and IBM's AS/400 operating system. NDS will also interface with Microsoft's Active Directory. In addition, Cisco will support NDS in its Internetworking Operating System (IOS) software for routers and switches. Cisco is also committed to supporting Microsoft's Active Directory in its IOS.

Active Directory has only recently been released, and as a result, it has a number of bugs to work out. Novell faced similar problems when it first released NDS. Microsoft's Active Directory does support LDAP. However, with the exception of Cisco's IOS, there has not been a rush by other vendors to implement Active Directory.

The products listed above are by no means an exhaustive list of the available network system directory products. These products offer the ability to link various directory services together to varying degrees, but none offers the ability to handle dissimilar and disconnected directories enterprise-wide from one end of an organization to the other. A relatively new concept to emerge in recent years is that of the *metadirectory*. The term metadirectory services refers to a category of enterprise director tools that integrate existing disconnected directories. Metadirectories accomplish this by surmounting the technical and process issues associated with integrating dissimilar and unrelated systems and architectures.

While Novell and Microsoft both tout their directory systems as meta-directories, they are in fact "network system" directories only. It is true that they link to other directories through LDAP, but they don't really fit the definition of a metadirectory—primarily because the systems that are linked together are similar and, while they address technical issues, they do not address process management.

The appeal of metadirectories is that they offer the ability to share information that is common to all other subdirectories, regardless of the platform or architecture. In addition to reducing the cost of management, this also assures data integrity across an entire enterprise.

The ideal metadirectory lets an administrator make a change in one directory and have that updated or propagated throughout all system and application directories. A metadirectory will ultimately provide this centralized approach, while letting the owners of information maintain control over their own directories.

As an example, when a company utilizing a metadirectory system hires a new employee, the information for the new employee would be entered into the human resource management system (HRMS), and that would propagate to other directory services creating a network login, an e-mail account, and access to various applications. Even the organization's PBX, building security system, and parking space allocation would be synchronized by the metadirectory; in fact, all of the enterprise's directories would be synchronized. The information is entered locally, but the access level for each system is controlled centrally by the metadirectory.

Due to their hierarchical nature, directories are very efficient at providing quick answers to queries. This makes directories well-suited in a policy-based management scenario. However, directories are by no means the only choice. A database structure is an appropriate alternative under certain circumstances.

A database architecture does have inherent scalability limitations. In addition, there are advantages to the synchronization process with directories over the replication process that is required when employing databases.

Replication requires a much higher level of uniformity and integration between servers. For the replication of the database to be successful, it is also necessary for servers be able to interface much more tightly. This implies that a higher level of trust between servers is required, which can have security implications. By contrast, the synchronization process is more in line with performing a file export. The server simply dumps a flat file.

One of the likely applications for directory services will be in the area of network security management and the storing of digital certificates. Many observers see directory services in general and metadirectories in particular as a means to manage an organization's public key infrastructure. Chapter 3 discusses the benefits of an X.509 public key infrastructure. However, to be effective the digital certificates need a distribution process. A metadirectory offers this capability. One company, Texas Instruments, is presently using an X.500/LDAP directory to store X.509 certificates.

While policy-based management can have advantages it also holds risks. When Windows 2000 was first released there was much debate about the security of Active Directory. When utilizing Active Directory Services, there are dangers associated with loosely defined policies or the granting of broad administrative privileges to managers and administrators, which can result in gaping holes in an organization's network security. At the very least it can result in potential exposure of confidential information. Due to the design of Active Directory, administrators who have been restricted from accessing particular network objects can actually take ownership of the restricted objects with a few clicks of a mouse. Microsoft's response to the flaw was to recommend that multiple domains be implemented with Active Directory, which defeats the purpose of implementing the directory service. It is amusing to note that Microsoft's initial response to the flaw was to call it a "feature" of Active Directory. I guess it's true that any software bug sufficiently advanced becomes a feature.

However, Active Directory is not alone in containing risks associated with loosely defined policies. The same danger is associated with any policy-based system and can result from poorly defined or implemented policies. With Active Directory, the risk is heightened by the concern that organizations will attempt to implement it with the same broad privileges that they had implemented NT domains. Active Directory and NT domains are two entirely different systems with different approaches to security and implementing them in the same manner can have disastrous results.

Segmenting LAN Traffic

Ethernet is the most commonly implemented LAN protocol. With the Ethernet protocol, any device on a network segment can monitor communications between any other device on that same network segment. Whenever possible, organizations should segment their networks for both security and performance purposes. Segmenting networks prevents packets from traversing the entire network. Network segmentation is a process of separating a large network into several smaller networks. This can be accomplished by grouping associated users together on a hub or similar network device. A hub is a network device with multiple ports into which other network devices are plugged. A hub acts as a conduit for packets traveling from one device to another. When a packet arrives at one port, it is copied to the other ports, so that all segments of the LAN can see all packets.

There is a performance advantage to this approach, due to the fact that the packets stay within a segment and do not traverse the entire network. The network segmentation reduces traffic on the entire network and reduces the physical distance a packet must travel. The security comes from the fact that it is necessary to have physical access to a segment to sniff the specific segment packets. Without network segmentation all network traffic is available to a network sniffer.

As an alternative to standard hubs, consider using Ethernet switches, also called switching hubs. Switching hubs are employed for switched Ethernet. Switched Ethernet provides the same throughput as standard Ethernet (10 Mbps) or Fast Ethernet (100 Mbps) but uses what is referred to as microsegmentation. Switched Ethernet establishes virtual dedicated connections between devices. The advantaged to Switched Ethernet is that the dedicated connection restricts who can see the traffic. This improves network throughput, because the packets are only forwarded to the required port and not to all ports. This can be accomplished be replacing traditional Ethernet hubs with Ethernet switches. The trade-off is that Ethernet switches are more expensive than the traditional Ethernet hub.

Honeypot Systems

One technique that many administrators employ is the use of "honeypot" systems. Honeypots are decoy or lure systems. They are basically deception systems that contain phony services, files, and applications designed to emulate well-known holes with the goal of entrapping hackers. They are designed to attract hackers, hence the name "honeypot." The honeypot is intended to make hackers believe that they have discovered a real system. The system is designed to lure a hacker into a "safe" network or server that impersonates important applications or information. When the hacker enters the honeypot the trap is sprung and the alarm is sounded. For it to work properly, the system has to be interesting enough to occupy the hacker long enough so that a security administrator can trace the hacker.

Honeypots are usually deployed in conjunction with IDSs. As a result, companies like Cisco and Network Associates offer them as part of their IDS products. Network Associates' CyberCop Sting actually simulates an entire network with multiple routers and host systems. What looks like an entire network is actually the CyberCop software running on a single workstation. The software is designed to monitor and report any activity to the simulated devices on the fictitious network. IDSs are discussed in greater detail in Chapter 15. There is also an open source freeware program, aptly name the Deception ToolKit, available from Fred Cohen & Associates at www.all.net/dtk/. The Deception ToolKit requires a C compiler. It also requires that the system on which you wish to run it also be running TCPWrapper.

Static IP Addresses Versus Dynamic Host Configuration Protocol (DHCP)

DHCP enables network administrators to centrally manage and automate the assignment of IP addresses for an organization's network. This means that a computer with a DHCP client can dynamically obtain an IP address from a remote server (DHCP server). Each time a workstation logs into the network it is assigned an IP address. An alternative would be to use preassigned static IP addresses that each system would be individually configured to use. Many organizations that deploy TCP/IP for internal corporate networks also use DHCP for IP address assignment as opposed to using static IP addresses. This is especially true if the organization's network has many nodes.

The major advantages of DHCP include simplicity of configuration for the clients, more efficient assignment of IP addresses, and ease of administration. With DHCP administrators don't have to bother configuring each individual workstation with the various IP addresses, because DHCP will do that automatically when the end user boots up on the network. Since the IP address assignment is dynamic and temporary, administrators no longer need to worry about tracking what IP addresses have been assigned and which IP addresses are becoming available due to retired systems. In addition, DHCP is ideal when there are more nodes or systems than IP addresses.

The major disadvantage of DHCP is that the assignment of IP addresses is temporary. From a security standpoint this can make system identification difficult. I have worked in environments where DHCP was employed on the corporate network. At one organization where I was employed all business units except my particular work unit used DHCP. My work unit employed static IP addresses. We did this to use IP addresses to control and monitor access to our central systems. Employing static IP addresses made it easier to identify foreign IP addresses attempting to access our systems. When our log files indicated that an unauthorized IP address had attempted to access our systems we could rarely track down the culprit, because DHCP was employed. The environment was a large network with tens of thousands of nodes, with many subnets spread out over a very large geographic area. The best we could do was narrow it down to a particular building or sometimes a particular floor in a building at a particular facility.

I discussed this situation with the organization's Information Protection Team, the computer cops for the company, and they agreed that DHCP did present some problems. However, the general feeling was that, from an administrative standpoint, the advantages far outweighed the disadvantages.

There are other alternatives to DHCP, such as Reverse Address Resolution Protocol (RARP) or Bootstrap Protocol (BOOTP), that essentially function the same way. These protocols are almost nonexistent in the corporate environment, but you may find them employed in an academic environment.

If you work in an environment that employs DHCP on the network, you need to take it into consideration. This is particularly true if you do any filtering based on IP address. The filtering can take place at the router, through a protocol filter like TCPWrapper, or even at the application level. It is possible to assign a range of IP addresses to a group using DHCP, so if you are limiting access based on IP addresses it does not necessarily require that you use static addresses—just plan accordingly.

9

Media and Protocols

Network Media

Every network, regardless of the protocol, must operate over some media. There are several options from which to choose when selecting the most appropriate media for an organization's network needs. Too often security is given little consideration when selecting the media for a network design. There are different types of physical media available with various characteristics. The various media is sometimes categorized as guided or unguided. Table 9.1 lists some of the network media choices available. The term unguided may be somewhat of a misnomer. With the exception of radio-based wireless, no network media is truly unguided. Microwave, infrared, and satellite, while not confined to the path of a physical media, are certainly guided. Media can also be categorized as terrestrial and nonterrestrial. Copper and fiber are terrestrial in that tehy are usually underground or physically anchored to terra firma in one manner or another. Microwave and satellite are nonterrestrial in that they are not bound by the same physical limitations.

Table 9.1
Network Media Choices

Guided	Unguided
Twisted pair	Microwave
Coaxial cable	Infrared
Fiber optic	Satellite
	Wireless

Twisted Pair

Twisted-pair cable is made up of pairs of wires insulated from each other and twisted together within an insulating sheath. The twisting of the wire pairs produces a mutual shielding effect. This effect cuts down on the absorption and emission of electromagnetic interference. There are two main types of twisted-pair cable, shielded twisted pair (STP) and unshielded twisted pair (UTP).

It is very easy to tap both STP and UTP cabling. In some cases it is not even necessary for physical contact to occur with the tap for it to be effective. This is because there is residual electromagnetic emanation from the cable as the signal traverses its length. Sensitive devices can detect and interpret the minute variations in the emanation.

Twisted pair is also susceptible to electromagnetic interference. This is particularly true of unshielded twisted pair. Electromagnetic interference can reduce network performance. If the interference is strong enough it can effectively disrupt the operation of a network.

Coaxial Cable

Coaxial cable consists of a copper core of solid or strand wire surrounded by an external sheathing of woven copper braid or metallic foil. The cable derives its name coaxial, or coax for short, from the fact that the braided sheathing and the core have the same axis.

There are two types of coaxial cable, thick coax and thin coax. Thick coax cable was used in the first Ethernet networks. Thick coax is about as thick as a garden hose and is usually yellow in color. There is also thin coax cable, sometimes called "thinnet." Thin coax is usually black and is about the thickness of a pencil.

Like twisted pair, coax cable is susceptible to tapping, and the tap does not even need to make physical contact with the cable. However, it is less susceptible to electromagnetic interference, as a result of the sheathing.

Due to the fact that all copper cables radiate electromagnetic energy, they are relatively easy to tap. In the book *Blind Man's Bluff*, authors Sherry Sontag and Chistopher and Annette Drew tell the story of how U.S. submarines were able to tap Soviet communications cables. These cables were within Soviet territorial waters in what the Soviets thought were secure areas. The taps were performed during the 1970s and 1980s by placing a device on the cables. The result was an intelligence gold mine.

Fiber

Fiber-optic cable is made of glass and carries laser or LED-generated light impulses. This light contains digitized data that can be rapidly transmitted hundreds of miles. Fiber-optic cable can send information much faster than existing copper-based cable and can also carry considerably more information than copper cable.

Fiber-optic cable offers several other advantages over traditional copper cable. It has superior transmission quality and is immune to electromagnetic interference. Fiber-optic cable is also much smaller and lighter than copper wire. There are two types of fiber cable for networks, multimode and single-mode.

Fiber is the most secure of all the cable media, because it is very difficult to tap. Unlike copper cable, tapping a fiber cable requires invasive measures, since the light traverses the cable in a focused linear beam and does not radiate. Tapping a fiber cable usually requires that one cut the cable and insert a special device. As a result, any attempt to tap a fiber cable would be detected immediately, because it would interrupt the beam. However, it has been reported that if you can get physical access to an optical fiber and bend it at a sufficient angle you can actually tap the signal without invasive measures.

Microwave

Microwave communications are used for line-of-sight transmissions. Line-of-sight transmissions require an unobstructed view between devices. Microwaves operate at the high end of the radio frequency spectrum. Microwave communications can be intercepted in the line of sight of the transmission. In addition, microwaves penetrate physical structures such as walls. As a result, encryption should be employed when transmitting sensitive data with microwave technology.

It has been said that during the Cold War, in days when relations between the United States and the Soviet Union were fraught with intrigue, the Soviets always built their embassies on the highest geographic point they could find, so that they could intercept microwave transmissions. Conversely, the Soviets never let the United States build its Moscow embassy on high ground. It has been reported that the Soviets also bombarded the U.S. embassy with microwaves to jam any microwave listening devices installed in the embassy.

Microwave communications are also susceptible to interference and are relatively easy to disrupt through a denial-of-service attack. Even natural phenomena such as rain, heat thermals on a hot day, or fog can disrupt microwave transmissions.

Speaking from personal experience, I can tell you that microwave transmissions can be unreliable on very hot days. At a company at which I worked, we used microwave transmissions to connect to our branch offices. On hot sunny days the microwave communications with one particular office often went down. Our telecommunications equipment would kick into dial backup mode. I always attributed this problem to the fact that there were a number of large black asphalt surfaces between the two microwave towers. On hot days the black asphalt would heat up and fill the air between the two towers with heat thermals. Luckily, we didn't experience too many very hot days.

Infrared

Infrared communications utilizes noncoherent infrared light. Infrared is also a line-of-sight medium, but it is relatively secure since infrared light does not penetrate solid objects, such as walls. As a result, it is not necessary to worry about infrared transmissions going beyond the confines of your office. To function, the network transceivers must actually be in the line of sight of each other with no obstruction. However, it is possible to bounce infrared transmissions off of a white or lightly colored object, such as a wall.

Satellite Relay

Since satellite communications can be easily intercepted, they should be considered not secure. As such, measures should be, and usually are, taken to encrypt data for transmission and to authenticate the origin of individual transmissions.

While copper media has risks associated with it, due to the fact it radiates energy, unguided media has even more risks. It is important to remember that when trying to sniff a network half the battle is getting the tap on the network. As a result, unguided or nonterrestrial media is not as secure as guided media. With guided media you need to have some physical access to place the tap. With unguided media, it is only necessary to be in the line of sight to intercept the transmission.

Wireless

The term "wireless" is inclusive of many technologies that don't necessarily belong in the same category. Some wireless technologies are employed for LANs, and some are employed for WANs. Technically, microwave and infrared are wireless and have been in use for years. Microwave is usually considered a WAN technology, and infrared is considered a LAN technology. For this discussion, the term wireless will be used in reference to more recently developed standards and technologies. It is also confusing when attempting to categorize wireless technology as a protocol, a media, or a standard. For the purpose of our discussion, wireless will be covered in the media section.

Wireless (LAN)

Most of the wireless LAN products on the market today are based on the IEEE 802.11b standard. This is a relatively new standard. Wireless LANs offer limited mobility, but their main appeal is that they do not require the cabling that traditional Ethernet LANs employ. This makes them particularly attractive to small and new offices. However, they generally do not have the throughput of standard Ethernet.

There are two basic components of a wireless LAN. The first is an access point, which is a device that is usually connected to a standard wired LAN, usually through a hub. The second component is a wireless LAN adapter that is connected to the PC. The LAN adapter communicates with the access point, usually through radio-based transmissions.

Most of the products on the market have a maximum operational range of 100–300 ft. The maximum throughput is 11 Mbps, although most operate at speeds significantly less than that. The 802.11b radio standard operates at the 2.4 GHz frequency band level. For media access control (MAC) the 802.11b standard has specified three different options, frequency hopping spread spectrum (FHSS), direct sequence spread spectrum (DSSS), and infrared. The MAC is part of the IEEE 802.X standard that specifies the link layer. The MAC is the media-specific access control protocol that deals with electrical signals and includes token ring, Ethernet, and CSMA/CD.

There are a number of security issues involved with radio-based wireless LANs. First, the 2.4-GHz band is subject to interference. Common appliances, such as microwave ovens and cordless phones, operate at the same frequency. In addition, because the transmissions are radio-based they can be intercepted by anyone with the proper receiver. When products were first released, most manufacturers argued that spread-spectrum technology effectively masked radio signals or that employing frequency hopping made it difficult, if not impossible, to lock onto a signal, so interception was not a risk. However, this approach relies on security by obscurity, which is not a recommended model for network security.

An optional component of the 802.11b standard is wired equivalent privacy (WEP). WEP adds encrypted communications between the wireless LAN client and the access point. Most of the more recent products include WEP as a standard feature.

While interception of communications with wireless LANs is a risk, even greater is the risk associated with some unauthorized person gaining access to the LAN. Anyone within a couple of hundred feet of the access point device has the potential to tap into the network. In an office building environment that means most anyone on the same floor, the floors above and below, someone out on the street in a car, or even in the next building over. Since the access is radio communication, there is no need to make a physical connection. To minimize this risk, most wireless LAN products use some method to authenticate clients. Usually they employ an ID or security code. It is strongly recommended that organizations utilize this kind of feature if they are planning on deploying a wireless LAN. However, I suspect some very smart hacker will eventually devise a way to spoof these ID or security codes. Wireless LAN products on the market today include offerings from 3Com, Aironet-Cisco, Compaq, and Lucent.

Wireless (WAN)

The next big thing in WAN networking technology will be wireless networking. I expect that over the next 10 years wireless networks will be the fastest growing segment in terms of new installations. I am lumping several technologies into this category. Personal Communications Service (PCS) is usually the technology most often referred to when talking about wireless WAN networking. Three different digital technologies make up PCS. They are Code Division Multiple Access (CDMA) IS-95, Time Division Multiple Access (TDMA) IS-136, and Global System for Mobile communications (GSM) 1900. There is also Cellular Digital Packet Data (CDPD) technology that is employed for handheld devices. In addition, there are analog options, such as Frequency Division Multiple Access (FDMA) technology. There several are other developing and competing technologies out there as well.

The appeal of wireless is obvious. The ability to use a laptop to send data, e-mail, or fax while away from the office can enhance productivity. Many people are using it just to be able to surf the Web while on the road. At the same time, wireless technology can reduce the necessity to invest in physical network infrastructure (cabling), thereby reducing overall costs. However, the risks associated with wireless technology is even greater than with traditional unguided media. Wireless differs from traditional unguided media, such as microwave, in that it radiates in all directions. As a result, it doesn't even require one to be in the line of site to intercept a transmission. Presently, there are several consortiums working to enhance wireless technology security.

The underlying application and the sensitivity of the information will dictate the security requirements when employing wireless technology. At a minimum it is recommended that some form of encryption be employed.

Plenum Cabling and Risers

Regardless of the type of cable you choose to deploy for your LAN, you need to consider how the cable is actually installed. This is particularly true for organizations that are in multenant premises with shared facilities. Most organizations fall into this category, since few are large enough or affluent enough to have their own building. When installing cable in buildings with other tenants and shared facilities, it is necessary to consider the security implications of running cable in plenum areas and up building risers.

The plenum area is the exposed area above suspended ceilings, through which can be pulled cable that houses conduit, pipes, ceiling supports, and air ducts. Cable pulled in these areas is referred to as plenum cable, because it must meet specified code requirements for flammability and smoke discharge. If the cable does not meet the requirements, it can't be pulled in plenum areas.

A building's design largely dictates how cable is installed. Ideally, cables should be installed utilizing some form of trench system that is designed for the horizontal distribution of cables on each floor. Figure 9.1 depicts how the trench system is used to house cables for transport across a floor. Utilizing a trench system ensures that the cables are never exposed to the floor below, which exposes them to possible risk.

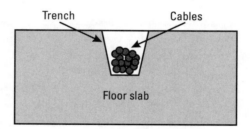

Figure 9.1 Floor trench system.

In most office buildings that employ a trench system, the trenches criss-cross the floor or radiate out from a central closet. Figure 9.2 depicts a cross-section of a trench system, which illustrates how a trench system allows cables to be pulled without protruding into the plenum area in the floor below.

By contrast, buildings without trench systems often require boring holes through the floor in order to achieve the horizontal distribution of cables. This can result in network cables being exposed in the plenum area in the floor directly below. Figure 9.3 is cross-section example of a building that does not employ a trench system. The network cable protrudes into the floor below and above the suspended ceiling.

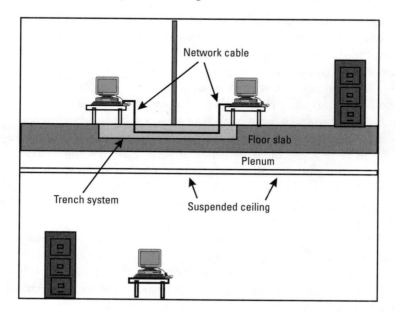

Figure 9.2 Floor trench system and plenum.

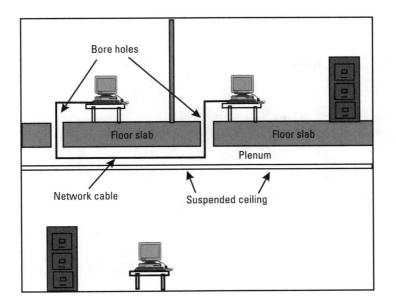

Figure 9.3 Plenum cable.

The risk associated with having network cables exposed to the floor below is that they can be tapped. At the very least, you run the risk of having the cables cut by exposing them in this manner. The risk is compounded if the floor below is occupied by another organization. Some organizations utilize pressurized conduit to minimize this risk. The conduit is filled with pressurized gas and is monitored by a pressure alarm. If the conduit is penetrated the pressure drops, and an alarm is triggered. However, as stated previously, invasive measures are not always required to tap copper cables. Placing the tap near the cables can work if the tapping equipment is sensitive enough. The pressurized conduit would be more effective in protecting fiber-optic cable since fiber does require invasive measures to tap it.

Another concern is cabling in building risers. A building riser is a vertical shaft or conduit that is used to transport circuits from the minimum-point-of-entry (MPOE) to a customer's wiring closet. The MPOE is the demarcation point for circuits installed in a premise, usually by the local telephone company. The local telephone company brings the circuit to the MPOE. The MPOE is usually in the basement of a building. It is the customer's responsibility to get the circuit from the MPOE up to the proper floor for horizontal distribution. This is accomplished through the building riser. Figure 9.4 illustrates this concept. The riser is usually in a wiring,

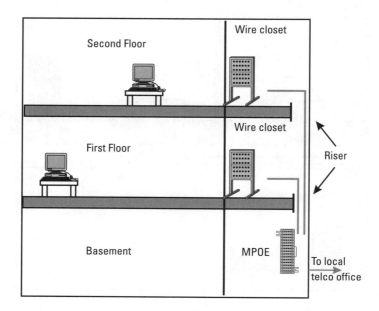

Figure 9.4 Building riser.

electrical, or communications closet. The closets are on every floor, stacked on top of each other.

The security concern associated with cabling in risers is that the cables can pass through many floors before reaching their final destination. The floors through which they pass may or may not be occupied by the same organization. Access to the closet and cables is available on every floor. Just as with plenum cable, the risk once again is that they can be tapped or inadvertently cut.

The sensitivity and criticality of the information should dictate whether plenum and riser cabling is really an issue. If it is an issue, then consider pressurized conduit; also consider encrypting your network communications to ensure confidentiality even if your cables are tapped.

WANs

WANs are usually used to connect geographically dispersed offices. Basically, a WAN connects all of an organization's LANs, so that they can share information and resources. There are many options available to connect an organization's offices into a WAN. As discussed in Chapter 1, WAN implementations can be divided into two very broad categories. One approach utilizes point-to-point dedicated lines and the other uses packet-switched technology over a shared network.

Dedicated Lease Lines

A dedicated leased line, sometimes referred to as a dedicated or leased circuit or a virtual private line, is usually a specially conditioned point-to-point circuit that connects two locations. However, a lease line can be multipoint circuit as well.

A dedicated circuit is obtained from a carrier or service provider for the exclusive use by the customer and is used to connect two sites that are geographically distant from each other. Examples of dedicated lease lines can include 56K circuits, ISDN, fractional T1s in 64K increments, or full T1 (1.54-Mbps) and up.

A dedicated WAN connection typically uses a single circuit to connect two locations. Figure 9.5 illustrates a WAN utilizing single circuit connections. Typically for each location added to the network it is necessary to add a circuit.

As long as dedicated connections use terrestrial circuits and guided media, they are relatively secure, since the dedicated lease lines are provided for the exclusive use of the customer. The major security concern is from the service provider itself or if the carrier uses other carriers to provide the service.

Packet-Switched Networks

An alternative to dedicated circuits is packet-switching networks. Packet switching refers to protocols in which messages are divided into packets

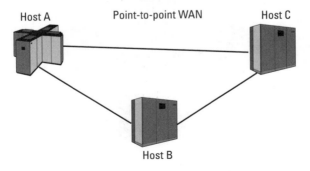

Figure 9.5 Point-to-point circuit.

before they are sent. Each packet is then transmitted individually and can even follow different routes to its destination. Once all the packets that make up a message arrive at the destination, they are recompiled into the original message.

Most modern WAN protocols, including TCP/IP, X.25, and frame relay, are based on packet-switching technologies. In contrast, normal telephone service is based on a circuit-switching technology, in which a dedicated line is allocated for transmission between two parties. Circuit switching is ideal when data must be transmitted quickly and must arrive in the same order in which it's sent. This is the case with most real-time data, such as live audio and video. Packet switching is more efficient and robust for data that can withstand some delays in transmission, such as e-mail messages and Web pages, although now even protocols such as frame relay and TCP/IP are being used for voice and video transmission.

Figure 9.6 illustrates the concept of a packet-switched network. Typically, a packet-switched WAN is a shared network like the Internet. Even if you are using a service provider's private frame relay network you are using a network shared by many of the service provider's customers. Accordingly, concerns about the interception of data or protection of systems should be much greater in this environment.

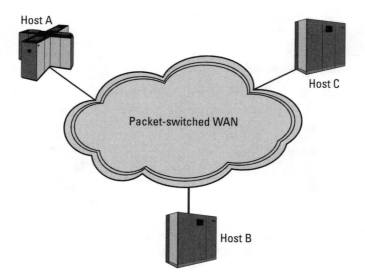

Figure 9.6 Packet-switched cloud.

X.25

X.25 is one of the most widely used packet-switched protocols, particularly outside of North America. X.25 utilizes error detection and correction and is a connection-oriented service, which insures that packets are transmitted in order. X.25 was developed back in the 1970s when circuit performance was notoriously noisy. As a result, communications needed the error detection and correction that X.25 provides.

X.25 utilizes switched virtual circuits (SVCs) and permanent virtual circuits (PVCs). SVCs work much like telephone calls in that a connection is established, information is transferred, and then the connection is released. A PVC is similar to a leased line in that the connection is permanently in place.

In the United States, X.25 has largely been usurped by other protocols such as frame relay that are more efficient and provide greater throughput. The newer protocols are able to provide the greater throughput because they don't have the overhead that is associated with X.25's error detection and correction. This is largely due to the fact that the digital circuits used today are much more reliable and less noisy than circuits used 20 or 30 years ago. As a result, error detection and correction are not needed. X.25 is used extensively overseas because the quality of circuits in some countries is not as good as in the United States and other industrialized nations. However, in the United States, X.25 is still used extensively in ATM and POS networks.

Frame Relay

Frame relay is a widely implemented packet-switching protocol that offers an alternative to virtual private lines or leased lines. It is used primarily for connecting geographically dispersed offices on a WAN. Since it is a packet-switching protocol, it is not well-suited for voice communications, so it is used primarily for data.

Like X.25, frame relay is available in two flavors, PVC and SVC. A PVC is a fixed point-to-point circuit that ensures all packets take the same path. A SVC does not use a predefined path; it uses whatever path is available.

Frame replay is an inexpensive alternative to leased line networks. In addition, it has the advantage over a VPN on the Internet in that it can offer a committed information rate (CIR), which guarantees network performance. Meanwhile, the performance of an Internet-based VPN is subject to the volume of traffic accessing the Internet. Chapter 11 discusses VPNs in more detail.

Asynchronous Transfer Mode

Asynchronous transfer mode, a network technology based on transferring data in cells or packets of a fixed size, is sometimes referred to as cell relay. The cell used with asynchronous transfer mode is relatively small compared to packets used with more mature technologies. ATM uses a fixed route between source and destination. By contrast TCP/IP divides messages into packets, and each packet can take a different route to the destination. ATM's fixed route and small, constant cell size allow asynchronous transfer mode equipment to transmit video, audio, and computer data over the same network and ensures that no single type of data inundates the network.

From a security perspective, the important thing with X.25, frame relay, or ATM is the underlying protocol (i.e., IP over frame relay or ATM). That is where the encryption typically occurs.

For example, security is an issue with X.25, frame relay, or asynchronous transfer mode, because it switches data over shared lines. Frequently the data is switched over lines that are not even owned or managed by the service provider with which the customer contracted. While private networks utilizing X.25 or frame relay may be safer than sending data over an unsecured network, such as the Internet, one should not assume that there are no risks. The information can be monitored anywhere along the route. The risks include physical security, internal attacks, and international connections.

Frame relay, for example, can use both in-band and out-of-band channels. The out-of-band channel is often used for network management functions. Very often, TCP/IP and SNMP are employed as the out-of-band protocol. If these circuits are connected to your routers, there is a potential risk. We will discuss SNMP and routers in more detail in Chapter 10. If these frame relay circuits utilizing TCP/IP for network management are connected to your routers, you should ensure that measures are taken to prevent the inherent weaknesses of TCP/IP from being exploited to compromise your network.

Frame relay and X.25 providers usually offer PVC service with a predefined point-to-point route. While this can make network management easier and reduce the risk of a security breach, it can have drawbacks. Since a PVC uses a fixed route, it is known where the information is coming from and where it is going. Therefore, it is easier to intercept or interfere with the information during transmission.

While SVCs are not subject to the same risks as PVCs, they have risks of their own. Since SVCs use dynamic routing, it is unclear on which route the data travels or on whose equipment the information passes through.

In addition, with dynamic routing you run the risk of information passing through more "hops," thereby being subject to more potential interception or monitoring.

Most large frame relay service providers will scoff at the possibility of such risks, because the network is "privately" owned. However, smaller service providers and even many of the large service providers use local providers in their networks. This is particularly true with international connections. As a result, you really have no way of knowing over whose network your data is traveling. Anywhere along the path the data can be, and frequently is, monitored, if for no other reason than for network management.

Even the large frame relay service providers that can provide end-to-end private network connectivity are not entirely safe, because it is their private network! (Not yours!) Consequently, it is necessary to determine if the risk warrants encrypting the information that traverses the X.25, frame relay, or ATM network.

Cable Television

Many individuals use cable TV modems to connect to the Internet. In addition, some companies use cable TV to connect their offices. The lure of cable is that it offers 1.5 Mbit per second throughput for a relatively small fixed monthly rate. However, cable TV is basically a large broadband network. As such, it is simply a bus architecture, which means that as traffic on the bus increases, your response time can degrade. In addition, because cable is a shared medium, every cable subscriber has access to the network making it vulnerable to network sniffing. Remember half the battle is being able to the get the physical access to the network to sniff the network. Every cable subscriber has physical access to the network.

Devices on the cable network that are unprotected can be accessed. For example, if the cable connection is not properly configured, using MS Windows, it is possible to view other Novell and Windows systems on the cable network using Windows' Network Neighborhood. If a Windows system on a cable network is sharing enabled, it is actually possible to access the files on its disk drive.

In addition, it is necessary to consider the inherent vulnerability that certain operating systems, such as Microsoft's Windows 95, 98, 2000 and Sun's Solaris have in their implementation of the ICMP Router Discovery Protocol (IRDP), which was discussed in Chapter 2. Hackers can exploit this vulnerability by rerouting or modifying outbound traffic as they choose. A requirement for a successful attack using this vulnerability is that the attacker must be on the same network as the targeted system. With cable access, every subscriber on the local loop is sharing the network. They, in effect, have access to the network on which your system resides.

If you employ a cable TV network for Internet access, turn off sharing on your Windows system and use some method to firewall your system. If using cable TV to connect remote locations, employ a firewall to protect your systems and use a VPN tunneling protocol to ensure the confidentiality of the data passing on the network.

Another major difference between cable modem connections and standard ISPs is the fact that cable subscribers can be assigned a static IP address. With standard ISP connections that use dial-up modems, the IP address is dynamically assigned, just like DHCP. The IP address can change with each connection to the ISP. However, cable modem subscribers have a static IP address that never changes. The fact that the IP address never changes makes it easier to find and target a system on the Internet.

x Digital Subscriber Line (xDSL)

xDSL refers to the different variations of the DSL technology, such as ADSL, HDSL, and RADSL. Basically, DSL provides an Internet connection that is always on. There is no dialing up into an ISP. Just as with cable modems, the appeal of xDSL is the relatively high bandwidth at a low monthly cost. Typically xDSL connections provide from 1.544 Mbps to 512 Kbps downstream and about 128 Kbps upstream. When compared to a dial-up analog connection that can provide a maximum of 56 Kbps you can see why xDSL would be so attractive.

However, DSL also has many of the same risks associated with cable modems. Just as with cable modems, DSL can employ static IP addresses. As a result, once your system is identified, it can be easily found again. In addition to the risk associated with using a static IP address, some DSL and cable service providers have been known to use DNS to associate subscriber's names to the assigned IP address. This can cause serious privacy issues and make it much easier to identify your particular connection. For example, let's say a hypothetical service provider called xyzisp.com has assigned me the static IP address of 209.37.67.203. The service provider then creates a DNS entry of johncanavan associated with 209.37.67.203, so that the complete entry is johncanavan.xyzisp.com. This DNS entry can make it much easier to track my activity and for someone to find me on the Internet.

In addition, because DSL is an "always-on" connection, the exposure of your own system is greater. You are essentially on a very large network.

If you can see others on the network then they can see you too. As such, you need to take steps to ensure that your system or systems are secure from unwanted access.

A colleague of mine had installed an ADSL connection to the Internet at his home. The ADSL circuit was connected to a Linux system that he had recently set up. While my colleague was very knowledgeable with several operating systems, he was a novice when it came to UNIX and its variants such as Linux. One day he received an e-mail from a system administrator of a university informing my colleague that his system had been used to launch a number of probes and attacks on the university's systems. Apparently, a hacker had compromised my colleague's system and had been using it as a platform from which to launch attacks on unsuspecting victims.

Once the university had determined that my colleague was not actually the hacker, but one of the victims, he received several e-mails offering assistance. They instructed him what to look for, such as files that are hidden or use blank spaces in for a name. For example a file that might be named " .dat." These would not normally show when performing a simple directory listing. It turned out that the hacker had stored several hundred megabytes worth of files on my colleague's system—source code, scan logs, executables, the works. Many of the files had been stolen from other systems.

After determining that his system had been thoroughly compromised, someone offered my colleague the best advice to secure his system. That advice was to format his hard drive. Once a system has been compromised as badly as my colleague's was, the only thing you can do is format the system and reload from the original distribution media. Considering this story, if you choose to implement DSL, please take precautions to secure your system.

The Internet

If you are reading this book then I assume you already know about the Internet. In fact, unless you have spent the last 10 years on a desert island, you are likely know that the Internet is a large TCP/IP network that can be used to connect remote sites in a relatively inexpensive manner. To connect to the Internet you can use most any of the interfaces or protocols discussed above. ADSL, cable, frame relay, dedicated circuits—alone or in combination—are used to connect to the Internet, usually through an ISP.

However, the Internet is an unsecured network, and measures must be taken to secure data traversing the network, to safeguard company network resources, and to provide authentication for communications.

Chapters 11 and 12 discuss some of the technologies used by organizations that connect their private networks to the Internet, specifically VPNs and firewalls.

Redundancy and Alternative Connections

One last consideration with WANs is redundancy in communications. The concern here is with the alternatives when the primary connection to the outside world goes down. Fortunately, there are numerous ways to build redundancy into a WAN or at least to include a secondary means of communication; simply plan accordingly.

10

Routers and SNMP

Router Issues

One cannot discuss network security without at least touching on routers. Routers are a critical element of both the Internet and corporate network infrastructures. They control the flow of data packets on a network and determine the best way to reach the appropriate destination. On corporate networks, they are often used to separate network segments. In addition, border routers are often the first-line of defense in firewall configurations and are a key component of most VPNs.

Routers are network devices that operate at the network layer (layer 3) of the OSI model that are employed to connect two or more networks. They serve three primary purposes. First, they route network traffic based on predetermined rules or routing tables. Second, they segment frames for transmission between LANs. For example, they can frame 10-Mbps Ethernet LAN frames for transmission on a 16-Mbps token ring LAN or a frame relay connection WAN. Third, routers provide the ability to deny or block unauthorized traffic. This can be accomplished through filtering commands that limit certain protocols (i.e., http, ftp, snmp) or by employing access lists that control the IP addresses that are allowed through. Figure 10.1 illustrates the basic concept behind a router.

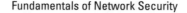

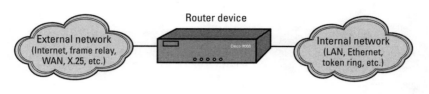

Figure 10.1 Basic router configuration.

Even though routers are ubiquitous, they tend to be overlooked when security measures are developed. No security measures can be considered to be comprehensive unless they include control and management of routers.

Risks

It is important to understand that routers are subject to many of the same risks associated with computers. In fact, the first routers were actually modified computers. A router has an operating system that needs to be configured and, like any OS, that can be subject to bugs. Just as with computers, proper password controls are critical to router security. Routers should not run unnecessary services or protocols. Routers can be effected by denial-of-service attacks. They need to be monitored, just like computers.

How well the router is configured and maintained is critical to the availability of the network. In many ways an incorrectly configured router is an even greater risk than an incorrectly configured computer. An incorrectly configured computer usually only affects local users of the system. An incorrectly configured router can affect everyone on the network. As an example of the possible severe consequences that can result from incorrectly modifying routing tables, in 1997 a major portion of the Internet was practically shut down by the incorrect routing tables of a small backbone service provider. The service provider had sent incorrect routing tables to other backbone providers that essentially sent all network traffic to the small provider. The problem took three hours to resolve, during which time it is estimated that 30–40% of Internet traffic was lost. It can have a crippling effect on one's network if a hacker is able to gain privileged access to your routers. A simple denial-of-service attack launched against a router can cripple a network.

Cisco IOS

The dominant player in networking today is Cisco Systems. They have approximately 80–90% of the market for routers, switches, and hubs. The vast majority of routers on corporate networks and on the Internet are Cisco products. To illustrate how similar routers and servers are when it comes to security we can use Cisco's IOS.

IOS is the operating system that Cisco routers run. An example of one of the concerns that IOS shares with computer operating systems is the concept of the banner or message of the day. IOS can be configured with a banner. Just as with a server, you run the risk of providing information in a banner that could be useful to a hacker. Of course, this should be avoided.

Cisco's IOS supports multiple password levels and encrypted passwords. However, the default at installation is not to encrypt the password. This is important because if the password is not encrypted it is readable in the configuration file if you do a "show startup" or "show run." In addition, it is a common practice to store router configuration files on network tfpt servers. This is done so that the network administrator can update the non-volatile RAM (NVRAM) on the router from the copy of the configuration file on tftp server. For example, an administrator may use the configuration file on the tftp server to reload a "clean" configuration file onto a router if he or she garbled the existing file in NVRAM. A tftp server is designed to facilitate access and as such is notoriously easy to hack (see below). As a result, if the password were stored in the configuration file in an unencrypted format, it would not be too difficult for someone to view the file and obtain the password. In addition to the risk of password disclosure associated with using a tftp server, you also run the risk of unauthorized modifications being made to the configuration file stored on the tftp server.

> Trivial File Transfer Protocol (tftp) is considered not secure, because it doesn't require password authentication. If a host runs the tftp service without restricting the access in some manner, an attacker can read and write files anywhere on the system. For example, it is possible to obtain the password file from a system run the tftp service. The steps are listed as follows:
>
> $ tftp anyhost *(IP address or alias)*
>
> tftp> get /etc/passwd /tmp/passwd.
>
> tftp> quit
>
> Generally, it is a very bad idea for any server to run the tftp daemon. This protocol is an example of an unnecessary service that a computer should not run.

Even if the password is securely encrypted, there are programs available to decrypt Cisco login and enable passwords from a Cisco configuration file or to sniff the password on the network. These programs are easy to find. For example, at the SolarWinds Web site (www.solarwinds.net) it is possible to download a program that can decrypt Cisco-enable passwords. The program is available for Windows 95, 98, NT, and 2000 and will decrypt series 7 non-SECRET passwords. Figure 10.2 shows how simple the program is to use. Simply enter in the encrypted password and out pops the decrypted password.

SolarWinds also offers a tool that allows you to reset the enable password for a Cisco router and change any Cisco configuration parameter via SNMP. While this tool has legitimate uses, it can also be used as a tool for hacking. SNMP will be discussed in more detail later in the chapter.

Cisco Discovery Protocol (CDP) is an example of a protocol that should be disabled on most routers. CDP protocol makes it very easy for hackers to gather information about routers on the network. The CDP protocol broadcasts platform and protocol information to other devices on the network. This information can be useful to any potential hacker. By default, CDP is enabled on a router and its interfaces when IOS is installed. It should be disabled unless there is a specific purpose for running it.

This is not meant to be a lesson on the configuration and commands for Cisco IOS but is simply offered as an illustration of the similarities between servers and routers. Servers are normally protected behind firewalls on the internal network, while routers, due to their unique function, are often exposed to the outside world.

Cisco Secure Integrated Software (SIS)

One of the optional offerings from Cisco is their Secure Integrated Software (SIS). This option, which was formerly called the IOS firewall feature set, does not come with the purchase of basic IOS. The package is a minor plenitude of useful enhancements to IOS that can be used to secure a border

Figure 10.2 SolarWinds' Router Password Decrypt. (*Source*: SolarWinds.Net. Reprinted with permission.)

router and provide secure connections over the Internet. For a relatively minor incremental cost, a Cisco router can be configured to provide firewall and rudimentary IDS capabilities. The firewall capabilities include state inspection and application-based filtering. The IDS is rudimentary in that only specific attack signatures are recognized, and there is no real-time notification. The Cisco SIS package also provides a VPN solution that supports IPSec and L2TP. The VPN software comes with client software that can be installed on a PC workstation to interface with a router. We have found the Cisco SIS package to be robust in terms of feature and functionality. It is an effective initial tier in a multitiered defense.

Simple Network Management Protocol (SNMP)

Due to the security problems inherent in its original design, SNMP is also considered to be an acronym for "security's not my problem." SNMP was developed to allow for the remote monitoring and management of network devices. Unfortunately, hackers can exploit those same facilities for monitoring and managing network devices to gain access to a network. The SNMP standard was developed by the IETF about 10 years ago in an effort to develop a single management server protocol that could manage all network devices regardless of the make of the network device. SNMP also provides the ability to obtain statistical information on the performance of an SNMP network device. For example, network administrators can use SNMP to get information on number of bytes in and out of a particular device.

The graph in Figure 10.3 is an example of the type of information that can be gathered employing one of the many monitoring tools that are designed to be used in conjunction with SNMP. In this example, I am using Multi Router Traffic Grapher (MRTG) to graph the data from a router.

Weekly graph (30 minute average)

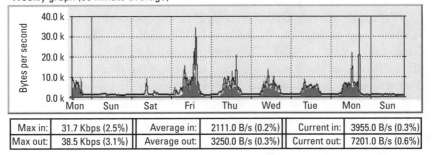

Figure 10.3 Network activity graph.

MRTG communicates with the routers using SNMP and can be utilized to monitor the traffic load on routers. MRTG reads the traffic counters on the routers and logs the traffic data. MRTG also generates HTML pages containing GIF images, which provide a visual representation of the traffic. MRTG was developed by Tobias Oetiker and Dave Rand utilizing Perl and C and is available for download at the URL www.mrtg.org. This is an example of the relatively innocuous information that can be obtained through SNMP.

SNMP provides the capability to manage a network device through what is called an agent. Any SNMP-managed device—whether it is a router, hub, server, or printer—must have an SNMP agent that the SNMP server monitors and queries.

When SNMP was first developed, no consideration was given to security. As a result, SNMP can be a very useful tool for a hacker attempting to compromise a network device. SNMP version 2 (SNMPv2) is a little more secure, but many installations are still running the earlier version. SNMP version 3 (SNMPv3) is under development and is supposeed to provide even more security.

SNMP's authentication is very weak and not very secure. You have to ask yourself what the designers were thinking when they came up with the process. SNMP uses passwords called community strings or community names for the authentication process. It's the standard "something you know" or password authentication. However, the community string passes on the network in the clear. In other words, the community string is transmitted unencrypted as cleartext. This vulnerability can potentially allow a hacker to compromise a device and gain privileged access to the device. A sniffer on the network can easily intercept the community string in transit. As discussed in Chapter 2, the three sources of vulnerability are poor design, poor implementation, and poor management. This is an example of a vulnerability whose source is poor design.

To make matters worse, every SNMP request and response contains the community string. The fact that it is transmitted so often makes it very easy to sniff on the network. This is even worse than the cleartext password vulnerability associated with logging into a system over a network using telnet, rlogin, or a terminal emulator. Even with telnet or rlogin the password only passes in the clear once when you first log into a system. With SNMP the community string is transmitted every time a request is sent to the device.

There are tools that are easily obtained that allow hackers to gather SNMP information on the network. SNMP Sniff is an SNMP packet sniffer that will listen on a network and intercept any SNMPv1 and SNMPv2 information that passes by. This can be very useful for gathering information about devices on the network, including community strings.

If a hacker captures the community string he or she can modify or delete router configurations, change routing tables, crash your network, or open up the entire network to the outside. If SNMP network devices are not properly configured, it is relatively easy for hackers to obtain information on the devices. This includes routers and information in routing tables. In addition, with SNMP versions 2 and 3 management servers and agents tend to be proprietary, so you need a specific vendor's software to manage that vendor's devices; this results in limited interoperability.

If you have to employ SNMP then be sure to use access lists on routers and limit manageability to selected IP addresses. While this is not foolproof it does provide some measure of protection. In addition, you should never use the default community string that comes standard with a router. It is amazing the number of installations that have SNMP running when they don't need the protocol. Often the error is compounded by using the default or "public" password.

Detecting or discovering devices on a network configured with the default SNMP password is a straightforward process. You can walk the IP addresses manually, testing each node's response. There are also tools available to automate and speed up the process. For Mac users there is SNMP Watcher. SNMP Watcher can be used to query network devices for information about their configuration, activity and errors. SNMP Watcher is a freeware program from Dartmouth College.

Another tool that allows you to scan a range of IP addresses looking for devices running SNMP is SolarWinds' SNMPSweep. With this tool you only need to specify a range of IP addresses, and the program will check each node to determine if it is configured for SNMP and if it is using the default community string. Figure 10.4 shows an example of the results of an SNMP scan that I performed on a small network that I have at home using SNMPSweep. In the example only one of the systems named NTSERVER has SNMP configured with the default or public community string. You can tell that by the fact that the system NTSERVER displays information on the system name, machine type, and description. If it weren't configured with the public community string then it wouldn't have returned the detailed information to the query.

Figure 10.5 illustrates the additional information that can be obtained through SNMPSweep with a few clicks to the mouse. In Figure 10.5, I am able to view information on the user accounts that have been set up on the

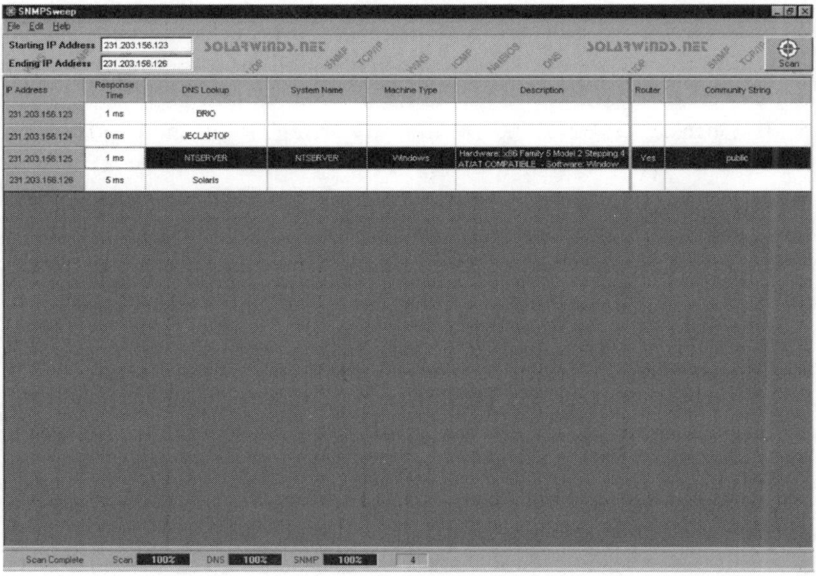

Figure 10.4 SolarWinds' SNMPSweep. (*Source:* SolarWinds.Net. Reprinted with permission.)

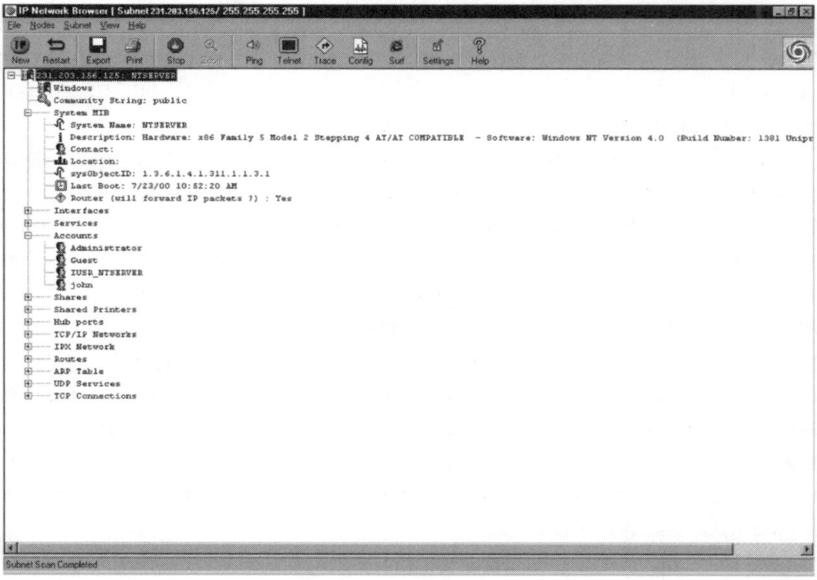

Figure 10.5 SolarWinds' SNMPSweep.

Windows NT server. Knowing the user accounts can be useful information to a hacker.

I could just as easily run a scan on a broad range of IP addresses on either the Internet or a corporate network. In fact, I have. It is surprising to find the number of devices that are configured with the public community string. If I were a hacker, I could use that information to compromise the devices.

Generally, when it comes to routers and servers, most organizations are contentious about either turning off SNMP or not using the default community string. However, certain network devices tended to be deployed without much thought to SNMP security. This can be due either to the fact that the device is not thought to be critical or because those deploying it don't know that it is configured for SNMP by default. This is particularly true for devices on an internal company network. Scanning internal networks I have often found printers, printer servers, terminal servers, UPSs, and other special devices configured for SNMP with the default community string. For example, devices such as HP JetDirect printer servers are often overlooked. While a JetDirect box is not as important as a router or a server, it would still be a nuisance to have someone change the configuration. On the other hand, a network-enabled UPS is critical to the network, and allowing someone to reconfigure or shut it down would have a detrimental effect on the network.

Where possible, limit access to SNMP devices to read-only functionality. This will at least prevent unauthorized individuals from gaining control of a device and modifying the configuration. Also, send authentication traps, so you know when someone is trying to access your SNMP-enabled devices. An SNMP trap is a means of reporting an event, such as a failed attempt to log into a router. This will at least give you some warning that someone is attempting to access the network device. If available, use a VPN to encrypt the connections between devices. Chapter 11 details VPNs.

11

Virtual Private Networks

Encryption on the Network

Chapter 5 discusses the way in which encryption is employed on the WWW, specifically how confidentiality, integrity, and authentication are achieved with SSL when used in conjunction with public key cryptography and digital certificates. SSL is just one example of how encryption can be employed to secure connections on an untrusted network. A VPN is another example of a widely implemented use of encryption to secure connections on an untrusted network.

Before going into a detailed discussion of VPNs, we need to cover some basic concepts related to encrypting a network connection. To begin, when using encryption to secure a connection between two or more systems, it can generally be handled in one of two ways: node-to-node or end-to-end.

Node-to-Node Encryption

Node-to-node encryption is also referred to as link-to-link encryption. Referring to the OSI model, the data link layer is concerned with node-to-node or link-to-link connections. As a result, if you encrypt the packet at the data link layer, it must be decrypted by the data link layer recipient before passing it up to the network layer to determine how to forward the packet.

When encrypting at the data link layer, a packet has to be decrypted and re-encrypted for each node-to-node hop along the route. Node-to-node encryption operating at the data link layer requires compatible devices, sharing a protocol, and a key management process for every device on the network. Figure 11.1 illustrates the concept of node-to-node encryption.

If the devices on the network are not compatible, they will not be able to relay the packets they receive. This is an issue that must be considered, because if the network is large, management requirements will be significant.

End-to-End Encryption

As an alternative, end-to-end encryption operates at the upper layers of the OSI models and can encapsulate data into standard network protocols. As a result, no special considerations are necessary for the intermediate hops along the network. The encryption and decryption of the encapsulated data is done at either end of the connection. Figure 11.2 illustrates the concept behind end-to-end encryption on a network.

However, a consideration with end-to-end encryption is that the further up the protocol stack you move the encryption, the more information you may be providing a potential eavesdropper. As you will see, as you move

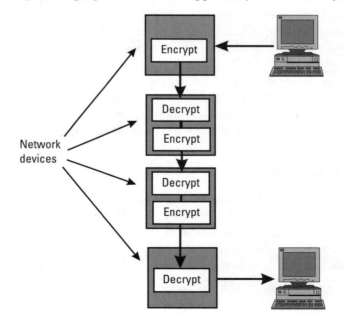

Figure 11.1 Node-to-node encryption.

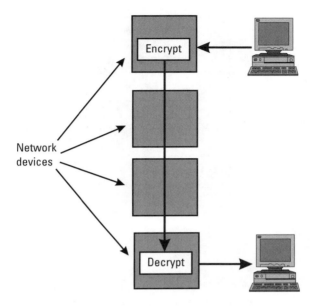

Figure 11.2 End-to-end encryption.

the encryption higher up the protocol stack, more information is revealed about the sender, the recipient, and the nature of the data.

Where to Encrypt

The level of security achieved differs depending on where the encryption takes place. The level of security required should dictate where your encryption is performed. Referring again to the OSI model (Figure 11.3), if you encrypt at the network layer (layer 3), information identifying the devices or machines can be intercepted. For instance, information on the IP addresses of the source and destination can be monitored. This information can be used for network traffic analysis. As we have discussed, network traffic analysis in itself can provide a wealth of information that can be utilized by individuals or entities sniffing the network.

If the encryption takes place further up the protocol stack at the transport layer (layer 4) then someone eavesdropping on the communications can tell which port you are communicating with on the recipient system. From that information, eavesdroppers can surmise what protocol you are using.

For example, if you are communicating with port 161, then you are most likely using SNMP for network management. If you are

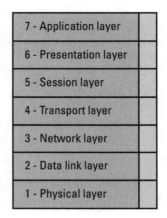

Figure 11.3 OSI model.

communicating with port 25 then you are probably using SMTP for e-mail. Knowing the protocols that are running on a device or system can be used to plan an attack.

A TCP/IP port is a logical connection to a server that usually handles a specific service or protocol. TCP/IP network servers often provide a variety of services or protocols such as SNMP, HTTP, or SMTP. Each of the available services "listens" for an outside connection on a particular port number or uses a specified port number. Table 11.1 lists examples of well-known ports numbers and their associated services.

The port numbers range from 1 to 65,535, with the privileged ports ending at 1,024. Nonprivileged ports range from 1,025 to 65,535. Sometimes the port numbers are displayed at the end of a URL. For example http://www.someurl.com:81. In this example the server is using port 81 for

Table 11.1
Well-Known Port Numbers and Associated Services

Port	Service
25	Simple mail transport protocol (SMTP)
53	DNS
80, 81	HTTP
161	SNMP

the particular URL address. It indicates the port number that the TCP/IP connection is using on the Web server.

At the application layer (layer 7) even more information is available. If e-mail is encrypted and transmitted at this level it may be secure from disclosure and modification, but anyone monitoring the transmission will know you sent e-mail, to whom you sent it, and where. As a result, when implementing encryption on a network you have to determine where you need the encryption to take place and what is an adequate level of security based upon the sensitivity of the data.

Virtual Private Networks (VPNs)

A VPN is a means of transporting traffic in a secure manner over an unsecured network. A VPN usually achieves this by employing some combination of encryption, authentication, and tunneling. "Tunneling" (sometimes called encapsulation) refers to the process of encapsulating or embedding one network protocol to be carried within the packets of a second network.

There are several different implementations of VPN protocols. There are at least five generally recognized VPN protocol "standards." I use the word standard here somewhat loosely. There are also several proprietary products available on the market. The four most commonly employed protocols are listed as follows:

- Point-to-Point Tunneling Protocol (PPTP);
- Layer 2 Tunneling Protocol (L2TP);
- Internet Protocol Security (IPSec);
- SOCKS.

PPTP

PPTP is a tunneling protocol supported by Microsoft for connecting Windows NT clients and servers over remote access services (RASs). PPTP is one of the more widely implemented VPN protocols if for no other reason than it was one of the earliest. PPTP operates at the data link layer (layer 2) of the OSI model and can be used to create a VPN between computers running the Windows operating system.

PPTP is basically an extension of the Point-to-Point Protocol (PPP), the Internet standard for transmitting network layer datagrams (i.e., IP packets) over serial point-to-point links and is used by TCP/IP routers and PCs to send packets over dial-up and leased-line connections. PPP was developed as a replacement for Serial Line Internet Protocol (SLIP). When you dial into an ISP's dial-up service you are using a PPP dialer to connect to the ISP.

PPTP does not provide the actual encryption. Instead the encryption for the PPTP tunnel is provided through Microsoft's Point-to-Point encryption. Microsoft Challenge Handshake Authentication Protocol (CHAP) is the preferred setting for clients supporting Microsoft encryption. CHAP actually uses RSA's MD4 algorithm to ensure integrity and the RC4 algorithm for confidentiality of the data.

To establish a connection, the CHAP server sends a unique random challenge to the client. The challenge is used by the client to encrypt the client's password. The password is then returned to the server to login the client.

PPTP has been submitted to the IETF for standardization. It is currently available only on networks served by Windows NT, 98, and Linux.

Sniffer programs are available at hacker sites, such as L0pht.com, that they claim will sniff PPTP authentication and output the challenge and password hashes. Also available are programs that purport to exploit a flaw in MS-CHAP to get the password hashes without the overhead of cracking the challenge/response.

PPTP is not secure because MD4 has been broken, and the hashing algorithm has been proven not to be one-way. However, when transmitting on an open network PPTP is vastly superior than using nothing at all.

L2TP

L2TP is an IETF standard that combines features from Cisco's Layer-Two Forwarding (L2F) protocol and Microsoft's PPTP. Since L2TP's basis is PPTP, it too is an extension to the PPP. As its name implies, L2TP operates at the data link layer (layer 2). As such, it is used for node-to-node communications. To function across the network from end-to-end, all network devices or nodes must be L2TP-compliant.

IPSec

IPSec, a set of protocols under development by the IETF to support secure exchange of packets at the IP layer, is utilized to implement VPNs on the

Internet and intranets. IPSec operates at the network layer (layer 3) and supports two modes, transport mode and tunnel mode.

IPSec Transport Mode

Transport mode encrypts only the data or information portion (payload) of each IP packet; it leaves the header untouched. Transport mode provides end-to-end encryption since the header information is untouched. As a result, no special setup is required for the network devices.

Transport mode is usually used for secure communications between hosts. With transport mode, someone sniffing the network will not be able to decipher the encrypted payload. However, since the header information is not encrypted, sniffers will be able analyze traffic patterns.

IPSec Tunnel Mode

Tunnel mode encrypts the entire packet, both the header and the payload. The receiving device must be IPSec-compliant to be able to decrypt each packet, interpret it, and then re-encrypt it before forwarding it onto the appropriate destination. As such, it is a node-to-node encryption protocol. However, tunnel mode safeguards against traffic analysis since someone sniffing the network can only determine the tunnel endpoints and not the true source and destination of the tunneled packets.

The sending and receiving devices exchange a public key information using a protocol known as Internet Security Association and Key Management Protocol/Oakley (ISAKMP/Oakley). This protocol enables the receiver to obtain a public key and authenticate the sender using the sender's digital certificates. Tunnel mode is considered more secure than transport mode, since it conceals or encapsulate the IP control information.

SOCKS

SOCKS is an accepted IETF protocol standard that is designed for handling TCP traffic through a proxy server. Currently, there are two implementation of the SOCKS protocol in use, SOCKS version 4 (SOCKS4) and SOCKS version 5 (SOCKS5).

As one would expect, SOCKS5 is the most recent version. The major difference between the two versions is that SOCKS5 provides additional security through authentication. NEC is a major proponent of SOCKS5 and has one of the most widely implemented SOCKS5-based products.

SOCKS5 is compatible with most TCP applications. It also provides rudimentary firewall capabilities, because it authenticates incoming and outgoing packets and can provide network address translation (NAT). NAT is a process that hides the IP addresses of systems on the internal network from the external network.

Implementation

There are various approaches that one can take when implementing a VPN solution on the Internet. The configuration can be router-to-router, server-to-server, server-to-router, workstation-to-server, or workstation-to-router. One low-cost approach might be to use to Windows NT servers employing PPTP with xDSL, frame relay, or fractional T1. Figure 11.4 illustrates this approach employing xDSL with the minimum hardware configuration. While this approach can be inexpensive, I would implement additional firewalls to protect the systems. Additional routers, firewalls and IDS would be required to protected the individual systems and prevent unauthorized access to the network.

We've actually used the Cisco package discussed in Chapter 10 to connect small branch offices to a central office over xDSL. As an example, a one-person office located several thousand miles away from the central headquarters was connected using Cisco's VPN software. Figure 11.5 illustrates the configuration installed to connect the branch office.

The client VPN software was installed on a workstation at the branch office. The client VPN software uses 3DES for encrypting the data portion of the IP packet. The VPN client interfaces with the VPN software on the Cisco router. Since only the data portion of the IP packet is encrypted, the VPN is an end-to-end connection, as illustrated in Figure 11.5.

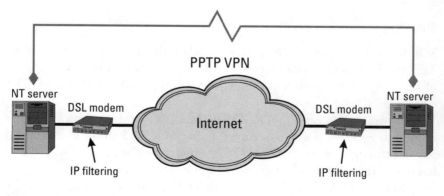

Figure 11.4 PPTP VPN.

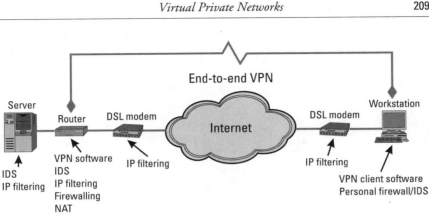

Figure 11.5　Client-to-router VPN.

In the actual installation the xDSL modems, which are actually routers, perform IP filtering, as does the Cisco router. The Cisco router performs other firewall functions as well, such as protocol filtering. The router also has an IDS installed and performs NAT to mask the IP addresses of the internal network. In addition, the gateway server on the internal network performs IP and protocol filtering and is running IDS software. Finally, the client workstation runs a personal firewall/IDS software.

It is important to recognize that there are vulnerabilities within this configuration. For example, it can be subject to IP spoofing. However, to be successful, spoofing would require knowledge of the internal network addressing scheme and vigilant monitoring and IDS would detect the initial attempts.

The major rational for deploying this type of configuration is cost. The cost to deploy an Internet VPN using xDSL is perhaps one-third the cost of using frame relay. When compared to a point-to-point T1 circuit, the savings is even greater. In the above example, the major incremental expense was the Cisco router and software package. We could have just as easily put another router at the branch office. In fact, this would have provided additional security and administrative features. However, we chose not to do so because of cost.

12

Firewalls

Firewalls

Firewalls are a fundamental component of any perimeter defense. Contrary to popular belief, a firewall is usually not a single system; it is actually a collection of components. A firewall is usually placed between two networks to act as a gateway. The principal requirements of an effective firewall are described as follows.

1. It must act as a door through which all traffic must pass (incoming and outgoing).
2. It must allow only authorized traffic to pass.
3. It must be immune to penetration or compromise.

Figure 12.1 illustrates the basic concept behind a firewall. In its basic form, a firewall acts to prevent unauthorized network traffic originating from an untrusted network from accessing a protected internal network. The

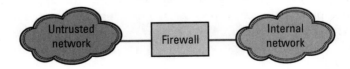

Figure 12.1 Illustration of firewall concept.

origin of term "firewall" derives from construction vernacular for a wall that must be able to withstand fire for a prescribed period of time. In construction, the purpose of the firewall is to provide enough time so that people can either escape or extinguish the fire. An Internet firewall has to be able to withstand a lot of heat, just like its namesake in construction.

As a rule of thumb, an organization should never connect the company's network or systems to an external network, such as the Internet, without a firewall—unless it doesn't care if those systems or network get trashed. A firewall is a combination of hardware and software that protects the company's network and computers from possible intrusion by hackers from the external network.

When implementing security measures to protect an internal network from an untrusted external network you have to make sure the measures you have taken are an adequate response to the perceived threat. Some companies believe that simply placing a router, that is performing packet or protocol filtering, between the internal and external networks is sufficient protection. In general, this is not adequate protection. It is far too easy to circumvent router-filtering systems. In addition, the traditional router was not really designed for protecting networks. They were designed to "route" network traffic. Even though many of the newer routers are much more sophisticated in their capability to protect a network, I would still think twice before relying on a router alone to protect my internal network from an external untrusted network.

Firewalls Pros

Firewalls are general good at keeping unwanted and unauthorized traffic from passing (in or out). They are also an efficient method of providing Internet access to internal users. A firewall can provide NAT for systems or networks that don't have an IP address. They can (sometimes) monitor for and notify you of attacks and network problems. At the very least, firewalls are effective at maintaining logs of all activity that pass through, connections to, or attempts to connect to the system. These logs can be used to identify abnormal events.

Firewalls Cons

One of the drawbacks of a firewall is that it represents a single point of failure. It is the high-tech equivalent of putting all your eggs in one basket. If you make a mistake configuring the components of your firewall you may be allowing unauthorized users through. It takes knowledge, experience, and skill to configure a firewall. In addition, if the firewall goes down, your connection to the outside network is down. A denial-of-service attack that effectively shuts down your firewall shuts down your network connection to the outside world. At the very least, a firewall tends to degrade network performance between the outside network and the inside network. This is because a firewall examines traffic going in and out; this process of examination takes time, which can slow network throughput.

Firewalls are also not quite as smart as would be desirable. As a result, they can only control and monitor traffic so far. They will still allow some things through that can hurt you, and they can stop some things that you do want to pass through.

A firewall by itself does not assure a secure network. A firewall is only a tool. Firewalls need to be configured properly, and they need to be monitored. Vigilance on the watch is still required. Many organizations assume that if their network is behind a firewall they only have to monitor the firewall and not be concerned about the systems sitting on the inside network, or they assume that if their network is not connected to the Internet, they don't need to be concerned about hackers. Nothing could be further from reality.

Firewalls are of no use tracking activity on the internal network. While a firewall does make it somewhat more difficult for someone from the outside to get in, the majority of attacks on corporate systems come from the inside—not from the outside. Sometimes the biggest threat to an organization's systems and networks is from its own employees. Critical systems should be configured to monitor logins, failed logins, and all network activity. Most every computer and NOS has utilities for monitoring this kind of activity. For example, Windows NT Server has the Event Viewer. Most versions of Unix allow you to monitor logins through the wtmp file and record failed login attempts. Unix, in particular, can be configured to record all sorts of activity that can be reviewed for security purposes.

In addition to the threat from within an organization, firewalls can be circumvented by outsiders, so it is important that critical systems be configured to monitor network and login activity. If the firewall—as your first line of defense—fails, then intrusions might be detected in the logs of the individual systems.

Remember, just because a system is on an internal network doesn't mean it is safe. There may be some external access point that you aren't even aware of somewhere on that network. It only takes one opening to the outside for a hacker to have access to an entire internal network. As a result, you should defend your systems as if they were connected to an external network.

Many organizations are lulled into a false sense of security by the existence of firewalls. Putting your systems inside a moat of firewalls does not ensure security. Since many of the threats will come from within the boundaries of the firewall, don't just rely on the firewall. You must monitor internal systems every day. This is where having knowledgeable and experienced staff is very important.

When developing firewall access policies, there are two general approaches that can be employed. The first is to deny anything that is not explicitly allowed. The second is to allow that which is not explicitly denied. Obviously, the first approach is the more secure.

Types of Firewalls

Firewalls can be categorized in several different ways. They can be categorized by the layer of the OSI model at which they operate, by the technology they implement, or by the general approach they employ. When using the different approaches employed by firewalls, you can separate them into two different categories, filtering firewalls and proxy firewalls. Many firewall implementations use a combination of both approaches.

When categorizing firewalls based on the level of the OSI model at which they operate, there are three basic types of firewalls:

- Network level;
- Application level (proxy server);
- Circuit level (proxy server).

Network Level Firewalls

A network level firewall operates at the network level of the OSI model, hence the name network level firewall. A network level firewall is usually a screening router or specially modified computer that "filters" or "screens" each incoming packet to determine whether to pass it on through to the network. Network level firewalls typically employ one of two different filtering approaches:

- Static packet filtering;
- Dynamic packet filtering/stateful inspection.

Static Packet Filtering

A static packet filtering firewall employs a process of filtering incoming and outgoing packets to deny or authorize access. The criteria to deny or authorize access can be based on the network address of the packet and other rules as defined by the network administrator. The most widely employed static packet filtering firewall is the common router. The filtering rules employed to determine whether to deny or authorize a packet are non-dynamic. In other words, they don't change. The rules are static, hence the name static packet filtering firewall.

Stateful Inspection/Dynamic Packet Filtering

Stateful inspection also occurs at the network level of the OSI model. A stateful inspection packet filtering firewall also filters packets, but it can modify the rules according to need. The rules are "dynamic" in that they can change, as conditions require. For example, a stateful inspection firewall remembers outgoing packets and permits any corresponding incoming packet responses to pass through. It only allows in traffic that is a response to a request that originated from the inside network.

Proxy Servers

Application level and circuit level firewalls are two different implementations of a proxy server. A proxy server "stands in" for both the client and a server during a connection. A proxy server acts as the "man in the middle," so that there is no direct contact between a client on an internal network and a server on an untrusted network.

Technically, the proxy is not the firewall. The proxy runs on the firewall. This is an important distinction. The firewall stops the traffic from flowing through, while the proxy allows the controlled access. The proxy is only a software solution to allow communication between two networks in a controlled manner.

Application Level Proxy

Application level proxy firewalls are sometimes referred to as application level gateways. This is because the purpose they serve is to provide a gateway between a trusted and untrusted network through which information can pass. An application level proxy operates at the connection level through interactive proxies that control the establishment of connections. Typically, the proxy also authenticates the user and authorizes the source and destination addresses and permits or denies the protocol.

To function, the server requires proxies for each protocol (i.e., FTP, HTTP, and telnet). The application level proxy must know the particular application for which it is providing the service. There are generic proxies available that can be employed for obscure protocols, but utilizing them can have a detrimental effect on throughput. To optimize performance, proxies specifically designed for the various protocols should be employed.

Circuit Level Proxy

A circuit level proxy functions by creating a "circuit" between a client and a server without interpreting the nature or substance of the request. To function, a circuit level proxy requires that a client system run a special client software. One of the most widely used circuit services is SOCKS, which is discussed above.

Packet Filters Versus Proxies

Generally speaking, packet-filtering firewalls tend to provide better performance, in terms of throughput, than proxy firewalls. That only makes sense if you think about how the two differ in their functioning. Packet filters simply inspect the packets and pass them through, while proxy firewalls require much more setup and overhead. In general, proxy firewalls tend to provide better protection than packet filters. However, I am sure there are many individuals and vendors who would take exception to both of the previous statements. In terms of protocols, general network level firewalls are more effective at handling protocols such as telnet and SMTP, while proxy firewalls are better at protocols such as FTP and HTTP.

Firewall Configurations

There is no one way of implementing a firewall. There are many different ways to deploy the components that comprise a firewall. There is little difference whether the approach employed uses packet filtering or proxies. Many organizations use a combination of packet filtering and proxies in their firewall configuration. The most widely implemented architectures are listed as follows:

- Screening routers;
- Bastion hosts;
- Dual-homed hosts;
- Screened hosts;
- Screened subnets.

The architectures listed above are general concepts, and they are neither all-inclusive nor mutually exclusive. They are examples that I use to illustrate the practical application of the theory.

Screening Router

The screening router is probably the simplest approach you can use for fire-walling your network. If you are connecting your company network to the Internet you will probably need the router anyway. Usually, the router is supplied by your ISP. Routers can provide a cheap and useful level of security by allowing you to filter connections based on the IP address and the protocol. Most router software comes standard with the ability to filter traffic. There are also public domain software packages available on the Internet that enable you to create your own router.

One popular freeware is IPFilter. IPFilter runs on several versions of UNIX and can give a host system IP-filtering capabilities. The source code can be downloaded from a number of locations. One site is the University of Australia at http://coombs.anu.edu.au/~avalon/ip-filter.html. Another low-cost alternative for PC-based systems is Drawbridge. Drawbridge can convert most PCs with two network cards into a packet-filtering router. To find a copy to download simply use one of the many Internet search engines. Just be sure of the reliability of the site from which you choose to download.

Figure 12.2 illustrates the way the screening router functions. Basically, the router examines each packet as it attempts to pass through. This examination can occur for both incoming and outgoing packets. Based upon the rules loaded in the router, it either passes the packet on through or drops it. Screening routers are sometimes referred to as border routers because they sit on the border separating two or more networks.

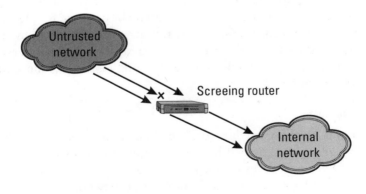

Figure 12.2 Screening router function.

A screening router is not sufficient to protect an organization's network connected to the Internet. As stated before, routers are designed to route traffic, not to be firewalls.

Bastion Host

A bastion host is somewhat more complicated than a screening router. In architectural terms, a bastion is the outer part of a castle. It is usually a part of the castle that sticks out exposed and is used to defend the castle. In the movies, the bastion is the part of the castle from which they would pour the boiling oil down onto the soldiers who were laying siege to the castle.

A bastion host gets its name from the fact that it is the part of the network that sticks out exposed and is used to defend the network. A bastion host is the outer defense of a network that does not allow traffic to pass.

With a bastion host you generally want to run a stripped-down version of the operating system, regardless of the operating system. If possible, you should modify the system kernel to remove utilities and functions that are not needed. Only those services that are needed should be run, and all other executables and services should be removed. By doing so you reduce your exposure to certain operating system vulnerabilities. For example, if you don't need *ftp* or *ping* on your bastion host, then don't have them running. If you leave the various utilities functioning, they will be used by hackers.

In general, IP routing should be disabled on a bastion host. It is not uncommon for internal users to actually log into the bastion host to access the outside network. There are, of course, risks associated with that approach in that unauthorized individuals may be able to compromise a username and password. As a result, it is very important that systems on the internal network should not trust the bastion host.

Since the bastion host is the system that is most accessible to the outside world, you should monitor it constantly and be prepared for the fact that it may be compromised. In today's environment, a bastion host by itself is not enough. Other measures, such as a screening router, should be placed between the bastion host and the internal network. Figure 12.3 illustrates the concept of a bastion host.

Dual-Homed Host

A nonrouting dual-homed host can be thought of as a type of bastion host. Generally, a dual-homed host is a computer with two network cards installed. One network card is connected to the outside network, and the other network card is connected to the inside network. It is called "dual-homed" because it sits on two networks at once.

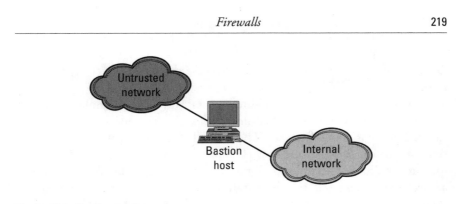

Figure 12.3 Bastion host.

A dual-homed host can perform the function of a router. However, for the dual-homed host to be effective, the IP routing function should be disabled. The direct flow of IP traffic between the networks should be blocked. Traffic between the networks should be controlled by proxies.

The major vulnerability of dual-homed hosts can be the administration. It is easy to make mistakes configuring such a system and that can create holes in the system that allow unauthorized traffic through. Figure 12.4 illustrates a dual-homed host.

Proxy Server

A "proxy" is a substitute or a surrogate for something else. With a firewall, a proxy is a program that acts as a substitute for another program. A proxy server is designed to prevent a connection from one entity directly connecting to another entity. Instead, the connection is stopped at the firewall, and a proxy application is forwarded. At no time are the two entities in direct contact. In effect, the proxy firewall is identical to the man-in-the-middle attack

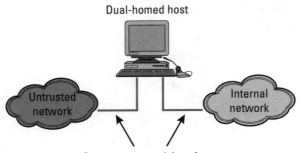

Figure 12.4 Dual-home host.

described in Chapter 2. However, in this case the proxy server is protecting the entities on the internal network.

A proxy server can be configured several ways. For example, it can run on a simple bastion host or a dual-homed host. It is important to remember that the proxy is not the firewall. The firewall security is provided by the bastion host or the dual-homed host. The proxy operates on a host that has IP forwarding disabled and blocks all traffic from passing. The proxy is actually a mechanism designed to allow traffic through in a controlled manner. Figure 12.5 illustrates the concept behind a dual-homed host proxy server.

Screened Host

Another option is to deploy a screened host. Figure 12.6 illustrates a screened host. With this configuration, the host is the only part of the firewall directly connected to the internal network. The host is protected by a screening

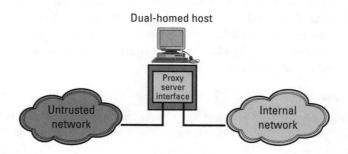

Figure 12.5 Dual-homed host proxy server.

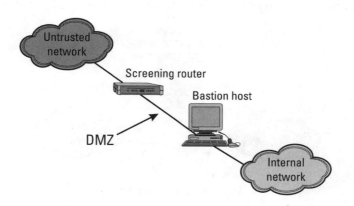

Figure 12.6 Screened host.

router that provides packet filtering. The router will only allow certain types of connections or traffic through to the bastion host. The router is configured so that the only system on the internal network from which it will accept connections is the bastion host. This setup can be configured so that the host is the only system on the internal network to which the router and outside systems can establish a connection or see.

The section of the network between the screening router and the host is referred to as the "demilitarized zone" (DMZ). The term derives from the buffer zone that separates North Korea and South Korea. In Korea, the DMZ is a no-man's land that is intended to separate the belligerent parties. It provides an added measure of security. With firewalls the DMZ provides the same function. The DMZ is neither part of the internal nor external network. Generally, the DMZ is a buffer zone between the screening router and the bastion host. However, you can have multiple buffer zones, as we will see when we look at a screened subnet.

Generally speaking, a screened host provides a greater level of protection to the internal network than does a dual-homed host alone. A dual-homed host represents a single point of failure, whereas a screened host uses a two-tiered approach.

Screened Subnet

With a screened host configuration, if a hacker manages to get through the screening router and is able to compromise the bastion host, there is nothing to stop the hacker from compromising the rest of the network. That risk is mitigated with a screened subnet.

A screened subnet adds an additional router, so that it sandwiches a bastion host between two routers that separate the internal network from the outside network. This establishes a separate subnetwork that acts as a barrier between the internal and external networks. This separate subnet is a buffer that acts as a DMZ that provides additional protection for the internal network. Figure 12.7 illustrates a screened subnet configuration.

With a screened subnet, the exterior or border router communicates only with the outside network and the bastion host on the subnet. The exterior router is never allowed to communicate directly with the interior router or the interior network. The interior router communicates only with the interior network and the bastion host. The two routers never directly communicate with each other.

In this configuration, both routers perform packet filtering. The bastion host has IP routing disabled and runs proxy services. With this type of configuration, the external router is frequently provided by ISPs.

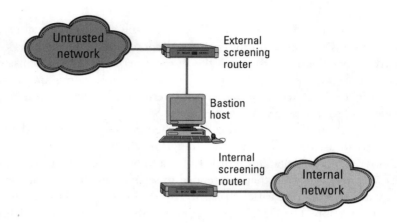

Figure 12.7 Screened subnet configuration.

Restricting Users Access to the Internet

When discussing the functionality of firewalls most people usually concern themselves with how well firewalls keep people from getting into the company network. However, one of the most important functions firewalls provide is restricting inside users from getting out.

A firewall can be setup to restrict internal users from accessing particular sights on the Internet or from accessing the Internet at all. Firewalls can restrict access based on the URL or the content of the Web sight. One such program is Secure Computing's SmartFilter software. SmartFilter is not a firewall in itself; it is a software product that can work as part of a firewall. Remember that a firewall is a collection of components that work together. (This is not a recommendation of the software, but simply an example of one of the products out on the market.)

With SmartFilter, end users' Internet access is controlled through a database of URLs. The SmartFilter software contains more than 1,000,000 nonbusiness-related URLs. It also provides the ability to download updates to the database. In addition, the database can be customized by each organization.

For example, in the past using SmartFilter, I have attempted to access the URL www.anonymizer.com, which is the Anonymizer Web site—discussed in Chapter 6. The URL for the Anonymizer is listed in the database as a restricted site. As a result, the message comes back that SmartFilter has denied access to the site. In this case, the denial reason is erroneously listed as "sexual content."

Actually, the Anonymizer doesn't contain sexual content. However, the reason many organizations block access to the Anonymizer and other sights like it is partially because firewalls have a hard time with encrypted connections. The Anonymizer site uses SSL to provide anonymous browsing capabilities. With most corporate firewalls, to allow a user on the internal network to connect to an outside site with SSL, a "tunnel" has to be established. This tunnel allows SSL connections to pass through the firewall. The firewall cannot monitor or examine the contents of the SSL connection, because it is encrypted. In this case the only thing that firewall is able to know is the source and destination address.

As a result, if an end user on the inside of the firewall goes out through the firewall to a site that has been configured for SSL, the monitoring software cannot inspect the packets. Normally, this would not be an issue. For instance, if you are connected to an Internet banking system to perform transactions, there is no harm. However, if you use SSL to go to a site such as the Anonymizer that offers anonymous browsing capabilities, then you can leapfrog to another site to view and download whatever you choose regardless of the monitoring software on the firewall. As a result, www.anonymizer.com is frequently a restricted site for organizations that monitor and control Internet access.

Firewall Products

There are so many available firewall products on the market and the companies merge or change so frequently that it does not make sense to try to list them here—they might be obsolete by the time of publication. Many brands of routers provide firewalling capabilities and built-in VPN capabilities. There are, of course, UNIX-based, NT-based, and even Mac-based firewalls. In addition, there are products with proprietary operating systems and special dedicated firewall devices. One popular example is the Cisco PIX box.

For small offices or the home connection, there are also many "Internet-in-a-box" products on the market today that offer a simple to use configuration interface. These Internet appliances can be multifunction systems that offer firewall capabilities and simplify the process of connecting to the Internet. Available products include the Whistle InterJet, the Cobalt Qube, FreeGate OneGate, and the WindDance Breeze. These systems can provide a mix of e-mail services, FTP server capability, NAT, DHCP, DNS, and even VPN.

Generally, these systems range in price from about $1,000 to $3,000. Some come with built-in routers, and some do not. If you are considering one of these systems, you need to take into account whether or not you will have to purchase a router.

Firewall Alternatives

For those who don't have a lot of money to spend, there are some inexpensive alternatives to purchasing a firewall. Some of these are described in the following sections.

TIS Firewall Toolkit

One well-known alternative to buying a firewall is to use Trusted Information System's (TIS) firewall toolkit. The TIS Toolkit was developed by Marcus Ranum, while at TIS. Ranum, who is well-known in the network security field, was also the architect of several other firewall products, including the TIS Gauntlet firewall. While the toolkit was developed several years ago, it is still widely used. The TIS toolkit is a set of basic proxies that provide the most commonly required functionality for a firewall. The source code is available to download, but there are some restrictions, and TIS requires that you register a copy for download. It is also available at other sites (although I'm not sure if those sites are legal).

The TIS toolkit information and download is available from TIS at the URL www.tis.com/research/software. The TIS toolkit can run on Linux, which can also be downloaded. Since the toolkit and Linux are available on the Internet, all you would need is a powerful Pentium-based system to build a relatively inexpensive firewall. However, this is not a task for beginners. The way you configure the toolkit determines the level of security. It is not a simple "plug it in and it works" process. The installer has to know what he or she is doing and what he or she wishes to achieve.

Because the TIS toolkit has been around for so long there is a lot of information about it available on the Internet and a fairly large user community. There is even a Web site dedicated to providing and sharing information about the TIS toolkit. The URL is appropriately www.fwtk.org, and it is depicted in Figure 12.8.

Juniper Firewall Toolkit

Another low-cost alternative is the Juniper firewall toolkit. The Juniper toolkit is actually a commercial product. However, no license is necessary for copies that support up to five simultaneous connections. Juniper provides basic proxy capability. I believe the source code is also available.

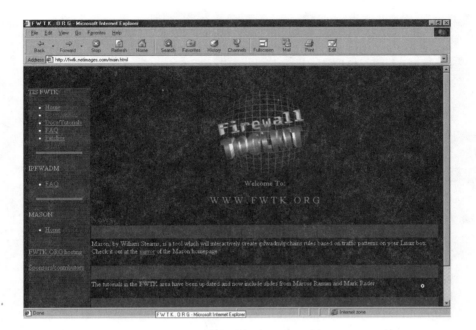

Figure 12.8 TIS toolkit Web site. (*Source*: www.fwtk.org. Reprinted with permission.)

Information regarding the Juniper firewall toolkit is available at the URL www.obtuse.com/juniper.

Freestone

I know very little about Freestone—other than the fact that it is the freeware version of a commercial product called Brimstone. SOS Corporation developed both Freestone and Brimstone. For information on Freestone, the best place to start would be the SOS Web site (www.soscorp.com).

Like the TIS toolkit, both the Juniper and Freestone firewalls require that you know what you are doing. Building a firewall requires knowledge and experience. If you don't have the knowledge and experience, then consider a commercial product—and, even then, I would still recommend you get some help or advice first.

Connecting critical networks and systems to the Internet is a job for properly trained personnel, not amateurs, nor is it the type of circumstance where an organization can allow the staff to learn on the job or grow into the position. The possibility of an attack is too great, and the potential harm to an organization is too high.

If an organization does not have knowledgeable staff, mistakes can be made in the setup and configuration of any firewall system. In fact, many successful hacking attacks have been attributed to incorrectly configured firewalls and routers.

It is also important that firewalls be monitored and that those monitoring them know what they are looking at when reviewing logs and reports. Knowledgeable and experienced personnel are crucial to being able to recognize and detect attempts to compromise a network or systems.

Organizations that don't have the personnel resources necessary for this type of position should consider outsourcing the responsibility for a firewall. Companies such as AT&T, Exodus, and UUNET offer managed firewall services. This type of arrangement has worked very well for some companies. Be warned though that with this type of arrangement you are placing a great deal of trust in the hands of the company selected to function as the firewall. You are trusting their technical skills and the reliability of their personnel. Accordingly, you need to be sure of the company with which you are doing business. Even if you choose to outsource the firewall function, I would recommend taking additional measures to harden your internal systems.

It is somewhat ironic that some organizations would never think of outsourcing the responsibility for their firewall because of security concerns, while they don't hesitate to outsource the entire organization's computer operations or WAN management to reduce operating expenses. Where is the logic in that thinking?

Personal Firewalls

The rise in popularity of broadband access from home, such as cable modems, and the introduction of xDSL technology has resulted in the development of a new class of firewall, the personal firewall. Cable and xDSL with their "always on" technology offer increased speed but with increased risks. These risks, which are discussed in Chapter 9, offer new challenges to the home user on the Internet. The greatest risk is the fact that with technologies such as cable and XDSL, hackers can gain access to a Web surfer's system. Personal firewalls were developed to mitigate this risk.

Personal firewalls are software products that act to safeguard an end user's computer on the Internet by monitoring attempts to access or probe his or her system. For instance, if a hacker attempts to "ping" or "finger" a computer running one of these personal firewalls the command is denied and the end user is notified of the attempt. The various personal firewalls can monitor for specific ports, protocols, IP addresses, and URLs. Some also provide virus detection capabilities and content filtering for Web sites.

Many of the available personal firewalls provide the ability to configure the software to allow or deny connections based upon a specific set of rules. For example, one can load in a specific group of IP addresses, so that when an unauthorized IP address attempts to connect to a system employing one of these software products, the system denies the connection and notifies the end user. Once notified, the end user can take appropriate action.

There are several products on the market that offer personal firewall capabilities. Symantec's Norton Internet Security 2000, McAfee's Personal Firewall and Software Builders' PC Secure are three examples. There are also some very good free systems available for download on the Internet. One option is Aladdin Knowledge Systems' eSafe program, which provides virus protection, content filtering and personal firewall capabilities. Figure 12.9 shows the configuration desktop of eSafe. eSafe provides the capability to allow or deny traffic based on port, protocol, IP address or URL.

Another freeware program is ZoneAlarm from Zone Labs. Figure 12.10 illustrates the ZoneAlarm configuration desktop. ZoneAlarm provides the capability to allow or deny connections based on IP address, host name, IP range, or subnet. Figure 12.11 illustrates the type of warning message one

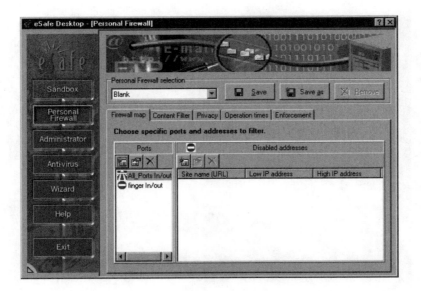

Figure 12.9 The configuration desktop of eSafe. (*Source:* Aladdin Knowledge Systems. Reprinted with permission.)

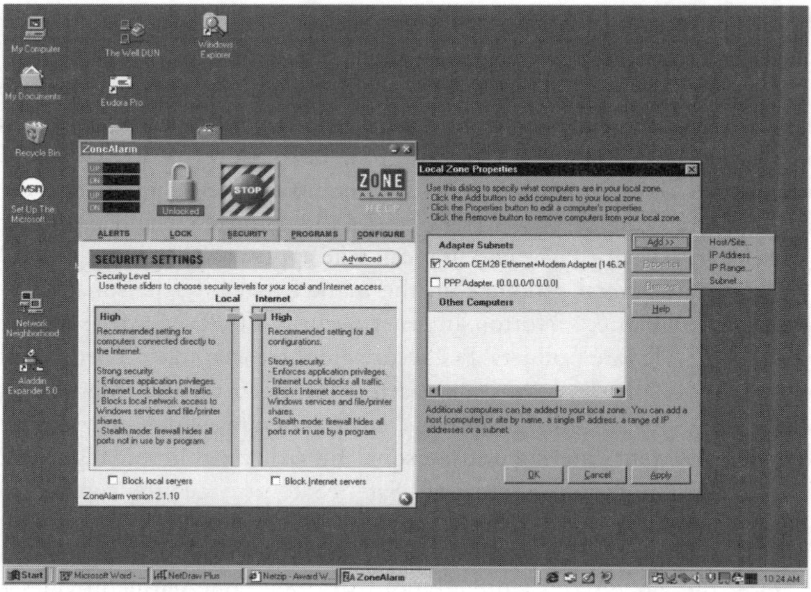

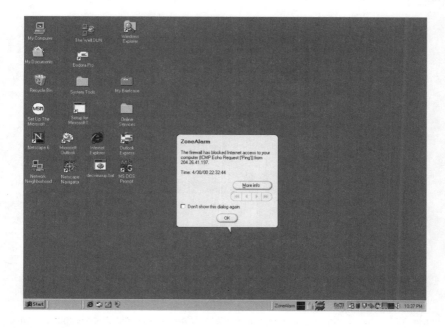

Figure 12.10 The ZoneAlarm configuration desktop.

Figure 12.11 ZoneAlarm warning message.

receives with ZoneAlarm. In Figure 12.11, I have used the "ping" command to test the IP address of a PC running ZoneAlarm. The ZoneAlarm personal firewall denies the ping attempt and displays a warning message identifying type of request and the originating IP address. In addition, the software denies the ping attempt so that the ping times out on the originator's end.

If you use a cable modem or xDSL to access the Internet, it is strongly recommended that you employ some kind of personal firewall to protect your system. Whether you purchase a system from a company like Symantec, McAfee, or Software Builders or use a freeware software, these systems provide an added level of protection that is well worth the expense or effort.

13

Biometrics

Identification and Authentication

As discussed in Chapter 1, there are three basic methods employed for identification and authentication. They are listed as follows.

- Something you know;
- Something you have;
- Something you are.

Generally, when we talk about a process of identification and authentication that relies on "something you know" we are talking about a system that employs passwords. As discussed in Chapter 7, passwords have many drawbacks: While passwords are inexpensive to implement and easy to establish, they are expensive and cumbersome to maintain. Speaking from personal experience, probably 50% of all calls handled by help desks are users who have forgotten one password or another and are locked out of a system. According to Gartner Group, an IT consultant currently located in Stamford CT, large organizations spend more than $340 per year, per user, on resetting passwords. That represents a significant cost to a large organization. If an organization has tens of thousands of employees, then the cost of password maintenance runs in the millions of dollars each year.

Chapter 7 also discusses identification and authentication processes that rely on "something you have." Generally, the something you have that provides the identification and authentication is a token card, smart card, or some kind of electronic badge. While these schemes can provide superior security when compared to the typical password process, the devices can be lost or stolen.

Biometric Identification and Authentication

When we talk about an identification and authentication scheme that relies on "something you are," we mean biometrics. Biometric authentication is the process of using some physical characteristic, trait, aspect of physical being, or behavior to authenticate one's identity. The most commonly known example is the process of employing fingerprints to identify an individual. For years government agencies like the FBI have been using fingerprints to identify individuals and perform background checks.

Biometric authentication usually fits into one of two general categories. The first is physical characteristic recognition (PCR), which relies upon a physical characteristic such as a fingerprint, retina or iris scan, voiceprint, or facial geometry for identification and authentication.

The second category is behavioral characteristic recognition (BCR). BCR relies on a behavioral characteristics such as how a person types at a keyboard, writes, or signs his or her name. In general, PCR is much more widely implemented than BCR.

With most biometric authentication there is usually a registration process. This entails the process of registering or enrolling some physical trait such as a fingerprint, voiceprint, or retina scan. During the registration process a template for the trait being registered is created. The template is typically a mathematical representation of the physical trait.

The template is then stored in some fashion (usually in a database in an encrypted format) to be retrieved at a later time for comparison to the user's actual physical characteristics to authenticate the would-be user's identity.

Let's say that the biometric system is used to identify and authenticate users of a network. When the user wants access to the network, he or she scans the physical trait again (fingerprint, retina, etc.). Then the same process used to create the template is used to create a mathematical representation of the physical trait, either at the reader or the server. It is then compared to the template that is stored on the server or station. If the two match, then the end user is given access to the network.

This is just an approximation of the process. I'm sure individual vendors' processes will vary according to the system design.

Biometric Identification Reliability

When considering a biometric authentication system, there are two critical characteristics that you should review before deploying any system. They are listed as follows.

- False acceptance rate (FAR);
- False rejection rate (FRR).

The FAR is the rate at which a system incorrectly accepts or recognizes a would-be user as authorized to access the system when in fact he or she are not. In other words, how often does the system let someone in that it should keep out? Most manufacturers of biometric authentication devices list the FAR for their products. If not, you should be able to request it from the manufacturer. Very often the FAR is listed as a percentage.

The FAR for any biometric identification and authentication system should be closely scrutinized. A manufacturer may list a FAR that appears to be very small, but the numbers can be deceiving. For example, a FAR of only 1% means that one time out of 100 a system will incorrectly accept an unauthorized user. That false acceptance rate percentage is much too high. A FAR of 1% means that if a hacker makes 100 attempts he or she will be successful at least one time. Even a FAR of 0.1% is too high to be acceptable. That means that one in 10,000 attempts will be incorrectly accepted. Those odds are much more in favor of a hacker when compared to the odds of the hacker guessing a password eight characters in length.

For example, even if you exclude the 26 letters of the alphabet and all special characters and use only numbers for an eight-digit password, you would still have over 99,999,999 passwords. That means there is less than a 1 in 99,999,999 chance of accessing the system by guessing the password. However, with a biometric identification system with a 0.1% FAR there is a 1 in 10,000 chance of accessing the system by mistake.

Another important characteristic of any biometric identification and authentication system is the FRR, the rate at which a system incorrectly rejects a legitimate user. While it is not as critical as FAR, the FRR is important to the successful deployment of any biometric authentication system. If the FRR of a system is too high, it can cause end-user frustration. The frustration can lead users to circumvent proper authentication procedures to avoid the biometric system. It can ultimately create security holes or lead to the system being scrapped.

When evaluating any biometric authentication scheme you need to take into account how it will handle the natural changes people experience. This is particularly true for PCR biometric systems. For example, suppose your system employs face recognition and you have a person who had a beard but decides to shave it. Will he then be locked out of the system? As people age, their physical characteristics can change. Whatever system is employed needs to be able to update a template with the subtle changes that naturally occur every time it authenticates the would-be user.

To be truly effective, any biometric system must also be sophisticated enough to detect fraud. In other words, it has to be very hard to fool. As a result, the underlying technology used for any system has to be multitiered. For example, a system employing only optical imaging for fingerprints, face recognition, or hand geometry may not be able to detect lifted or faked characteristics if the owner is deceased. The more sophisticated systems look at several elements of a physical characteristics. For example, a hand reader may not only compare the hand geometry but will also check temperature and even check for blood pressure. This multitiered approach makes it much more difficult to fool a system with something like a plaster cast of a hand.

Backup Authentication

An effective biometric system needs to be able to handle temporary physiological changes. If you are employing fingerprints for authentication, what happens if an end user badly burns his or her fingers? What happens if someone breaks his or her hand, and your system is based on hand geometry? Someone with a cast on his or her hand will be unable to gain access through the hand reader.

You need to consider the backup methods to authenticate users in the event the biometrics fail. You also need to consider how easy it is to activate the backup authentication method. You could find yourself locked out without an alternate authentication method. If you have a backup method, such as a password, what's to stop someone from using it all the time, or what's to stop someone from compromising the backup process and circumventing the biometric system altogether? A biometric system that can be circumvented is worthless. What's the point of going through the time, trouble, and expense of installing a biometric identification and authentication scheme to protect your network only to have someone with a password break in and compromise the network?

Environmental Conditions

Another element that must be considered before implementing a biometric authentication system is the environment in which it will operate. Water, noise, moisture, and dirt can adversely impact the operation of some biometric authentication systems. A factory floor where workers get their hands dirty with grease or where the conditions are very wet would not be the best environment to install a fingerprint reader or hand reader. A fingerprint reader or hand scanner would be equally ineffectual in an environment where workers wear gloves. Similarly, a retina scanner or face geometry reader would not be advised in an environment in which individuals must wear protective eyewear or masks. In addition, voiceprint readers would not work well in noisy environments. These types of issues have to be considered before deploying biometric systems.

User Acceptance

To achieve a successful deployment of a biometric authentication system, it is important to gauge user acceptance of the technology being used. Users may be uncomfortable with retina scanners and find recording of fingerprints an invasion of privacy. Consider how invasive the technology will be and whether users will accept it before implementing it. As one would expect, the more invasive the technology being deployed the more uncomfortable the end users become. While retina-scanning technology may be more reliable than fingerprint readers, end users are almost always more comfortable with the fingerprint readers.

Another issue that needs to be considered before deploying a system is general hygiene. This is more of an issue with biometric devices that are used to authenticate employees at a central location, such as a main entrance to a restricted facility. It may sound funny, but what better way to pass germs to all your employees than to have each and everyone of them touch a hand scanner? All it would take is for one employee to get a cold to have it spread to everyone. Would you want to touch a hand scanner or fingerprint reader knowing that the person who used it before you has a bad cold?

Of course, the same hazard is associated with other, more mundane objects, such as doorknobs and elevator buttons. However, it is inevitable that users' suspicions of a biometric system will be greater when first introduced.

Security of the Biometric System

Another critical factor with biometric identification and authentication systems is how it handles communication and storage. You have to look at how a particular system is implemented. For example, if it is deployed on a LAN, does the biometric identification system communicate with a server for authentication? If it does, then security in the communications between the reader and the host server is very important because biometric systems can be susceptible to replay attacks. Can the communication be tapped? Is the communication encrypted? Even if it is encrypted, what's to stop someone from using a replay attack?

For example, Alice identifies herself to the network using a fingerprint reader on her keyboard. The mathematical representation of her fingerprint is sent to the server for identification and authentication. However, Bob has placed a sniffer on the network and has captured the mathematical representation of the fingerprint in transit to the server. Now Bob has that information and can transmit it to the server at anytime and gain access to the network as Alice. Even if the transmission were encrypted Bob would still be able to capture and copy it to be transmitted at a later time. Of course, there are many ways that a vendor can avoid this problem. One method would be to use some timestamp in an encryption algorithm. Another method would be to store the template on the local system. However, that would only work for end users with workstations with local storage. In addition, storing the template on a local hard drive would introduce other security issues.

If the templates are stored on a server you also need to consider how they are stored and the security employed to prevent them from being compromised. These are the types of issues that an administrator needs to take into account before deploying any biometric identification and authentication system.

Interoperability

Another issue that is much more difficult to resolve and I believe will be around for a while is the fact that there is no interoperability between biometric systems. Every single product on the market is proprietary. It is also difficult to find a product that has operating system interoperability. As a result, if you work for a large organization, you will be hard pressed to find a system that can be deployed across the entire enterprise.

Costs Versus Savings

The cost to deploy these systems is also a significant factor in the lack of wide acceptance of biometric identification and authorization. However, when you take into consideration the cost associated with maintaining passwords there could be real savings associated with deploying a biometric identification and authentication system.

If you use the Gartner estimated cost of $340 per user per year to administer passwords as your starting point, you should be able to justify an equal amount per user for a biometric system. If you work for a company that employs 1,000 people, that amounts to $340,000 per year. That savings would be realized every year, not just the year in which the system was purchased. Most companies capitalize large IT expenditures and amortize them over three to five years. If you amortize the system over three years, your company would realize a savings of $1,020,000 over the three-year period. For that amount of money you should be able to deploy a fairly comprehensive biometric identification and authentication system.

In spite of its potential benefits, biometric identification systems have had only modest success in being deployed. Too many obstacles still prevent wide acceptance in the corporate environment. However, biometrics have made inroads in government organizations, the military, and utilities. In government, many law enforcement and security agencies have or are implementing biometric identification systems. The U.S. Army recently initiated a study to determine the feasibility of using biometric recognition systems to replace passwords for accessing computers and weapons systems. As for utilities, presently the majority of U.S. nuclear power plants employ biometric identification and authentication systems.

Biometric identification systems hold great promise but still have a long way to go. In addition, biometric identification and authentication is not the panacea that some observers believe it to be. Nevertheless, when used in conjunction with other identification and authentication methods, such as passwords, tokens, and public key encryption, biometrics could greatly enhance system and network security.

14

Policies and Procedures

Policies and Procedures

For most organizations, network and system security policies and procedures serve the purpose of ensuring information security. They achieve this by defining what constitutes information security, why it is important, and how to maintain it. In addition, the policies and procedures define the acceptable levels of information security. Before you can do so, however, you must first put in place a process that enables you to determine what is an adequate level of security for any given organization.

You should recall from the discussion in Chapter 1 that the elements of information security include confidentiality, integrity, availability, authentication, and access control. All five elements need to be addressed by whatever policies and procedures are implemented to address information security. In general terms, security policies are the set of rules and procedures that regulate how an organization manages, uses, protects, and distributes all information that directly or indirectly pertains to that organization.

Policies Versus Procedures

Policies should always be developed before procedures. The development of procedures should flow from the policies. Policies should be concerned with what assets to protect and why they need to be protected. They are generally broad in their scope and are designed to set the tone and direction. In general, they can be thought of as the documents that spell out the *what* and *why* of information security for an organization. Procedures, on the other hand, must be much more precise and detailed. Procedures should be concerned with the specific measures necessary to protect the organization's assets. They can be thought of as the documents that spell the *who, when,* and *how* of information security within an organization.

Information Security Policy Objectives

There are various reasons for an organization to develop network and system security policies and procedures. Some are obvious, while others are not so obvious. Some reasons concern the direct benefit that an organization gains from having policies and procedures, such as preventing or detecting fraud or deterring hackers. Other benefits are indirect in that the policies protect the organization from potential liability or save it from possible embarrassment. Below I have listed some of the objectives generally associated with network security policies.

- *Managing risk:* The primary goal of any policy concerning network and system security is to manage risk. It is almost impossible to completely secure an organization's information assets. As a result, an organization needs to identify the risks that its faces and develop measures to minimize the impact of those risks.

- *Ensuring business continuity:* The ongoing operation of the organization should be a fundamental goal of the policies developed by any organization. It is interesting to note how many organizations' policies tend to spell out what *cannot* be done in great detail but do a very poor job of addressing what *must* be done to ensure the operation of the organization. Organizational policies and procedures should ensure business resumption by outlining the appropriate actions necessary in response to an incident or disaster.

- *Defining responsibilities, expectations, and acceptable behaviors:* For any policy or procedure to be effective, those individuals subject to the policy or procedure must understand what is required of them to comply. Compliance to a policy cannot be achieved without reaching an understanding of what constitutes compliance. In addition, employees need to understand their responsibilities and how their responsibilities may vary depending on the circumstances.

- *Discharging fiduciary duty and complying with any regulatory requirements:* Most organizations are subject to rules or regulations governing the responsibility of the corporate officers and regulating the operation of the organization. If a company is publicly traded, the corporate officers have a fiduciary duty to ensure the financial soundness of the organization. If they fail in that duty they can be held personally liable for the losses incurred. Most every organization is required to adhere to certain standards when it comes to accounting records and bookkeeping. Many organizations are also subject to federal, state, or local regulations that require certain measures be taken to protect the assets of the organization. Many organizations are subject to rules and regulations regarding the protection and disclosure of information pertaining to employees and customers. This is certainly true in the financial and health sectors. For many organizations, the absence of proper policies and procedures is considered automatic noncompliance.

- *Protecting the organization from liability:* The policies and procedures developed by an organization are often required to protect it from liability. In some cases, the existence of the policies and procedures are essential to demonstrate that an organization did not approve of an end user's actions or that an employee was or was not acting with the authorization of the organization.

- *Ensuring information integrity and confidentiality:* A key component of information security is protecting an organization's information assets. Ensuring the integrity and confidentiality of an organization's information is fundamental to that goal. Without information integrity, an organization cannot make sound business decisions. Without information confidentiality, an organization will lose its competitive edge through the loss of proprietary information regarding products, customers, and even partners and suppliers.

Developing Security Policies

For an organization's information security policies and procedures to achieve the stated objectives, it is essential that certain elements be included in the policies and procedures. These elements can be thought of as key measures for the success for an organization's policy and procedures. The elements are the stepping stones in the development process. They are listed as follows:

- Identifying the organization's assets;

- Defining the risks;

- Defining how information assets are to be managed;

- Defining how information assets are to be accessed and what process will be used for authentication;

- Defining clearly and in detail what does and does not constitute appropriate use of company owned electronic media and services;

- Clearly defining what kind of information may be accessed and distributed and by what means;

- Defining what controls are to be put in place;

- Notifying users of monitoring and auditing procedures, information disclosure, and consequences for noncompliance;

- Identifying those responsible for security enforcement and how policies and procedures will be enforced;

- Developing steps to be taken in the event of noncompliance with policy, a security breach, or a disaster.

The first step is to determine responsibility for information security policy development. Too often, the IT unit is given sole responsibility for this task. However, if the policies and procedures are to be comprehensive, it will require the active participation of all business units. Development of information security policies must be a collaborative effort between the IT unit and the other business units within an organization. Any policy or procedure implemented without the active participation and "buy-in" of other business units faces an uphill battle.

The most critical factor in the success or failure of any information security policy is support from senior management: The policy developers must be empowered by senior management with the authority to implement the measures necessary to protect the organization's information assets. I cannot stress this fact strongly enough. Without the support of senior management any policies or procedures implemented are doomed to fail.

I have seen teams attempt to implement procedures only to see their effort undone by senior management's failure to back them when they encountered resistance. It was a no-win situation for the team. They were charged with the job of developing and implementing security procedures but not empowered with the authority necessary to succeed. As a result, they were ultimately seen as the bad guys and targeted by everyone's wrath. Basically, they had been set up to fail. If the group developing policies does not have the active support of senior management it is best not to even attempt the task.

Senior management needs to do more than just support the development and implementation of policies and procedures. Senior management needs to support a culture of information security within an organization. There needs to be recognition of the need for information security within every organization. Unfortunately, in most companies, information security is too often looked upon as something that can be dealt with after everything else. It is not recognized as a required core competency of the company. This fallacious mind-set can put an organization at risk.

Consider the following example: A student in one of my classes recounted a story indicative of the value that most companies place on information security. The student worked for a large software company that marketed a well-known database. During a cyclical downturn in business, the company went through a round of what was euphemistically called "rightsizing." While most business units experienced moderate cuts in personnel, the information security and the business resumption planning groups were devastated. Essentially, both units were dissolved, and all personnel were laid off. Obviously, the company did not see information security and business resumption as a critical business activity.

As another example, at a company where I once worked, I submitted to senior management a recommendation that the company develop a policy to address "pretext calling." Pretext calling is a widespread practice used by information brokers to gain information on individuals from unsuspecting companies. Generally, an information broker poses as someone or some entity that is related to or associated with the individual with whom the targeted company does business. The targeted company could be a hospital, a financial institution, an insurance company, or even a school or government agency. The information broker usually gets a little bit of information from each contact. The information gathered is cumulative. With each contact the information broker gets more information, which in turn can be used to gain even more. Many companies are being hit by pretext calling. Even though the information broker lies and misrepresents himself or herself to the targeted company, this practice is not illegal. Companies are unwittingly giving out information on their employees, customers, and clients. It is not only bad for the customer, but it is bad for business. In addition, a company could find itself liable for how that information is used. It certainly would not instill customer confidence to know that a company was giving out customer information to anyone who calls. For that reason, I recommended that a policy and procedure be developed to address pretext calling.

Specifically, my recommendation was that the company should develop a general information privacy policy. Part of the implementation of that policy would include a training program to educate our staff on how to identify pretext calls. I argued that it would provide our company with a competitive advantage in that we could state to our customers that their information was safer with us than with our competitors. In addition, it would protect the company from possible liability. Finally, it would provide the company with a response to customers who contacted us with requests for information on how we handled this type of occurrence. Senior management thought it was a good idea but not a high priority, and that is where it ended. No one wanted to invest the time to develop the policy. Without the active support of senior management, it would have been impossible to develop a policy and attempt to impose it on the other business units.

Another common occurrence is for organizations to develop policies for no other reason than to say that the policies exist. The policies are really only for show. Once a year, when regulators or auditors are on site, the company can point to the policy manuals gathering dust in the corner and proudly proclaim that they have all the required policies covered. Of course, the fact that no one even knows what the policies state or whether or not the company is in compliance with the policies is not considered.

An essential part of security policy development is the risk assessment process. It is important to go through a risk assessment process to determine what you want to protect, why you want to protect it, and from what you need to protect it. As described in Chapter 1, the steps associated with risk assessment include the following.

1. Identifying and prioritizing assets;
2. Identifying vulnerabilities;
3. Identifying threats and their probabilities;
4. Identifying countermeasures;
5. Developing a cost-benefit analysis;
6. Developing security policies.

The first step is to identify and prioritize assets and systems and then identify the vulnerabilities associated with those assets. When assessing vulnerabilities and the risks associated with them, it is important to weed out the possible threats from the probable ones. The process should be one of determining what threats are most likely and developing policies that address those threats and issues.

It is very important that the policies and procedures implemented within any organization should be real world-based. In other words, the policies and procedures should exist for the purpose of enhancing a preexisting process or function. As such, they should take into account the constraints of the real world and not try to achieve the apex of security. For example, it would be overkill to require all e-mail to be encrypted. You should not require passwords to be changed every week or require them to be 15 alphanumeric characters in length. While it might be very secure, it would not be logical to implement a hand scanner for biometric identification in an environment, such as a "clean room," where technicians wear special suits, including gloves.

As a rule, security policies and procedures that interfere with the operation of an organization are of little value. Those types of measures are usually ignored or circumvented by company personnel, so they tend to create security holes rather than plug them. If you make a process too arduous or annoying, people will ignore it. If you make the process of gaining access to a room too difficult, people will prop open the door. If you make passwords too hard to remember, people will write them down. All security measures (not just security policies), whenever possible, should complement the operational and business needs of an organization.

The steps involved in information security policy implementation are fairly straightforward:

1. Developing a written security policies and procedures manual;
2. Developing an end user awareness and education program;
3. Developing a process for policy enforcement and procedure implementation;
4. Developing a process for the periodic review and updating of policies and procedures.

Policy and Procedure Manuals

For a security policy to be practical, it must be documented. The plan must also be made available as a reference to all those subject to the policy. The policy and procedure manuals need to be kept current and updated with any necessary changes. Modifications to systems, personnel, business priorities, and other environmental factors must be reflected in the plan. That means regular and frequent reviews of the policy.

Policy Format

There are many different ways in which one can format the policies. The type of format is relatively unimportant as long as the policy is understandable and achieves the desired results. The most important thing is that policies are formalized and documented in some way. A policy should include, at a minimum, the following elements.

- *Policy statement:* This section should state the general policy, what the policy says, and what it entails. This section can be as short as a single sentence or as long as a page. If it goes beyond a page, perhaps you are attempting to cover in a single policy issues that should be covered by more than one policy.

- *Purpose:* This section should state why the policy is needed. Examples of the purpose for a policy could include something to the effect that the policy is to protect the company or employees, ensure the continued operation of the organization, or protect the financial health of the company.

- *Scope:* This section should cover how far the policy extends. The scope should spell out the circumstances under which the policy applies. It can also include the time frame, specific hardware or software, and/or events under which the policy is effective.

- *Compliance with policy:* This section should include a detailed explanation of what does and does not constitute compliance with the policy. The section can include examples, but be careful to word it in such a way that it allows you to include instances that may not be listed in your examples. The section should include wording to the effect "*examples include, but are not limited to ....*" Being too specific in detail may make the definition too narrow.

- *Penalties/consequences:* This section should explain the consequences for noncompliance with the policy. Specific punishments associated with noncompliance should be listed. If the consequences for noncompliance can include termination, then it should be clearly spelled out in this section of the policy. This section serves as a warning to employees and can protect an organization in the event that it finds itself in court as a result of terminating an employee for noncompliance with a policy. The fact that the organization had clearly warned all employees of the consequences can diminish any argument that an employee may have for termination without cause.

Policy Awareness and Education

A policy is of no value if no one knows what it states. End users and personnel must understand management's expectations and their responsibilities in regard to complying with an organization's policies. End users and employees must also understand the consequences for noncompliance. This aspect is very important for protecting the organization if litigation results from noncompliance.

The existence of a policy may be required to take punitive action against end users or employees who have acted in an unacceptable manner. Organizations that don't have a policy clearly defining unacceptable behavior may have no recourse.

Having a policy in place that prohibits certain types of behavior can also save an organization from liability for the actions of its end users or employees. The absence of a formal policy and an awareness process may make it difficult to hold an employee accountable in the event some inappropriate behavior on the part of the employee is discovered. With a written policy, an organization can demonstrate that any derogatory actions taken by an end user or employee were not in compliance with accepted behavior and were therefore not condoned by the organization.

Organizations should consider obtaining written acknowledgment from end users and employees stating that they have read and understand the organization's information security policy. This could be done as part of the general orientation for newly hired personnel or as part of the registration of new end users.

Policy Enforcement

Compliance with policies needs to be enforced. The only way to ensure compliance is through monitoring and auditing. Those responsible for enforcing the IT security policies must have the support of senior management. If an organization's IT security policy is to be successful, it also needs the support of all business units within the organization.

Security Policy Suggestions

Remember that the major emphasis of all policies and procedures is to prevent "bad things" from happening. It doesn't matter whether the bad thing is a mistake, disaster, or misdeed. Well-designed policies and procedures are flexible enough to address most "probable" threats. That is why risk analysis is such an import part of the process.

Policies and procedures should also assume that the preventative measures will occasionally fail. As a result, they should include steps to detect "bad things." It is particularly important that the procedures spell out in detail what steps are to be taken in the event that all other measures have failed to prevent some "bad thing" from occurring. In other words, it should detail how the organization responds to an incident.

When developing procedures one needs to address the basic elements of network and system security covered in Chapter 2. They are listed as follows.

- Identification;

- Authentication;

- Access control (authorization);

- Availability;

- Confidentiality (secrecy);

- Integrity (accuracy);

- Accountability.

At the same time, you need to incorporate all of the various elements of security into all aspects of the operation of an organization and to address all probabilities. This includes procedures to address physical security and natural disasters as well as hardware and software security. You also need to address media controls and communication security. Most importantly, you need to address the human variable in your procedures in an effort to minimize temptation and stupidity and ensure compliance.

The framework required to adequately address the needs of a particular organization will largely depend on the type of organization. Large corporations require extensive policies that cover all the possibilities, while most small organizations, which may use technology to a more limited extent—or at least have less of it—will require a much less extensive set of policies. Do not use a pound when an ounce will do the job. Overly complicated or detailed policies tend to create problems and are often ignored. Policies should be simple to understand and remember. The level of detail for each organization will vary, but the following sections provide some basic suggestions.

Use of Company-Owned Electronic Media and Services

With the advent of new technologies, organizations are finding themselves relying increasingly on electronic modes of communication and information storage. Most employees in an organization have access to one or more forms of electronic media or service. They include but are not confined to the following:

- Computers (PCs, workstations, minicomputers, and mainframes);
- E-mail;
- Telephones and voice mail;
- Fax machines;
- LANs, intranets, and the Web.

Every organization that uses electronic media and services should have a policy that clearly defines the acceptable use of these media and services as company property. The policies should not only exist to protect the organization but also to protect the employees of the organization. The policy should specify the acceptable personal use of company-owned IT facilities and services. The policy should also cover when it is necessary to obtain management's permission and the process to do so. This policy should cover all technologies that could be exploited to receive and distribute information. Company systems and networks should not be used to generate or distribute material that is illegal or immoral or that contravenes the principles of the corporation. Such a policy ensures that appropriate measures are enacted to protect company assets and to educate employees of their responsibilities. Often, an organization feels that developing a policy on the use of e-mail is all that is required. If the policy is to be truly effective, it must encompass more than just e-mail.

When it comes to developing such a policy, organizations can run the entire gamut from very liberal in their approach and loosely defined to very narrow definitions of what is acceptable use of company property with severe limitations on personal use. Each organization is different and the approach, and the philosophy that is brought to the task of developing a policy will vary greatly from company to company.

What Does the Policy Cover?

It is very important that employees or end users understand what technologies or kinds of technologies the policy covers. Accordingly, organizations need to explain what the company's electronic media and services are and what they entail. It is to their benefit and the benefit of their employees that they understand that the policy covers more than just e-mail.

Whose Property Is it?

A policy should state in clear terms that the electronic media and services are company property, not the employee's personal property. For example, employees very often become possessive about their PCs. They feel as if the PCs are their personal property and that no one has the right to access their PCs without first obtaining their (the employees') permission. It should be made clear that at any time, authorized personnel may review files on company-owned PCs, e-mail, or voice mail. This is not spying. Companies are, at times, obligated to perform such reviews to determine, among other things, whether there has been a breach of security, violation of company policy, or misuse of any company-owned media or services. Employees should be told that the company reserves the right to perform these reviews without prior notification of the employees. Make it clear to the employees that if they don't want the company to see something, they should not store it on company owned property.

What Is Acceptable Use?

An organization has to determine for itself whether it will allow electronic media and services to be used for non-company-related purposes. The most reasonable approach is to allow limited, occasional use for personal, nonbusiness purposes (as is the case with personal phone calls). It is also important that policies be consistent with one another. It does not make sense for a policy to forbid the use of company e-mail for personal reasons while completely ignoring personal phone calls, voicemail, and faxes. Whatever an organization decides, the decision needs to be relayed to the employees in clear terms that spell out what the consequences are for violating the policy.

An organization should also protect itself by stating in writing that it is prohibited to use any of the company's electronic services for any purposes that violate state or federal laws. This includes requiring compliance with all copyright laws. If the company develops software, then the policy should also cover patents, trademarks, and intellectual property.

In addition, a policy should prohibit the use of company-owned electronic services to transmit, receive, or store information or data of a harassing or discriminatory nature or that is derogatory to any group or individual. The policy should also prohibit any employee from using the company's electronic services to transmit, receive, or store information or data that is obscene or pornographic or that is defamatory or threatening in nature. This not only protects the organization; it protects the employees as well.

Hacking

The policy should also prohibit attempts by employees or end users to "hack" other systems. It should be made clear that attempts to hack or access information without authorization will not be tolerated by an organization, and there should be severe consequences for doing so. This policy should not only apply to attempts to hacking company-owned systems; it should also apply to the hacking of outside systems using company-owned or -leased systems or services.

In addition, the policy should define the employees' responsibility to ensure that their logins and passwords remain confidential and the steps that they are required to take if they suspect that their passwords have been compromised. It should be made clear that these steps are not optional or suggested but are a required part of their job function and that failure to comply with the policy can result in adverse consequences.

Unauthorized Software

Many organizations employ a cookie cutter approach to deploying desktop systems. Everyone gets the same image of a specific suite of authorized software. While this can be aggravating to the end users, it is a sound management practice. At the very least, this approach reduces the costs associated with the installation of desktop systems. This is particularly true when employing a package such as Microsoft's System Management Server (SMS), which essentially pushes an image onto the desktop from the server. This approach can also reduce an organization's support costs by reducing the number of applications that the help desk supports.

In general, it is a good security practice to have a policy that prohibits end users from installing software on their desktop systems without authorization from the IT group. This can prevent malicious programs from being introduced to the network. When it comes to installing software on servers, there should not only be a policy in place that bars such activity, but the access control mechanisms should be in place to prevent such activity.

In many environments, it may be prudent to implement measures that prevent end users from installing software on their systems or in any way altering their desktop configuration. For example, Windows NT desktop systems can be installed with the local configuration capability disabled. Some programs designed to secure the desktop, such as Full Armor, Fortres 101, and Fool Proof, can be installed with Windows 3.X, 95, and 98. These systems provide some level of protection, but they can be circumvented and, in some cases, may actually pose risks.

E-Mail

Employees should be made aware of the fact that e-mail is not a secure media. There is no guarantee that e-mail will remain private. They should also be made aware of the fact that e-mail transmitted on the Internet is particularly vulnerable to interception and disclosure. As such, information of an extremely sensitive or confidential nature should not be transmitted on the Internet unless the message is encrypted.

Every organization should reserve the right to review and disclose any employee's e-mail received or transmitted on or from company-owned electronic media or services. It should be made clear to every employee that this review and disclosure can be done without obtaining the employee's prior consent. This is not "big brother," it is common sense. A company has the right to protect itself. There have been a number of cases in the news media where the improper activities of an employee have landed an employer in court. The improper activities were later found to be detailed in the company e-mail. As a result, the company could be found libel for the employee's activities.

The results of a *Computerworld* survey regarding e-mail monitoring published in the magazine's October 1999 issue stated that 31% of the survey respondents had installed software that allowed for the active monitoring of e-mail and that another 21% were planning on installing software with that capability. Products such as Mailwall from Omniquad, MIMEsweeper from Content Technologies, and 2MA Messaging Manager from Re-Soft provide administrators with the ability to scan end users' e-mail for key words. These programs can scan both the e-mail subject and body for questionable, obscene, abusive, or illicit content.

Identification

Any policy covering the acceptable use of company-owned electronic media and services should also deal with the issues of identity authentication and impersonation. Employees should be cautioned about relying on the stated identity of the sender of e-mail or any other type of transmission. E-mail messages in particular can easily be forged. Any policy should also prohibit employees from any attempt to hide their identity or to falsely represent themselves or attempt to represent themselves as someone else, when transmitting, receiving, or storing e-mail or other electronic communications.

Communicate the Consequences

Finally, an organization should clearly define the consequences to any employee who knowingly violates the policy or allows another employee to violate the policy, so that there is no possibility of misunderstanding.

For an organization to develop this type of policy, senior management, IT, and human resources need to work together. Developing a comprehensive policy governing the use of company-owned electronic media and services can protect an organization and save it from legal troubles down the road. For that policy to be effective, it must encompass more than just e-mail. An organization has to make the policy broad enough to incorporate all of the technologies that it is presently using. At the same time, individual elements of the policy have to be defined narrowly enough to make them meaningful and understandable. In addition, the policy needs to be periodically reviewed to ensure that it includes newly implemented technologies.

Information Privacy

It is important that active steps be taken by all employees to ensure that information privacy is maintained. Corporate information pertaining to customers, employees, and company projects and products should be reviewed to determine their level of sensitivity. This is important from both a business and regulatory perspective. Disclosure of sensitive information can help competitors and scare away customers. In addition, a corporation may also be subject to regulatory requirements governing the disclosure of information. Web sites catering to children are subject to the Children's Online Privacy Protection Act, which is enforced by the Federal Trade Commission (FTC). Japan and most of the European nations have much stricter regulations than the United States governing the disclosure and sharing of personnel information by companies. As a result, a general policy is recommended. The policy should outline the requirements governing the actions of the organization for information privacy.

Finally, the policy of organizations that have employees who frequently present at conferences or who are offered speaking engagements should cover what can and cannot be disclosed by the employee in his or her presentation. The policy can go so far as to include some type of review process by the management of the material being presented. This is to ensure that no sensitive proprietary or customer information is inadvertently disclosed.

Information and Data Management

Depending on the environment in which you operate, you may want to consider classifying and prioritizing information by its level of importance or sensitivity. Correspondingly, the nature of the data will dictate the measures necessary to protect it. Determination of access levels should also be dictated by the sensitivity of the information or data.

Any policy should also define where information should reside and how it is to be moved, transported, or transmitted. The level of importance and sensitivity should be taken into account when these definitions are developed. For example, an organization may want to forbid information of critical importance from being copied to removable media such as floppies or tapes.

Information and data are valuable corporate assets and must be protected. Data can be defined as raw information, or information can be defined as meaningful data that has been organized in a coherent manner that allows for the reliable retrieval of data elements. One of the key components for the protection of information is to assign ownership. A policy on ownership should outline the responsibilities of the information guardian and the relationship with the custodian of the data.

Policies are also necessary to address the proactive management of information and data. Policies must address the availability of the data and ensure that the appropriate controls are in place and utilized. Development of these policies should entail the analysis of the risks and the establishment of appropriate classification and authorization standards for the data.

Information and data integrity is not just concerned with protecting information content. Integrity must also address the accuracy of the data elements. A policy concerning data integrity should identify the requirements for secure data storage and mechanisms for the backup of data, and the requirements for the procedures to preserve and test the accuracy of the data. In the appropriate environment, data integrity also includes data entry standards to ensure that information is entered in a consistent and uniform format.

To ensure data integrity, a policy should be enacted governing proper procedures to protect against the potential threat from computer viruses. The policy should cover requirements for virus scans and copying files from outside sources to company-owned systems.

Information and data management policies should also state that all files that reside on company-owned devices or media, such as PCs, removable disks, and tapes, are the property of the company. As such, the policy should prohibit employees from removing company information from the premises without authorization. This policy, while difficult to enforce, may be a useful legality to have in place. In addition, as a precaution, a company should reserve the right to examine, access, use, and disclose any or all information or data, transmitted, received, or stored on any electronic media, device, or service owned or paid for by the company.

Systems Administration

One of the biggest challenges in devising proper security procedures is determining how to deal with the control and monitoring of the administrators of the organization's various systems. For example, many organizations operate in an environment where an individual or individuals have access to or responsibility for all aspects of system administration. The organization may have a small IT unit where using delineation of responsibility and segregation of duties as a control procedure is not practical. How do you segregate duties when there is only one person in the department?

However, whenever possible, segregation of duties should be implemented. The individual or individuals responsible for the day-to-day administration should not also be the individual or individuals responsible for creating new accounts. In addition, the individual or individuals who create new accounts should not be responsible for determining the level of access given to those accounts. All new accounts should be reviewed by an individual not responsible for creating accounts. If possible, a distinction should be made between system administration and security administration. System administration functions should be audited at least annually.

All system changes and daily jobs performed by administrators and operators should be recorded in a log or schedule and should be reviewed daily. All system backups should be recorded and logged and the logs reviewed and retained. Backups should also be tested periodically, at least weekly. All security access changes should be documented, reviewed, and filed. A policy will also stipulate the records retention schedule and destruction of logs, schedules, and other documentation.

In addition, systems should be classified according to their confidentiality and criticality to the operation of the organization to determine appropriate security measures. System classification is also required for disaster recovery planning.

System auditing and validation should be addressed in some manner through policies. They can either be incorporated into existing policies or be in a separate policy. Chapter 15 discusses auditing in more detail.

Remote Network Access

Many organizations have requirements for remote network access. Sales staff, field engineers, and even delivery personnel and drivers often require access to an organization's network. In addition, with the growth in telecommuting, many employees are now working from home, rather than coming into the office. As a result, more employees require access to the company's systems from outside the corporate network. Any remote access to the corporate network should be tightly controlled and subject to stringent security measures. A policy for remote access should address issues associated with authentication and access control. At a minimum, the policy should require any connection to utilize some kind of secure ID procedure. Refer to the discussion in Chapter 7 regarding modems for more detail.

Another consideration is third-party access to the corporate network. Many organizations have vendors, partners, customers, or joint ventures that require access to the corporate network. Policies need to be developed to ensure that proper controls are implemented, maintained, and monitored for all third-party access to an organization's network.

Security of Telecommunications

Related to remote access are the issues associated with secure communications. Different modes of telecommunications are subject to different potential for disclosure. A policy should detail what measures should be taken when using each of the different modes of electronic communications, based upon the sensitivity of the information. Refer to Chapter 9 for a more detailed discussion of the issues associated with the different modes of telecommunications.

Physical Security

Physical access to IT facilities should be restricted to only those authorized personnel who need access to perform their job functions. A policy should define who are the appropriate individuals and what processes and safeguards should be enacted. Where appropriate, the policy should also cover company IT assets while in the possession of employees. The types of issues addressed should include computer room or network center fire suppression systems and environmental controls. For example, if the computer room is not monitored constantly, is there an automated system in place that pages someone in the event that the fire suppression system is triggered or the environmental controls fail?

Use of Standards

Policies should be developed that dictate a standard platform or common operating environment that is deployed throughout the organization. Adherence to the platform should be mandatory. In addition to reducing costs and administration requirements for an organization, standards can also protect data and infrastructure. Standards also aid in the interoperability and portability of applications in a distributed computing environment.

Standards should even be considered for the look of the desktop. Nothing is more annoying to someone from the IT group than to sit down at the system and find that all of the icons have been changed to nonstandard images such as flowers, bumblebees, and smiley faces. Nonstandard icons impede the support process. In addition, installing these nonstandard icons is a security risk in that it is an introduction of unknown files into the network. Consideration should be given to restricting local administration of all desktops to ensure that standards are maintained.

Reporting Noncompliance

Frequently, organizations educate employees and end users on their responsibility to report noncompliance but never put in place a mechanism to provide that capability. There are times when an employee may not feel comfortable reporting an incident of noncompliance. If the noncompliance involves a supervisor, systems administrator, or real criminal activity the individual may be apprehensive to report the occurrence for fear of reprisal. In this type of circumstance you need to be able to provide a way to report issues of noncompliance anonymously. Consider setting up a hotline for reporting such matters. To ensure the caller's anonymity, consider using an outside service or third party for this function.

Personnel-Related Policies

Introduction

There are several personnel-related policies that should be implemented which impact procedures in the areas of employee hiring, termination, and attendence.

Pre-Employment Screening

Before hiring someone for the IT group, check all references. Never assume simply that because a person gave references that the reference will be good. Talk to the references and question them about the candidate. Also consider a credit check. A bad credit rating or a history of bankruptcy on a potential employee's record may indicate someone who is not responsible or who is financially strapped. This is an indication that the person could be a potential risk, especially if he or she will be involved with systems that process financial transactions. Financial institutions, in particular, like to have employees who are financially responsible. If possible, consider drug screening. Many people consider drug screening to be an invasion of privacy, but when hiring new employees it can be a useful tool to weed out questionable applicants. The drug test can also be required if you wish to have the employee bonded.

Mandatory Vacation Policy

Every employee in the IT unit should be required to take at least five consecutive business days off each year. Also consider rotating job functions and responsibilities. This is something that should be considered for most every position in an organization. It is unfortunate, but most often the employee that embezzles from a company or is caught committing some fraud is almost always considered to be a model employee up until the crime is discovered. Such employees are often considered to be hard workers, because they almost never take any time off. The reason they never take time off is because if someone filled in for them while they were out, the irregularities would be discovered. As a result, they come into work everyday, sick or healthy, without fail, and always do their job.

For this reason, I recommend that organizations adopt a policy that requires each and every employee to take off five consecutive business days, so that someone else can perform their job function for that period. This may not identify every instance of employee misappropriation, but it will at least catch some.

New Account Policy

When an account is created for a new end user or employee the system administrator should not be the one to determine what level of authorization and access to assign the account. This policy would cover the process of notifying the system administrator of the new end user accounts and the level of access required. There should also be a follow-up review process. The follow-up review should be performed by someone other than the system administrator to ensure that the access level assigned to the new account was the authorized level.

Security Access Change Request

When an access level change is requested for an existing account, such changes should be documented and authorized by someone other than the requesting parties. When the access level change is effected, it should be reviewed by someone other than the system administrator who made the change.

Employee Termination Checklist

When an employee is terminated, either voluntarily or involuntarily, all access to systems should be deleted, and all keys, badges, files, or equipment should be recovered. If the employee was a system administrator all passwords should be changed, if possible. If it is not possible to change all passwords, then at least change the passwords for privileged accounts. If the employee had dial-in access, consider changing telephone numbers. Someone other than the system administrator should review that the employee's access to all systems has been removed.

Procedures also need to be developed to handle occasions when turnover takes place for critical IT employees. Specifications need to be developed to address hardware and software training for firewalls and network operations. The policy should seek to avoid allowing a situation to develop where one person has all the knowledge, and there is no succession plan in place.

Information Protection Team

Any corporate information security policy should include the formation of an information protection team. This team should be responsible for reviewing, monitoring, and enhancing policies and standards for the organization in regards to information security. The team's charter should include reviewing the security implications of any new major system prior to its implementation. The information protection team and its authority should be codified in an organization's policies and procedures.

Crisis Management Planning

Every organization's planning and procedures should include some kind of crisis management planning. Most organizations will need at least two sections to any crisis management procedure: One section should deal with disaster recovery planning, and the other section should cover computer security incident response planning. Chapter 16 discusses crisis management in more detail.

15

Auditing, Monitoring, and Intrusion Detection

It is stating the obvious to say that, in this day and age and for some time to come, organizations will rely heavily on computers and networks for their existence. As a result, the accuracy of those systems and people who use and maintain them are crucial to an organization's survival. Moreover, since people make mistakes and since some people can be dishonest or malicious, organizations need to regularly audit and monitor their computers and networks.

With the introduction of computers and networks, the concept of an audit has expanded to have multiple meanings. Historically, audits have had the effect of reducing reliance on administrative and procedural controls. In other words, the controls were not built into the process but were in the verifications that took place afterward. This does not mean that an audit negated the need for procedures and controls, but it would only catch any deviations from those procedures and controls after the fact. The residual risk was deemed acceptable to the operation of the organization, so that an audit was only required periodically. This orientation toward residual risk may have been acceptable in the past, but it is very dangerous in today's environment. As a result, in some contexts "audit" has become synonymous with "monitor."

This chapter covers three separate aspects of "auditing." First is the traditional electronic data processing (EDP) audit to which most IT departments are subject and which is usually performed with the assistance of an outside firm or by an internal audit department. EDP audits can review issues such as the controls for application development, records retention, copyright requirements, and general operational issues, but this chapter focuses on security audits. The second aspect of auditing examined in this chapter is system auditing and tools that are available to periodically check the integrity of either an individual system or a network in general. The third is intrusion detection, which is a process of ongoing auditing or monitoring of the security and integrity of an organization's systems and networks.

What Is an Audit?

Traditionally, an audit is an independent review of a given subject. Its purpose is to report on conformance to required standards. One of the functions that an EDP audit serves is to verify compliance to company policies and to ensure that required security procedures and practices are being followed. In addition, an EDP audit usually entails the process of monitoring and analyzing systems, networks, and end-user activity.

In addition to reviewing compliance to policies and procedures, an audit is concerned with risk assessment. An EDP audit assesses the risks to and associated with systems and networks to determine if the existing controls are adequate to protect the organization's assets. Some of the areas that a security audit would review include the following.

- Ensuring that desk manuals and procedures are up to date;
- Ensuring proper segregation of duties with proper reviews of work;
- Ensuring that adequate physical controls are in place;
- Ensuring that user authentication controls are adequate;
- Ensuring that audit trails are maintained;
- Ensuring that disaster recovery/business resumption plans are in place and tested regularly;
- Ensuring proper controls for application development and implementation;
- Ensuring that data integrity is monitored and maintained;
- Ensuring that general policies and procedures are followed.

An audit can be an opportunity to validate an organization's security policies and can provide IT with a chance to have an outside party test the security measures that have been implemented. It is not uncommon to employ a "tiger team" or "white hat hackers," as they are sometimes called, to test security measures. These are network security experts who test system and network defenses by attempting to "hack" into them. This hacking is done with the knowledge and consent of the organization that owns the network or systems that they are attempting to penetrate. Such individuals are usually hired consultants, but some organizations employ internal staff for tiger teams.

If an organization does business through a partner or a third party, then the organization's IT unit may need to audit that partner's or third party's security measures. This is particularly true if an organization uses a portal, colocation, or ASP vendor to provide Internet-enabled or branded Internet services to customers. It would be extremely risky for an organization to enter into an agreement with an ASP without first certifying all aspects of the ASP's computer operation, including security. When using a colocation or ASP service, a company can find itself the indirect victim of a denial-of-service attack directed at another subscriber of the service.

As mentioned above, there are many areas reviewed during an audit. Consequently, for large installations, it may be necessary to categorize the functions and audit the functions separately. For example, the functions can be categorized under the following headings:

- Operational audits;

- System audits;

- Activity and usage audits.

Operational security audits seek to ensure that proper controls have been established to identify deviations from established standards and policies. This type of audit is designed to mitigate vulnerabilities introduced by poor management.

There are several objectives for system security auditing. The first is to validate the system configuration. System security audits also seek to analyze the system configuration to mitigate vulnerabilities introduced by the faulty implementation of a system, network, or application. The types of things a system audit reviews or looks for includes, among other things:

- *Accounts without passwords:* It happens more often than you would think.

- *Adherence to and enforcement of password policies:* How easy is it to crack the passwords?

- *Shared accounts:* Are there accounts to which more than one person has the password?

- *Dormant accounts:* These accounts are often used by hackers and should be deleted.

- *Files with no owner:* These files are open to abuse, because anyone can take possession of them.

- *Files with inappropriate access rights:* These files are also open to abuse. It is very important that critical system files have the proper access rights.

- *Separation of duties:* Is there a process of checks and balances in place with proper reviews, or does one or two individuals have all the controls?

Even a secure system that is properly configured is vulnerable to attack, and auditing provides an excellent way of determining whether and how such attacks may take place.

Another reason for a system security audit is to monitor for attempted probes, attacks, and other unusual occurrences. Auditing a system can also assist in setting baselines for system usage, which are used to identify abnormal activity.

System monitoring relies heavily on system audit logs or event logs. General system log files record particular events including the following:

- Logins or attempted logins;
- Logouts;
- Remote system access;
- File opens, closes, renames, and deletions;
- Changes in privileges or security attributes;
- Changes in access control levels.

These log files are usually maintained on the server's or system's local disk drives and as such are vulnerable to alteration. It is generally a good practice to either move the log files to another server on a daily basis or simply print out the pertinent log entries to ensure a hardcopy record that can not be altered.

There are several software tools available to aid in the process of auditing a system. Two of the best known open source freeware programs are COPS and SATAN, which are discussed in Chapter 7. There are also a number of commercial products available from vendors such as Internet Security Systems (ISS), Secure Networks, Cisco, and Netective, just to name a few.

The key to an activity and usage audit is the establishment of baseline metrics to assist in identifying potential security problems. System activity audits seek to analyze deviations from the normal patterns of usage and other unusual activities. Baseline metrics should be established to assist in identifying potential security problems. The purpose is to identify abnormal usage and to identify possible attacks in progress. Exceeding these metrics or thresholds should trigger alarms in the system or should cause action to be initiated by whoever reviews the reports or logs. For example, baseline metric may reveal that a particular employee accesses data 20 times more than any other employee does? Why? What causes him or her to deviate from the normal behavior pattern?

Baseline metrics are also a key element of certain types of IDSs, which are discussed in more detail later in the chapter. However, this type of auditing does not require an IDS to be effective. Auditing of this nature is geared toward the application level, and most IDSs are generally geared toward the operating system level. It is usually not difficult to generate simple queries that identify anomalies in activity for a given period. Sometimes all it takes is a daily eyeball review of standard reports. Identifying anomalies for overall system activity on a daily basis is relatively easy. It is more difficult to identify anomalous behavior for a given operator over an extended period. An employee who accesses files 20 times more in a given day than any other employee would be easy to spot, but identifying anomalous behavior for a given employee over a period of time is more difficult because it requires comparisons to historical data. For example, a user account that logs in at an unusual hour for a given period might warrant investigation. However, one would not know if the hour that the login occurred was unusual unless there was historical data that indicated that the behavior was not normal.

Many applications have built-in logging capabilities that can be utilized for routine reviews. In general, it is advisable to log, monitor, and review transactions that require any kind of an override of system parameters. For example, in the financial industry it is normal for controls to be put in place for each employee that specify an upper dollar limit on transactions. These controls or system parameters may require a supervisor override if a transaction is over the specified amount. Most systems of this type generate a daily supervisor override report that is reviewed by a third party to ensure the legitimacy of the transactions and to serve as a precaution against collusion.

These types of reports are usually one of the first things examined by external auditors. External auditors examine them to ensure that the reports are, in fact, reviewed on a daily basis. Auditors will sometimes sample the transactions to ensure that they are legitimate. Auditors may also review whether the trigger mechanism that flags the transaction is adequate for the function.

Another auditing function that is frequently a standard feature of many system applications is data change tracking. This is the ability to identify the last operator that made a change to a data element, record, or file. The minimum characteristics that should be recorded include the following:

- Identification of the operator making the change;
- Type of change;
- File and data element;
- Date and time of a change;
- Whether the change was successful;
- What the element was before and after the change.

This capability can be particularly crucial when investigating fraudulent activity involving insiders, such as employees.

Audit Mistakes

Ideally, an audit should be seen as an opportunity to improve processes. Unfortunately, the reality is sometimes one of finger-pointing and recrimination. Based on personal experience, some of the more common mistakes that contribute to a difficult EDP audit are described as follows:

- *Not consulting with IT in the scheduling or planning process:* Nothing will ensure a difficult EDP audit like scheduling one during a period when the IT division is stretched to the limit working on projects. This results in the IT division feeling imposed upon and resentful of the untimely intrusion. The IT division's resources may already be stretched to the breaking point when they start getting requests to provide all sorts of information and reports for the auditors. On the other hand, the auditors feel that IT is not cooperating, because IT is not responding in a timely manner to the requests for information. This makes for strained relationships and almost ensures that a process that should be one of open communications becomes painful and difficult.

- *Auditors not properly trained to perform an EDP audit:* I've been involved in EDP audits where the auditors did not have the technical background necessary to adequately perform the audit. In these instances the results were mixed. In some cases, the auditors simply accepted everything they were told by the IT group to be factual and accurate. There was no process of independent verification. While this might make the process easier on the IT group, it is not a true audit and does not serve the needs of the organization as a whole. In other cases I've seen the lack of technical knowledge on the part of auditors make then insecure about information with which they are provided. In some cases I've seen it border on paranoia. Since the auditors had no way of independently verifying information with which they were provided, they doubted everything.

- *Leaving it up to IT to enforce unilateral changes within the organization:* It is not unusual for deficiencies in procedures to be identified, over which the IT unit has no control. For instance, access levels within applications may be administered by the IT unit, but those who determine the actual level of access may reside within other business unit. As an example, the ultimate authority as to who has what access to the HRMS is the director of human resources. The IT group supports the HRMS package, but it is human resources who owns it, and it is they who determine who will have access to what information. On more than one occasion, I have seen audit findings in a final report regarding issues over which IT had no control or say in the process. However, the items were still cited as deficiencies in the audit. The IT group is left to correct the deficiency, over the objections of another business group.

- *Doing it by the book:* Auditors sometimes fail to recognize one of the cardinal rules of network security, which is that security measures and procedures that interfere with the operation of an organization are of little value. Those types of measures are usually ignored or circumvented by company personnel, so they tend to create security holes rather than plug them. Whenever possible, security measures should compliment the operational and business needs of an organization. Some auditors have a tendency to site any deviation from standard recommended practices, even if the deviation makes sense operationally for an organization. Security is a balancing process—balancing the security needs with the business needs and the probable with the possible. Too often auditors concentrate on the possible and not the probable.

- *Audit report does a hatchet job on IT:* It is not uncommon for the final audit report to be unnecessarily harsh on the IT unit. This is often a result of the mistakes listed above. Misunderstandings, lack of communication, and general distrust often lead to harsh findings. This is very unfortunate, since the security audit is actually an opportunity to test, learn, and improve an organization's security. As such, it should be welcomed, but too often it is met with dread. The IT unit and the audit group need to work together in developing the final report, so that it is comprehensive and practical. It needs to be comprehensive in that no area is glossed over. It needs to be practical in that no audit recommendations should constrict or interfere with the operation of the organization.

- *Lack of management support to implement audit recommendations:* The surest way to ensure that an audit is a failure is for management to fail to support the implementation of the audit recommendations. Management support is critical when implementing policy changes, particularly when those changes meet with resistance. In some cases it may simply be a matter of management not allocating the resources necessary to implement the recommendations. Most organizations have projects with deadlines and commitments that existed before the audit. Implementing the audit recommendations is always something that is given low priority. Ultimately, the recommendations are never implemented, and the same findings are usually cited at the next audit.

Deficiencies of Traditional Audit Techniques

The unfortunate reality is that it is not possible to build a completely secure system or network. Procedures are sometimes ignored. Passwords are vulnerable, and technologies fail or are subverted. Even in an environment where everything functions according to plan, the systems are still vulnerable to abuse by privileged insiders, such as system administrators.

The ultimate goal of a network security scheme is to prevent successful attacks on a network. Traditionally, the primary tool for ensuring network security has been the firewall. However, firewalls are almost useless for monitoring activity on the internal network. Organizations are beginning to recognize the need to audit or monitor their internal networks simply because the majority of all attacks and losses involve insiders.

While traditional security audits may identify weakness in security measures or even expose security breaches, it is usually after the fact. Audit tools, such as COPS or SATAN, will only identify weaknesses in the configuration or implementation of systems or networks. Neither one of these approaches identifies problems as they occur; instead, they are concerned with residual risk. Traditionally, the residual risk was deemed acceptable to the operation of the organization, so that an audit was only required periodically. In today's Internet-connected environment the paradigm of residual risk is no longer valid. As a result, more proactive methods are required to audit or monitor networks and systems. Today there are new tools available that provide administrators with the ability to monitor network and system security on-line in real time.

Intrusion Detection

Competent system administrators have always monitored their systems for intrusions. The process usually entailed reviewing logs on a daily basis. Intrusions were sufficiently rare that after-the-fact reviews were usually adequate to address any possible problems. Unfortunately, times have changed drastically. After-the-fact reviews are no longer adequate; real-time or near real-time responses to intrusions are necessary. In addition, the volume of activity on the networks today dwarfs what was the norm 10–15 years ago. As a result, it is not humanly possible to review the amount of information in today's log files without some automated process. Without the automation of the review and monitoring process, it could be weeks before a system administrator knows about an intrusion to his or her system.

In general terms an "intrusion" can be defined as an unauthorized attempt or achievement to access, alter, render unavailable, or destroy information on a system or the system itself. Basically, an intrusion is somebody attempting to break into or misuse a system. Some observers differentiate misuse and intrusion. The term intrusion is usually used in reference to attacks that originate from outside an organization. Misuse is usually used to describe an attack that originates from the internal network. However, not everyone makes this differentiation.

Intrusion detection is the art of detecting unauthorized, inappropriate, or anomalous activity. The art of intrusion detection has been practiced by system and network administrators for years. However, intrusion detection has recently received more attention in the media largely due to the fact that so many companies are now marketing IDSs. Supposedly, these new IDSs can identify attacks in progress, generate real-time alerts, and even launch countermeasures or reconfigure routers or firewalls to counter an attack.

Intrusion Detection Systems (IDSs)

IDSs act much like security guards or sentries. They constantly scan network traffic or host audit logs. While the present batch of IDS products provide useful tools to augment an organization's network security, it is necessary to get past the marketing hype to evaluate a system's effectiveness. Presently, no single system provides truly effective end-to-end intrusion detection capability. In addition, IDSs are not a new concept. In Chapter 7, we discussed the TCPWrapper, a UNIX-based freeware IDS that has been around for many years.

Generally, IDSs fall into one of two categories:

- Network-based IDSs;
- Host-based IDSs.

While there are merits to both approaches neither method by itself is sufficient to monitor all threats. As a result, the current trend in the industry is to combine the two approaches.

Host-Based Intrusion Detection Systems

Host-based products reside on the host and are capable of automatically monitoring and denying services if suspicious activity is detected. They monitor activity on the individual host as opposed to monitoring activity on the network. Host-based IDSs still rely on system audit logs, much the same way system administrators do, but IDSs automate the process. Typically a host-based IDS monitors system, event, and security logs on Windows NT and the syslog file for UNIX. The host-based IDS uses system log files and the system's own auditing agents to monitor the system.

There are a couple of approaches that host-based intrusion detection software can employ. One is to employ a wrapper, like TCPWrapper. This approach wraps the various host network services in an extra layer or shell that interprets network packet requests to the various services. The other approach employs agents that run as separate processes and monitor the requests to host. Both approaches are effective at detecting anomalous activity or misuse of host systems.

One advantage to host-based agents is that they can monitor changes to critical system files and changes in user privileges. When a key system file changes, the IDS compares the files properties with known attack signatures to see if there is a match. One popular method for detecting intrusions involves verifying key system files and executables via checksums at regular intervals for unexpected changes. For example, Chapter 7 discusses using MD5 to monitor changes to system files and the Tripwire IDS, which also provides this function. The first time one of these systems is run, it generates a snapshot of the file attributes, including file sizes and access rights. This information is stored in a database. Each subsequent run of the IDS compares the attributes of the files on the disk to the attributes stored in its database. If the attributes have changed then an alarm is sounded.

Some host-based IDSs monitor TCP port activity and notify system administrators when specific ports are accessed or scanned. They can also monitor and record when physical ports are accessed. This can be useful if the port has a modem connected to it.

Perhaps the biggest drawback to host-based IDSs, such as TCPWrapper and Tripwire, is that the intrusion detection process is not real-time. Host-based intrusion detection programs, regardless of whether they use some wrapper or agent, generally identify intrusion attempts after they have been attempted or succeeded. The lag between the intrusion and its discovery can be substantial. By then it can be too late. This is a weakness with host-based IDSs in general. Another general weakness with host-based IDSs, like TCPWrapper and Tripwire, is that they don't have any capability to proactively react to an intrusion. Nor do they allow the system administrator to be proactive.

Another drawback to the host-based approach is that to secure the entire network, it is necessary to load the IDS on every computer. However, this aspect of host-based IDSs can also be a benefit. If you only desire to monitor one system, the cost of host-based IDSs is often lower than those for their network-based counterparts. As we have already discussed, there are freeware versions of host-based IDSs available on the Internet. In addition, host-based IDSs usually require no additional hardware, since they run on the system itself. Network-based IDSs very often require a dedicated system or device to function. This too increases the cost.

Another advantage to a host-based IDS is that it monitors specific systems and can identify non-network-based attacks. The host-based IDSs can monitor system file integrity, file permissions, and other file system parameters that a network-based IDS does not monitor. In addition, host-based IDSs can monitor terminal connections that bypass the network, and they can also monitor the specific activities of someone logged into the host and accessing files. In addition, a host-based IDS can monitor the activities of applications and processes running on the host. A network-based IDS can only monitor the network, not what is occurring on a specific host.

Network-Based Intrusion Detection Systems

Network-based IDS products run on the network and monitor activity analyzing patterns and reporting on suspicious activity. A network-based IDS usually employs a dedicated network server or device with a network adapter configured for promiscuous mode to monitor and analyze all traffic in real time as it travels across the network. The network-based IDS monitors packets on the network wire and attempts to discern the legitimate traffic from the malicious. Some vendors state that a dedicated server is not necessary for the functioning of their network-based IDS. However, in reality it would not be advisable to run an IDS on a general-purpose application server. Would you want your network's IDS running on the company's payroll server?

When compared to host-based IDSs, network-based IDSs have advantages and disadvantages. Depending on the system, a network-based IDS may be less expensive to implement. This is due to the fact that a network-based IDS is operating system–independent and is not required to be loaded on all hosts on a network to be effective.

In addition, host-based IDSs will miss many network-based attacks. Host-based IDSs do not examine packet headers, so they cannot detect denial-of-service attacks. Network-based IDSs are also much more stealthy than host-based IDSs. With a host-based IDS, if the system is compromised a hacker can readily see if there is an IDS present. It would be very difficult to determine if a network-based IDS was on a network simply by examining the wire. About the only thing a hacker could determine is that there is a device on the network running in promiscuous mode. A network-based IDS can also provide superior controls on event logs. With many host-based IDSs, the audit logs reside on the system locally. As a result, if the system is compromised, a hacker can manipulate the log files to hide his or her tracks.

Another weakness of network-based IDSs is the fact that they become less effective as network traffic increases. They work very well on an empty network, but as the number of packets increase, their effectiveness decreases to the point where they cannot identify any intrusions. This is a major weakness considering today's high transaction volume and the growth of fast Ethernet and switched Ethernet.

Knowledge-Based Intrusion Detection Systems

There are two general approaches employed for identifying hostile intrusions. One is knowledge-based, and the other is statistical-based. The two approaches are very different and employ different technologies.

Most of the IDSs deployed today are knowledge-based. Knowledge-based IDSs are sometimes referred to as misuse detection systems, expert systems, or model- or signature-based IDSs.

Knowledge-based IDSs rely on the ability to recognize known attacks. A knowledge-based IDS recognizes known intrusion scenarios and attack patterns. The knowledge-based IDS relies on a database of attack "signatures" or "patterns" that can be changed for different systems. For example, a host-based, knowledge-based IDS may monitor keystrokes for attack patterns. The IDS has a database of known keystroke patterns that are known to be a threat.

Knowledge-based IDSs employ many different techniques to identify intrusion patterns or signatures. For a host-based, knowledge-based IDS the process can involve monitoring keystrokes, reviewing files for changes and monitoring ports. The review of files can function much the same way as a virus scanner on a PC. The scan searches for known patterns or changes that have been made to critical files since the last scan. String signatures look for text strings that indicates a possible attack. An example of a string that might raise a red flag for a UNIX system would be someone examining the contents of the password file or hosts file using "cat /passwd" or "cat /hosts." You should always be suspicious of someone who wants to examine the password file or review what other hosts are on the network. When monitoring ports, a host-based, knowledge-based IDS can compare audit logs to the signatures of common techniques. As an example, a significant number of failed TCP connections to well-known ports may be an indication that someone is scanning ports, or a large number of unacknowledged SYN-ACK packets is probably an indication that the system is under a SYN flooding attack.

A network-based, knowledge-based IDS examines packets on the network. Packets are considered suspect if they match a known signature, string, or pattern. A network-based, knowledge-based IDS can examine the protocol stack for suspicious invalid or fragmented packets that violate the TCP/IP protocol. The ping-of-death with its oversized ICMP packets would be an example of a known signature. A network-based, knowledge-based IDS can also examine packet headers for dangerous or illogical combinations in packet headers. Another well-known header signature is a TCP packet with both the SYN and FIN flags set, signifying that the originator wishes to start and stop a connection at the same time. This can be an indication that a system is being probed by an intruder.

Knowledge-based systems that employ pattern matching simply translate known intrusions into patterns that are then matched against the system or network activity. The IDS attempts to match activity to the patterns representing intrusion scenarios. The IDS monitors the activity, accumulating more and more evidence for an intrusion attempt until a threshold is crossed. The basic approach underlying pattern matching is that if it looks like a duck, walks like a duck, and quacks like a duck, then it must be a duck. However, for pattern matching to work the patterns must be easily recognizable, and they must be distinguishing. In other words, they must not look like any other normal or legitimate activity.

The advantages of knowledge-based IDSs is that they usually have low false alarm rates. This is due to the fact that they usually watch for very specific signatures, strings, and patterns. In addition, because they watch for specific events they are able to report with some detail and certainty on the threat being faced, which makes it easier to determine the appropriate course of action.

The major disadvantage to knowledge-based IDSs is that they are only effective against threats with which they are already familiar. As a result, they are useless against new techniques for which they have no signature or pattern in the knowledge base. In addition, it is not a simple matter to create a signature or pattern for an attack. It is not easy to translate known attack scenarios into patterns that can be used by a knowledge-based IDS. It requires keeping the IDS up-to-date with new vulnerabilities and environments. Further, it requires time-consuming analysis of each new vulnerability to update the IDS's knowledge base. As a result, vendors don't update their databases as often as they should.

Another common weakness of knowledge-based IDSs is that they are ineffective against passive attacks, such as network sniffing and wiretaps. They are also ineffective against IP or sequence number spoofing, DNS-based attacks, session hijacking, and redirects. In addition, a knowledge-based IDS will not detect the fraudulent or malicious activity of a privileged insider if the activity does not match a known pattern or signature. This is particularly true if the activity is performed through an application. For example, fraudulently transferring funds from one account to another will not be flagged, since it would be within the normal parameters of the system.

Some of the better known network-based IDS products are from AXENT, Cisco, and Internet Security Systems (ISS).

Statistical-Based Intrusion Detection Systems

Statistical-based IDSs identify intrusions by developing base-line measurements for "normal" activity and assuming that anything that deviates significantly from the norm is an intrusion. In other words, intrusions are recognized by identifying deviations from normal or expected behavior of the system or the users. Statistical-based IDSs are also referred to as behavior-based IDS or just simply anomaly detection systems. The underlying philosophy is predicated on the concept that anything new, different, or unknown must represent a threat to the security of the system or network.

A statistical-based IDS (SIDS) develops a model for "normal" patterns of activity and behavior by collecting information from various sources. The SIDS learns what is normal by knowing what the patterns have been historically. It requires large quantities of information and data to develop an accurate and useful model. The more information the IDS can acquire, the more it learns and the more accurate the model. These models can be developed at the system, user, or application level. A model can be developed for any kind of activity that needs to be monitored. The models, which are based on historical information, are used to compare and validate the ongoing activity for a system, user, or application. When a statistically significant deviation is observed, an alarm is generated. In other words, anything that does not conform to previously learned pattern or behavior is deemed to be suspicious.

The major advantage of a SIDS versus a knowledge-based system is that a SIDS does not rely on a predefined set of known attack patterns or signatures. As a result, the SIDS can detect attempts to exploit new vulnerabilities. At least theoretically it can. SIDSs are also less dependent on operating system–specific mechanisms.

Another advantage to a SIDS is that it can detect the fraudulent or malicious activity of a privileged insider. For example, the fraudulent transfer of funds from one account to another could set off alarms if the user did not normally access that account, or if the dollar amount was over what was normal for the individual, or if it was done at an unusual time. In other words, the alarm would go off if the transfer were statistically significantly different from the user's normal activity or behavior.

There aren't many SIDSs on the market today—at least not for the standard vanilla corporate computer system or network. This is due to a number of factors. First, they tend to have a high number of false alarms. This is due to the fact that SIDSs consider almost any activity that is new or different to be a threat. Very few networks are static. In addition, developing user profiles may be difficult, especially in an environment where users work irregular schedules or there is a high turnover. As a result, it would be very difficult to implement a SIDS in an environment where changes to the users, network topology, servers, or applications are the norm.

SIDSs must also be flexible enough to modify their model as a user's or network's activity patterns change. However, this flexibility can actually be exploited to an intruder's advantage. If the incremental changes are minor and performed over an extended period, an intruder can "teach" the SIDS to accept fraudulent or malicious activity as "normal."

Another weakness of the SID approach is that regardless of whether the SIDS is taught over time that an intrusive activity is normal or whether it is simply an oversight on the part of the system, a SIDS will not recognize attacks of any kind that conform to behavior that it has learned to be normal. In other words, if it's not abnormal, then the SIDS will assume it is not an intrusion. This logic is often fallacious.

Another concern with SIDSs is how to determine what components to monitor for creating the models. The possibilities are endless and include file access, access time, network connections, volume of packets, and CPU utilization. In addition, determining when a deviation from the norm becomes statistically significant can be difficult. Like most things in network security, it is a balancing process.

Many of the SIDSs in use today utilize neural networks. A neural network is a type of artificial intelligence that can be trained to learn. The training usually involves feeding the neural network large amounts of data and programming a complex set of rules about data relationships. Once set in place, the rules can be adjusted by the neural network based on additional input. Neural networks "learn" from examples and additional input. A neural network is capable of learning from examples to find patterns in data from a representative data sample. The more examples or input the network receives the more it learns. Neural networks are able to predict future events based on past performance.

A neural network usually involves large parallel processing systems employing the concept of fuzzy logic. Neural networks are sometimes described in terms of knowledge layers, with more complex networks having more layers. These systems examine the inputted data and make determinations based on the complex set of rules and past examples.

Neural networks are being employed for credit risk analysis, predicting market trends, weather forecasting, and fraud detection. For example, VISA and Mastercard use neural networks to identify fraudulent activity. The neural networks comb the millions of daily transactions to identify anomalies in activity based on each "individual" cardholder's past patterns. This is an impressive accomplishment, considering the volume of transactions and the number of cardholders each company has in its customer base.

Defense In-Depth Approach

Like a firewall, an IDS should be seen as just one more tool in a defense in-depth approach. Security measures should be multitiered, and IDSs can serve as another layer of security. Before you deploy an IDS, however, make sure that you weigh the pros and cons and be sure that the vendor you pick has the system that best meets your needs. Some of the pros of IDSs are listed as follows:

- Can detect some abuses and intrusions;
- Can identify where attacks are occurring;
- Can be useful for collecting evidence;
- Can alert administrators that someone is probing;
- Can take corrective action against certain types of abuses or intrusions.

Some IDS cons are listed as follows:

- Misses many types of abuses and intrusions;
- Do not work well on high-speed or heavy-volume networks;
- Generates false alarms.

An IDS can add depth to your overall security, helping to identify possible intrusions and abuses, but an IDS by itself does not ensure security. IDSs have a long way to go before they are as effective as much of the marketing hype would have you believe. Network-based IDSs' inability to function effectively on noisy, high-speed, or high-volume networks is just one example of the limitations that IDSs have to overcome before they become truly effective. Even when they are functioning correctly, all IDSs still miss many specific and harmful types of attacks. The most effective approach to intrusion detection is to use a combination of network-based and host-based detection.

Future Directions

Intrusions or abuses usually are not confined to a single system or network segment. We now work in an environment where information is distributed over large networks that are centrally administered. As a result, it would be useful to have intrusion detection tools that employed a distributed approach where the host-based IDS communicated with the network-based IDS, and both notified central administration of any anomalies.

To this end, the IETF has formed a working group to study intrusion detection. According to the working group's charter, the purpose of the IETF intrusion detection working group is:

> "... to define data formats and exchange procedures for sharing information of interest to intrusion detection and response systems and to management systems [that] may need to interact with them."

One can only hope that the IETF's efforts lead to integrated end-to-end IDSs that are able to monitor for and react to intrusions and abuses for the entire enterprise.

16

Crisis Management

This chapter describes the planning process that every organization should go through to prepare for an event that threatens the operation or viability of the organization. Disaster recovery and computer security incident response planning can be thought of as two sides of a coin. The two topics are closely related and share some common methodologies and goals. Both are concerned with ensuring the availability and integrity of an organization's networks and systems.

Disaster Recovery Planning

From time to time, many businesses face a catastrophic event that can threaten the viability of the organization. Accordingly, every organization should formulate a set of procedures that details actions to be taken in anticipation of a catastrophic event. The procedures should be designed as if the catastrophic event is inevitable and is going to take place tomorrow. This type of plan is referred to as a disaster recovery plan. In some organizations, disaster recovery planning is called contingency planning or business resumption planning.

Some organizations believe that having hot site recovery services is the same as having a disaster recovery plan. A hot site is a facility that is designed to be activated in the event that an organization's computers or computer facilities are rendered inoperable. A hot site is preconfigured with the power, environmental controls, telecommunications, and computers necessary for an organization to resume computer operations with a minimal disruption in service.

In response to questions about their disaster recovery plans, colleagues have told me that they have contracted for hot site services or maintained redundant systems at another facility, as if all they need to care about was ensuring that the systems were covered. In these cases, the emphasis was on the hardware and software and not on the business and people. A disaster recovery plan is about the resumption of business operations, not just network and computer operations.

The requirements for a disaster recovery plan vary for each organization. However, for most organizations, the minimum objectives of a disaster recovery plan is to provide the information and procedures necessary to do the following:

1. Respond to the occurrence of a disaster;

2. Notify the necessary personnel;

3. Assemble disaster recovery teams;

4. Recover data that may have been lost as a result of the occurrence;

5. Resume processing as quickly as possible to ensure minimal disruption of an organization's operations;

6. Comply with any regulatory requirements that dictate the existence of a disaster recovery plan for the organization.

One of the key factors in the success of a business resumption plan is proper planning for the IT group. Most organizations today rely heavily on computers, networks, telecommunications, and IT in general. As a result, IT plays a key role in most organizations' disaster recovery planning. Usually, the IT unit develops its own separate disaster recovery plan, which details the actions necessary to minimize system downtime, thereby minimizing the disruption of the organization's operation. The IT plan is integrated with an organization's overall disaster recovery plan.

The topic of IT disaster recovery planning is expansive enough that it could easily fill a book. In fact many books have been written on the topic. This chapter aims to discuss IT disaster recovery planning from a business perspective and demonstrate how it ties into network security. It is important to remember that one of the key elements of information security is "availability." This refers to the availability of the information that is located on the systems and networks of the organization. Proper planning is necessary to ensure the availability of mission-critical systems. It is crucial in the planning process to determine what is an adequate level of preparation and what is a mission-critical system.

What Level of Preparation?

The extent to which an organization is willing to invest resources into IT disaster recovery planning should be directly related to the business of the organization. Different organizations have different recovery needs, with regard to IT. As a result, the plans developed by different organizations should reflect their needs. For example, a nonprofit organization that relies on fundraising for income could probably survive several, days if not weeks, of downtime. A bank, on the other hand, could find itself out of business if its systems were down for that period. Most banks could accept a few hours to a day or two of downtime as a result of a catastrophic occurrence, while a stock brokerage firm that trades on the NYSE or NASDAQ could find itself in financial ruin if its systems were down for a few hours and it was unable to trade. The amount of resources that go into IT disaster recovery preparedness is dictated by the operational needs of the organization and the organization's ability, or lack thereof, to survive downtime.

While it would be nice if every organization had unlimited resources to prepare for the immediate resumption of business after a disaster, like everything else in business, expenditures on disaster recovery planning must be justified through cost analysis. In the case of the nonprofit organization, there is little financial loss associated with the downtime itself. In other words, the inability to do business for a day or two has relatively minor financial impact on the organization. In such circumstances, it would be difficult to justify the cost of extensive disaster recovery preparation that included such things as redundant systems and telecommunications and hot sites. In contrast, the brokerage firm could most likely demonstrate that the inability to function, for even a short period of time, could potentially cost the company a significant amount of money. As a result, the brokerage firm could justify substantial expenditures for IT-related disaster recovery preparation and planning.

Disaster recovery planning decisions have to be made like most every other business decision. The cost of the recovery has to be weighed against

the losses incurred as a result of any downtime that may occur. When esti-
mating the cost of the downtime, it is important to include the soft costs as
well as the hard costs. The hard costs, such as lost revenue directly related to
the downtime, are the easy ones to quantify. The soft costs are the hard-to-
quantify items such as customer good will, level of service, and satisfaction
or consumer confidence. It takes a thorough knowledge of an organization's
business to be able to estimate the soft costs. Consequently, it may be difficult for an IT unit to estimate these costs alone. Therefore, participation
from other business units within an organization is vital to the process of
determining the costs associated with any downtime.

What to Restore First?

Just as different organizations have different recovery needs, different functions within an organization have varying levels of priority for recovery. Any
IT disaster recovery plan should assign levels of importance to each system
to ascertain which systems will be given priority when restoring services.
Mission-critical functions need to be identified prior to the occurrence of a
disaster, so that when a disaster does occur, IT does not waste time restoring
superfluous systems instead of those that are truly required. Once again, this
takes a thorough knowledge of the organization's business—and input from
outside of the IT unit. One approach is to gather this information through
an assessment team headed by IT but with the participation of management
and staff knowledgeable in the functioning of the organization and familiar
with the various systems and applications. This process should include for-
mally validating the teams' understanding of the organization's business.

Another approach would be to identify or assign ownership for each
application and obtain the owners' input. By working your way up the hierarchy of applications and systems, you should be able to assign priority to
each. This process should also include obtaining management's perspective
on how critical each application is to the conduct of business. The process of
prioritizing systems should be quantified, by performing a detailed analysis
of each application, to determine what the cost would be to the organization
to lose access to a particular function.

Review and Test

From a cost analysis perspective, successful disaster recovery preparation
is proportionate to the potential loss. From an operational perspective, a

successful disaster recovery plan is responsive to the business needs of the organization.

From a general management perspective, a disaster recovery plan must be kept current and updated with any necessary changes. Modifications to systems, personnel, business priorities, and other environmental factors must be reflected in the plan. That means regular and frequent reviews of the disaster recovery plan. For most organizations, the shelf life of a disaster recovery plan is about three to four months. In other words, that is how long it will take for the plan to become out-of-date and need revision. During the three to four month period, personnel will turn over, technologies will be introduced and/or retired, new products will be released, and business priorities will change. As a result, the plan will need to be revised to reflect these changes.

There must also be regular and comprehensive tests of any disaster recovery plan, and the results of any tests must be incorporated into the plan. Moreover, key personnel must understand their roles and responsibilities in the plan. If they do not, then the best-written plan in the world will be of little value to an organization when a disaster strikes.

Disaster Recovery Planning Case Study

As an example of why it is important to update such plans, a financial institution with which I had a business relationship undertook a comprehensive review of its then existing disaster recovery preparations. At that time, the business resumption plan was about eight years old. Since the time the plan was originally developed, individual sections of the plan have been updated to reflect changes in such things as personnel and technology, but the plan in its entirety has never been reviewed to determine whether it is still adequate for the financial institution's business model.

The purpose of the review was to ensure that the company was properly prepared to deal with a disaster, either limited in scope or large in scale, that interrupted normal business operations. For the review, a team was assembled to evaluate and revise the existing disaster recovery plan. The team included a cross-section of business units within the organization. Most of the team participants were also key members of the business resumption team. The idea was for the team to review and revise the plan as necessary to address the needs of the organization. As with any disaster recovery plan, the goal of the existing plan was the swift resumption of the operations of organization in the event of a disaster.

The first task was to review the existing plan from start to finish. The review of the existing plan only confirmed what many of the team already knew. That was that the organization's business model had changed significantly since the plan was first conceived, but that none of those changes was reflected in the plan. After a thorough review of the existing plan, the team came to the conclusion that simply revising the plan would not address the needs of the organization. The plan was so outdated, and there were so many deficiencies in it that the plan needed to be entirely rewritten. Some of the major shortcomings of the organization's disaster recovery plan are detailed as follows.

- *Remote delivery systems:* When the financial institution's disaster recovery plan was first developed years earlier, well over 50% of all business with customers was performed in the branches by tellers. When the plan was originally developed, the financial institution had few of the electronic delivery systems that were in place at the time of the review. Those that had been deployed years earlier were not used as extensively by the financial institution's customer base as those that were in place during the time of the review. As a result, the primary emphasis of the organization's disaster recovery plan, as it existed, was the resumption of branch operations. A review of how the financial institution was operating revealed that over 85% of all transactions were performed through one of the electronic delivery systems. As a result, the financial institution's disaster recovery plan needed to be modified to reflect a primary emphasis on the restoration of the systems that were providing services to customers. The original plan did not adequately address restoring the organization's call center operations, Internet banking, or banking-by-phone systems. As a result, it was necessary to drastically rewrite the existing plan to ensure the swift resumption of these electronic delivery services in the event of a disaster.

- *Geographic range:* Another problem with the plan was that when it was first developed years earlier, both the overwhelming majority of the customer base and all of the financial institutions offices were located in the San Francisco Bay Area. One of the basic assumptions of the plan was that any event large enough to disrupt the operation of the financial institution, such as an earthquake, would also affect the customers. This assumption was used to prioritize systems. For example, if our telephones were affected, then the assumption was that the customers' telephones would be affected. In this case, restoration of a system such as the bank-by-phone system would not be given a high priority. In addition, it was assumed that our customers, who would also be subject to the disaster, would understand if it required time to restore normal service. At the time the plan was conceived, the company was thinking like a small, community financial institution, and the plan reflected that mind-set. It was not necessarily a wrong mind-set, because at the time the plan was conceived, the organization was a small community financial institution. However, in the intervening years, the financial institution grew and expanded outside the San Francisco Bay Area. At the time of the review, it had offices throughout California, Texas, Oregon, New Jersey, and Arizona. In fact, over 40% of its customer base lived and work outside the San Francisco Bay Area. As a result, it could no longer be assumed that the customers would be subject to the same disaster that struck the financial institution. In addition, it could not and should not be assumed that the customers would be understanding if there were a major disaster in the San Francisco Bay Area. Customers outside the Bay Area would not care if there was an earthquake in San Francisco; they would still want access to the services that they expected the financial institution to provide. As a result, the financial institution needed to devise a disaster recovery plan that ensured the swift resumption of operations for all events, even if there was a major disaster in the San Francisco Bay Area.

- *Disaster recovery services:* In reviewing the changes that needed to be incorporated into the financial institution's disaster recovery plan, it was determined that the financial institution had outgrown the company with which it had contracted for "hot site" disaster recovery services. There were a number of reasons for choosing to review alternatives to the present service provider:

  - *Multiple hot sites (local versus remote):* The service provider that the financial institution was using at that time could only offer a single hot site, which was located out of state. In the event the financial institution was forced to activate its disaster recovery plan, it would have to transport personnel, media, and supplies to the out-of-state location. This would add 24–48 hours to the time it would take to resume computer operations. While this scenario might be acceptable in the event of a major disaster, such as an earthquake, it would not be acceptable if the financial institution experienced a very localized event such as a fire in the computer room or simply a failure of a major system. Under the scenario of a limited disaster, the financial institution would want the option of activating a hot site that would be accessible locally. Since the travel time would be minimal, a local hot site would substantially reduce the amount of time it would take the company to get systems back on-line. Ideally, the best service provider could offer multiple hot sites, with a choice of local and remote sites.

- *Possible contention for service:* Another issue was the fact that the company that the financial institution used for disaster recovery services had contracts with several clients in the San Francisco Bay Area to provide disaster recovery services. In the event of a major disaster, such as an earthquake, the financial institution would have to compete with the other Bay Area clients for time and resources at the single disaster recovery center.

- *Disaster recovery center's capacity:* After reviewing the facilities available at the disaster recovery center, it was determined that the service provider did not have adequate resources to handle all of its San Francisco Bay Area customers. In addition, the financial institution was utilizing ISDN circuits to communicate with the service provider's disaster recovery center. As a result, it required that there be a one-to-one relationship between our branch offices and the service provider's ISDN ports at the disaster recovery center. At the time the contract was originally signed for disaster recovery services, the financial institution only had a limited number of locations that required connectivity to the disaster recovery center in the event of a disaster. In the intervening years, the financial institution had grown and was continuing to grow. It was therefore concluded that at that time the existing disaster recovery center did not have adequate capacity to handle all of the financial institution's branch offices simultaneously. The situation would only become worse, since new offices were opening at a rate of two or three a year.

After a review of existing disaster recover preparations, it was determined that the financial institution needed a disaster recovery service provider with abundant capacity and the ability to provide multiple hot sites. Ideally, any service provider chosen would be able to offer both local hot sites, which can be activated for a limited event, and remote hot sites in the event the San Francisco Bay Area is affected by a major disaster.

Another conclusion of the existing plan review was that the present telecommunications configuration was designed for the resumption of branch operations and, as such, was not adequate for the electronic delivery systems. In addition, it was not flexible enough to address all contingencies. Nor was the present configuration as easy to implement as it should be in the event of a disaster. In the event of a disaster, the desire was to minimize the amount of intervention required to implement the backup telecommunications.

The financial institution needed to deploy a telecommunications configuration that encompassed the electronic delivery systems, that was flexible enough to address all contingencies, and that was relatively easy to implement. Accomplishing this goal would require the expenditure of funds to purchase new equipment and services.

Outsourcing Plan Development and Maintenance

Many organizations don't have the time, resources, and expertise to put together a comprehensive disaster recovery plan. Under these circumstances, an organization should consider outsourcing the process of developing a disaster recovery plan—and even the plan's maintenance. Generally, outsourcing the development of a business resumption plan includes the following.

- Project planning and orientation;

- Reviewing recovery strategies;

- Defining recovery plans and supporting documentation;

- Developing test programs;

- Developing and implementing plan maintenance procedures.

Any consultant hired to develop a plan should provide disaster recovery education to selected company personnel to enhance their ability to understand and respond to emergency outages and to prepare them to participate in the development of the organization's overall recovery capability.

The recovery plans developed by the consultant should define the detailed actions that the company must take to declare a disaster, notify appropriate personnel of the disaster, activate the recovery plans, and execute a timely restoration and recovery. The plan should also include testing programs that define primary and secondary objectives of the testing and the frequency of testing. In other words, each test can have a different objective. One can test telecommunications while another tests operational procedures.

Any disaster recovery plan should also include a maintenance program to ensure that the recovery plan remains up-to-date. The maintenance procedures should include periodic reviews of the technology platforms.

Typically, a plan is developed by collecting information through interviews, workshops, teleconferences, and questionnaires, as deemed appropriate by the consultant. The plan development process should also make use of existing documentation where applicable. Information collected is used to evaluate the ability of company's disaster recovery plan to meet the organization's business requirements. Upon completion and documentation of the disaster recovery plan, the company should validate its contents by performing a detailed and thorough walk-through.

Computer Security Incident Response Plan

Another aspect of crisis management planning is computer and network security incident response planning. Every crisis management plan should include a computer security incident response plan (CSIRP). This plan outlines actions that the company must take when there is fraud or misuse of company-owned electronic media or services, a theft or destruction of company information, or a penetration of, or attack on, company-owned systems and networks. The plan should address such things as what constitutes a security incident, identifying key personnel, a communication and notification process, as well as an escalation process. Needless to say, the information protection team should be a key component of any CSIRP.

Since security incidents occur with more frequency than disasters, organizations are finding that security incident response planning in some respects is more important than disaster recovery planning. In general, organizations experience few real disasters but deal with many security incidents. Denial-of-service attacks and virus outbreaks are becoming common. Most companies are willing to admit denial-of-service or virus incidents, but few are willing to disclose when their networks or systems are truly compromised.

General Recommendations

Just as with disaster recovery planning, there is no single CSIRP that fits all organizations. There is no universal CSIRP template that can be applied to an organization. Each organization's security requirements and needs are unique. However, the following sections outline some general recommendations for CSIRP.

Legal Counsel

The first step is to identify a computer security incident response team (CSIRT). This team can be different from the information protection team (IPT), but the IPT should have some representation on this group. In addition, since it may be necessary to take legal action against the parties responsible for the incident, it is a good idea to either have legal counsel on the CSIRT or at least have it readily accessible. The legal counsel may be necessary to determine whether it is possible to terminate or prosecute the individual or individuals responsible for the incident.

Liability

Legal counsel may also be required to assist in assessing an organization's liability for any computer security incident. The liability can come in many forms. An organization may be liable for the direct loss resulting from a fraud or destruction of company assets. An organization may find itself financially liable for the disclosure of information regarding customers, employees, or partners. An organization may also need to assess its liability as a result of a customer, employee, partner, or hacker using the organization's systems to launch an attack on another company's system.

I have read accounts of system administrators tracking the activities of hackers on their systems to gather more information on the hacker. Rather than shutting down the hacker completely, the administrator limits the damage and monitors the activity to gather evidence on the crime and to identify the perpetrator. Clifford Stoll's account in his book *The Cuckoo's Egg* is one example.

This kind of action or inaction can have risks, not the least of which would be an organization's liability should the hacker damage, steal, or misuse another organization's systems or information. If the hacker damages another company's systems, the question may arise, why didn't the first company stop the hacker when it had the chance? As a result, I recommend against this type of approach and suggest that if a hacker is detected, shut him or her down immediately. However, do gather as much evidence in the process as possible: Save audit and system logs to identify the origins and time of attack. Print out all logs to avoid having them altered or overwritten. Take detailed notes about what occurred, when it occurred, and any actions taken as a result. In addition, avoid using the compromised system or network for communications regarding the incident. It is possible that the hacker or hackers could intercept messages.

Retaliation

A CSIRP should not include any measures for retaliation. It can be tempting to retaliate against a spammer or to trace a hacker back to his or her system of origin. This kind of cyber-vigilantism is illegal and can result in additional liability. I have even heard some accounts where system administrators tracked down hackers, physically went to the hacker's locations, and threatened them with bodily harm. While this approach may provide a certain amount of satisfaction, I strongly recommend against it.

Another reason to avoid retaliation is that hackers often use the systems of other innocent victims from which to launch attacks. This masks their location and makes it difficult to trace the attack back to its true source. In this case, retaliating would only create another victim. In many cases, this is actually the true intention of the hacker. The hacker hopes for a retaliation to be directed against the system or network from which he or she is launching the attack. If an organization does retaliate it can find itself not a victim, but a perpetrator liable for its actions.

Triage

A CSIRP should include a triage process to handle all information regarding incidents. This triage process should provide the initial assessment and analysis and determine what if any escalation is necessary. Triage should act as the focal point for all information and funnel that information to the appropriate groups.

Sources for Information on CSIRP

As stated previously, it is not practical to use a cookie cutter approach to developing a CSIRP. However, there are many sources of information available that can provide some general guidelines to assist in the development of a plan.

The CERT coordination Web site has the "Handbook for Computer Security Incident Response Teams (CSIRTs)," which can be downloaded free of charge at the URL http://www.cert.org/nav/reports.html. Another useful document is "Expectations for Computer Security Incident Response," which is available from the IETF at the URL http://www.ietf.org/rfc/rfc2350.txt?number=2350. The SANS Institute also has publications with detailed recommendations for dealing with the various phases of an computer security incident. However, there is a cost associated with the publications, and they are not inexpensive. Information regarding the SANS publications is available at the URL http://www.sans.org/newlook/publications/incident_handling.htm. These and other available sources go into much more detail than I can in this limited space.

Most importantly, organizations need to spend some time planning what to do in the event of an attack, security breach, or fraud before it occurs. The time to start thinking about what to do is not during the crisis, but before.

17

Cookies, Cache, and AutoComplete

Today, millions of people use the Web every day for shopping, banking, education, business, and entertainment. An essential component of that process is the Web browser. Browsers such as Netscape's Navigator and Microsoft's Internet Explorer are the end user's interface to the Web. Normally when Web surfers think of browser security, if they think of it at all, it is in reference to SSL. People are usually most concerned about the interception of information—such as credit card numbers—as it traverses the network. However, there is exposure associated with files that reside on the local disk drive of the Web surfer's PC. These files are created, accessed, and manipulated by the Web browser and various Web servers every time a Web surfer uses his or her Web browser software. Very few people are aware of the potential risks associated with these files. At the very least they raise privacy issues. At the worst they expose the Web surfer to fraud from malicious Web sites or from the fact that the files can be accessed long after one has shut down the browser and logged off the Web.

This chapter will discuss some of the basic security issues associated with Web browser software. Specifically, we will discuss the internal functions of Navigator and Internet Explorer. We will look at how they work, what to look for, and ways to protect yourself when surfing the Web.

Cookies

Much has been written about cookie files and their possible uses and abuses. Essentially, cookies are text files that are stored on a Web surfer's disk drive by Web browser software, such as Navigator and Internet Explorer. Cookies are an invention of Netscape Navigator but were copied by Microsoft's Internet Explorer. The two browser software employ slightly different approaches when storing cookies. Navigator stores all cookies in a single file aptly named COOKIE.TXT. Internet Explorer creates a file for each cookie, but stores them in the WINDOWS\Cookies directory. A cookie is actually created by a Web server and passed to the browser. The cookie contains information pertaining to the Web site being visited that is stored on a PC's hard drive as a .txt file. By storing the information on the Web surfer's disk drive, Web sites avoid having to store information on their servers. Basically, cookies are used to track what sites you've visited. A cookie can be used to track the number of times you visit a site, to store the personal preference setting for a particular site, or to hold your authentication for a particular site.

For example, if the cookie file is tracking the number of times you visit a particular site, the cookie would be opened each time you browse the site and the counter stored in the cookie would be increased by one. This type of information can be useful for marketers and Webmasters to determine the number of return visitors a site receives. When customizing your preferences for sites like Yahoo, a cookie file would be created and stored on your PC's hard drive. The cookie information would be used to customize banner information that addressed your particular areas of interest or to determine whether to use frames or no-frames. Each time you visited the Web site, the Web server would open the cookie file and modify the information displayed according to the preferences stored in the cookie. When a Web surfer uses a site that requires a registration process, such as the NY Times or Amazon.com Web sites, the authentication information is written to a cookie and stored on his or her PC. With some cookies this can include usernames and passwords. The information stored in the cookie file is read by the Web server each time the Web surfer visits the site. The purpose is to save the end user the trouble of having to enter in the information each time he or she visits the Web site. Theoretically, only the Web site that created the cookie information can read or modify that information. In addition, not every Web site employs cookies, so you will not automatically receive a cookie when visiting a site.

Figure 17.1 shows the various cookies stored on my PC's disk drive under the WINDOWS\Cookies directory. In this case the files were stored

Name	Size	Type	Modified
anyuser@doubleclick(1).txt	1KB	Text Document	1/29/99 8:11 AM
index.dat	80KB	DAT File	1/19/00 4:59 PM
jcnv@206.138.64[1].txt	1KB	Text Document	9/1/99 3:52 PM
jcnv@247media.txt	1KB	Text Document	2/23/99 10:13 AM
jcnv@aaddzz[1].txt	1KB	Text Document	10/25/99 3:13 PM
jcnv@accendo[2].txt	1KB	Text Document	1/12/00 12:39 PM
jcnv@adobe[1].txt	1KB	Text Document	5/10/99 9:53 AM
jcnv@ads.admaximize[1].txt	1KB	Text Document	7/26/99 1:21 PM
jcnv@ads.cbc[1].txt	1KB	Text Document	10/14/99 4:42 PM
jcnv@ads.cimedia[1].txt	1KB	Text Document	10/29/99 9:46 AM
jcnv@ads.fairfax.com[2].txt	1KB	Text Document	4/30/99 11:06 AM
jcnv@ads.link4ads[1].txt	1KB	Text Document	7/21/99 10:58 AM
jcnv@ads.mirrormedia.co[1].txt	1KB	Text Document	5/4/99 4:36 PM
jcnv@ads.mm.ap[1].txt	1KB	Text Document	12/28/99 8:30 AM
jcnv@ads_enliven.txt	1KB	Text Document	12/21/98 4:34 PM
jcnv@adserver.americanbanker[1].txt	1KB	Text Document	6/24/99 1:23 PM
jcnv@adserver.faulknergray[1].txt	1KB	Text Document	5/17/99 11:56 AM
jcnv@adserver.janes[1].txt	1KB	Text Document	6/22/99 8:16 AM
jcnv@ad-venture[2].txt	1KB	Text Document	4/20/99 2:32 PM
jcnv@agency_grevbots(1).txt	1KB	Text Document	12/23/99 11:57 ...
jcnv@akl.txt	1KB	Text Document	4/1/99 8:01 AM
jcnv@altavista[1].txt	1KB	Text Document	4/28/99 1:53 PM
jcnv@amazon[2].txt	1KB	Text Document	10/29/99 8:12 AM
jcnv@antivirus[1].txt	1KB	Text Document	11/19/99 12:15 ...
jcnv@apbnews[1].txt	1KB	Text Document	10/15/99 8:42 AM
jcnv@apbnews[2].txt	1KB	Text Document	1/12/00 12:26 PM
jcnv@avenuea(1).txt	1KB	Text Document	12/23/98 12:00 ...
jcnv@bfast[2].txt	1KB	Text Document	9/13/99 8:51 AM
jcnv@bigcharts[1].txt	1KB	Text Document	12/24/99 3:36 PM
jcnv@billfishfoundation[1].txt	1KB	Text Document	1/10/00 2:19 PM
jcnv@books[1].txt	1KB	Text Document	4/21/99 9:05 AM
jcnv@boston.txt	1KB	Text Document	1/18/99 10:45 AM
jcnv@bouldernews[1].txt	1KB	Text Document	6/28/99 3:58 PM
jcnv@btglobal.txt	1KB	Text Document	12/29/98 9:33 AM
jcnv@catalog[1].txt	1KB	Text Document	6/17/99 10:35 AM
jcnv@cbnnow[1].txt	1KB	Text Document	8/20/99 10:41 AM
jcnv@cbs.sportsline[1].txt	1KB	Text Document	1/10/00 3:59 PM
jcnv@cbs[2].txt	1KB	Text Document	6/14/99 2:06 PM

1 object(s) selected   339 bytes

Figure 17.1 IE5 cookie files.

by IE5. The origins of many of them are easy to guess by their names. Others are more obscure. I have highlighted the cookie issued by the Amazon.com Web site. This cookie is used to authenticate my identity to the Amazon.com server during each visit to its Web site.

For example, in the past Amazon.com has used cookies to identify return visitors to its Web site. Essentially, the purpose of the cookie was to identify a returning customer without requiring the entry of information. If you were a first time visitor to the Amazon.com Web site, the page would display "Hello! New to Amazon.com?" If however you were a returning customer to the Amazon site it could identify you. For example, as a returning customer, I would simply type in the URL www.amazon.com and up would pop the Amazon.com home page saying "Hello, John E. Canavan." The site was able to identify me by the information that it had stored in the cookie on my disk drive at the time I originally signed up with Amazon.com. If I were to delete the cookie, the Amazon.com Web site would treat me as a first-time visitor. I had hoped to provide examples of the Amazon.com Web pages in action, but Amazon.com wouldn't allow me to use images of their Web pages.

Figure 17.2 shows the content of the COOKIES.TXT file that resides on my PC's disk drive. This is the file that is created by Netscape's Navigator. Navigator stores all of its cookies in a single file. Looking at Figure 17.2 you can see the sites that I have visited using Navigator include the NY Times, Double Click, Yahoo, and Netscape. The other information stored in the cookie files will vary from site to site.

The benefit of cookies files to Web surfers is dubious at best. Cookie files were developed for marketing and tracking purposes. Even for that purpose, their value is questionable because end users can access, change, delete, or block cookie information. However, the average Web surfer is neither aware of the existence of cookie files nor of the ability to manipulate them.

The risks associated with cookie files are obvious. Cookies can be an invasion of one's privacy. They basically let people know where you've been on the Web. If someone is able to access your PC they can view the cookies. If you've been to the Playboy Web site and if it issues cookies (I really don't know. Honest!), then playboy.com would clearly show in your cookies. I guess you could always say that you visited the site to read the articles.

The fact that cookies reveal this kind of information can be viewed as a good thing or a bad thing. Parents can use cookies to ensure that children

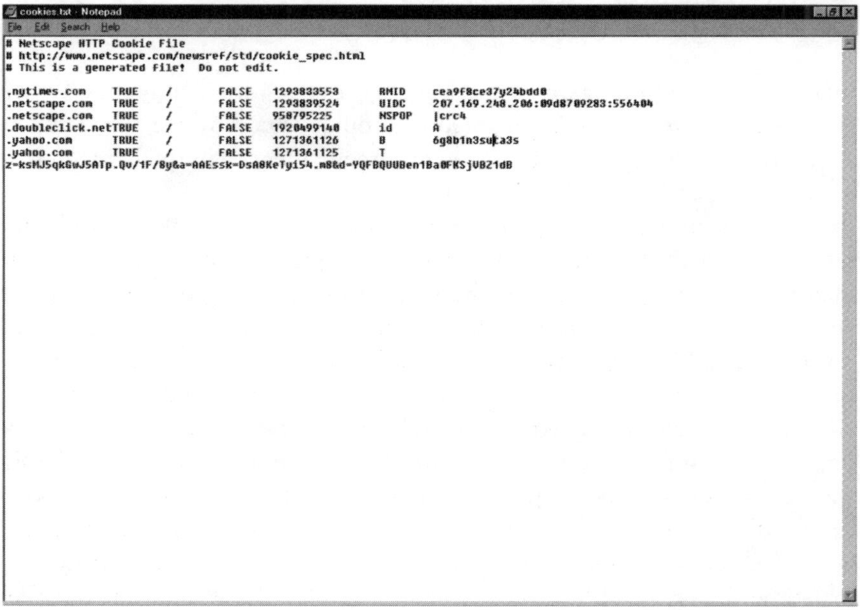

Figure 17.2 Navigator's cookie.txt file.

aren't accessing inappropriate sites, and companies can use them to check for policy violations. However, in either case it would be much more effective to put preventative measures in place rather then check after the fact.

In addition to the risks associated with someone having direct access to your PC there are risks from malicious Web sites. I stated earlier that "theoretically" only the Web site that created or issued the cookie should be able to access it. However, the reality is that from time to time, vulnerabilities are found in Navigator and Internet Explorer that allow for malicious Web sites to read, alter, and delete cookies issued by other Web sites. As a result, it is very dangerous for Web sites to store sensitive information in cookie files.

Imagine the risk associated with a Web server that uses a cookie to store credit card information for on-line transactions. Several free Web-based e-mail services use cookies for authentication. As a result, the operator of a malicious Web site has the potential to access the cookie, determine the e-mail service provider, steal the password, and access the e-mail account. At the very least, someone would be able to identify the owner of the cookie by visiting the issuing Web site. Referring back to the example of Amazon.com, if a hacker Web site had access to the cookie issued to me by Amazon, they could go to the site and up would pop my name.

There is also risk associated with using a site that simply allows the option of using cookies for authentication. I know of at least one on-line stock trading service that gives customers the option to use cookies as part of the authentication. I have seen first hand an instance where an end user went to the trading site and up popped someone else's name and account information. It is quite possible that the individual whose information was erroneously displayed did the correct thing and did not enable the cookies option, but the trading Web site read some information in the end user's cookie files that caused the incorrect identification. One may believe that he or she is protected by not using cookies only to find the poor design of a Web server application circumventing all precautions. In this case, the best protection is not to frequent Web sites that use cookies for authentication.

There are several options available to end users for controlling cookies. First, end users can configure your browser to prompt you before downloading a cookie. This gives end users the chance to accept or deny cookies depending on the site. They can also disable cookies altogether, so that your browser denies all cookies. This can be done with Navigator under Edit/Preferences and Advanced. For IE5 it can be found under Tools/Internet options and then clicking on the Security tab to custom level. Disabling cookies completely can cause problems, since some sites require cookies to be enabled to access the site. Unfortunately, the error message end users receive does not specifically tell them that they need to enable cookies. It is usually some nondescript message about the browser not being supported.

Another option to consider to protect yourself against this type of threat is disabling or prompting for Java, JavaScript, and ActiveX. Again, this will at least give you the option to accept or deny based upon your level of comfort with the site you are visiting. Keep in mind, however, that if you configure your browser to prompt you before accepting cookies, Java, JavaScript, and ActiveX, you will be prompted constantly.

There are also a number of utilities that can be used to monitor and control cookies. Programs such as CookiePal, CookieJar, CookieCop, McAfee's Internet Guard Dog, and Norton's Internet Security can all be employed for controlling cookies.

Cache Files

Cookie files are not the only files created on the disk drive of a Web surfer's PC when visiting a Web site. Both Netscape's Navigator and Microsoft's Internet Explorer also "cache" or store files that have recently been accessed at Web sites. This is referred to as caching, and the files stored on a PC's disk drive are referred to as cache files. The advantage to caching comes into play when reloading Web pages that have recently been viewed. The browser is able to load a page from the files cached on the local disk drive rather than having to reload it from the server. Loading files from the local drive is much faster than loading them over the network from the server. The cached files can include html files, graphic or image files such as gifs and jpgs, and text files.

The risks associated with cached files are similar to those associated with cookie files. Basically, they tell someone where you've been. However, viewing the cache files cannot only tell someone where you've been browsing, but they can actually allow them to view the files you browsed, since the html files along with their associated graphic or image files are cached on your hard drive when you browse most Web pages.

Figure 17.3 is an example of the files cached on my disk drive by Netscape's Navigator. The files are cached in a subdirectory aptly named cache and have nondescript names, but the extensions identify the file types. The files are easily viewed by simply clicking on them. Internet Explorer also caches files, but IE stores cache files under the temporary Internet files directory, which is a subdirectory of the Windows directory.

The fact that browsers cache the pages viewed on-line should be remembered when using the Internet to access bank and brokerage accounts

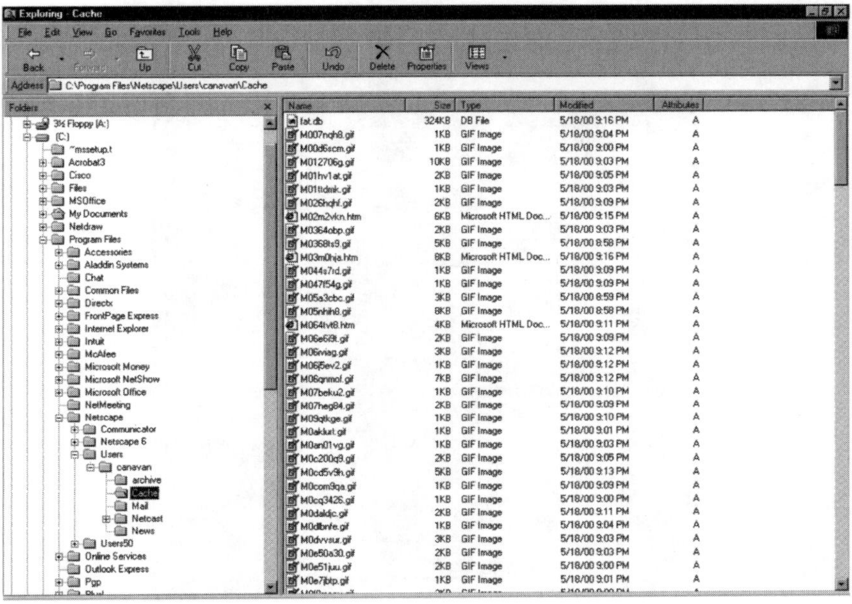

Figure 17.3 IE5 cache files.

for financial transactions. For example, all of the pages viewed when using an Internet banking system are stored in the PC's cached files. Those cache files can include account numbers and balances. If you use your Internet banking system on a PC that is shared by others, say at work, then anyone with physical access to that PC can potentially view information regarding your accounts.

Using Windows Explorer to access the directory where the files reside you can retrieve the cache files. In addition, Internet Explorer provides the ability to view cached files. Under Tools/Internet Options under the General tab you will find temporary Internet files. There are two buttons: One is delete files and the other is settings. This is depicted in Figure 17.4. If you click on settings, there is an option to view files.

Figure 17.5 shows the Internet Explorer cache files that reside on my PC's disk drive. It shows the file types and the location from which they originated. Figure 17.5 shows html, gif, and jpg files from the Yahoo and NASA Web sites.

In addition to the risk from individuals with physical access to your PC being able to retrieve information from your cache files, there is also the risk

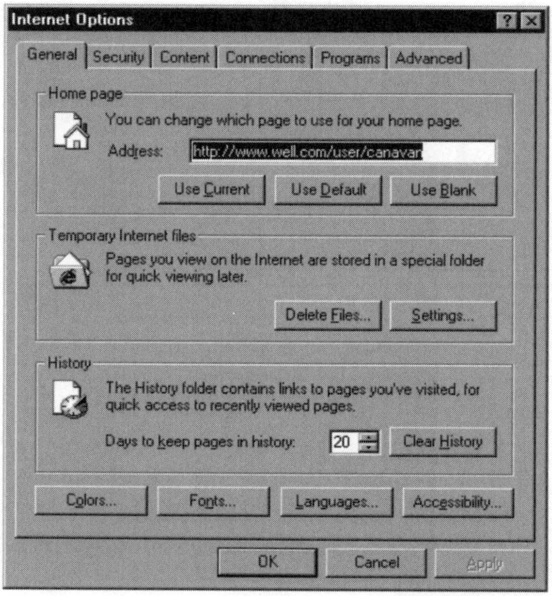

Figure 17.4 IE5 Internet options.

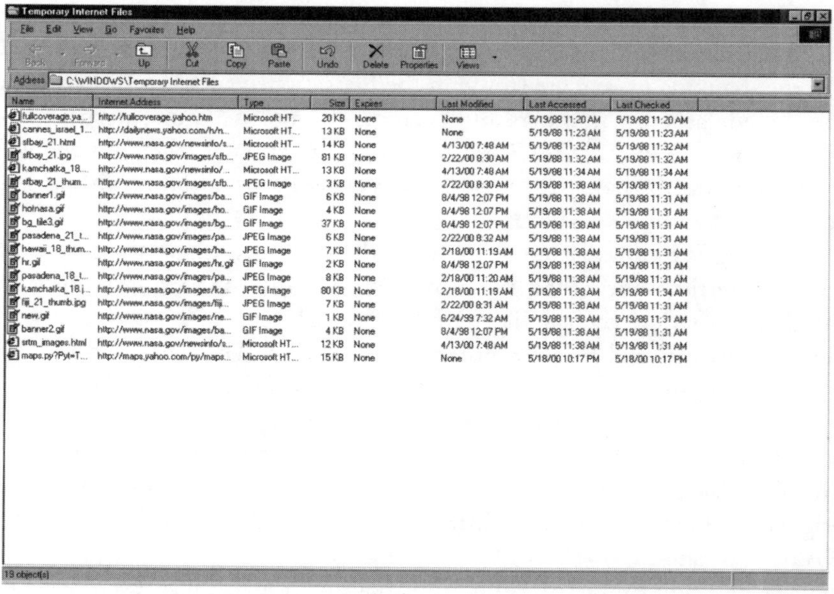

Name	Internet Address	Type	Size	Expires	Last Modified	Last Accessed	Last Checked
fullcoverage.ya...	http://fullcoverage.yahoo.htm	Microsoft HT...	20 KB	None	None	5/19/88 11:20 AM	5/19/88 11:20 AM
cannes_israel_1...	http://dailynews.yahoo.com/h/n...	Microsoft HT...	13 KB	None	None	5/19/88 11:23 AM	5/19/88 11:23 AM
sfbay_21.html	http://www.nasa.gov/newsinfo/s...	Microsoft HT...	14 KB	None	4/13/00 7:48 AM	5/19/88 11:32 AM	5/19/88 11:32 AM
sfbay_21.jpg	http://www.nasa.gov/images/sfb...	JPEG Image	81 KB	None	2/22/00 9:30 AM	5/19/88 11:32 AM	5/19/88 11:32 AM
kamchatka_18...	http://www.nasa.gov/newsinfo/...	Microsoft HT...	13 KB	None	4/13/00 11:20 AM	5/19/88 11:34 AM	5/19/88 11:34 AM
sfbay_21_thum...	http://www.nasa.gov/images/sfb...	JPEG Image	3 KB	None	2/22/00 8:30 AM	5/19/88 11:38 AM	5/19/88 11:31 AM
banner1.gif	http://www.nasa.gov/images/ba...	GIF Image	6 KB	None	8/4/98 12:07 PM	5/19/88 11:38 AM	5/19/88 11:31 AM
hotnasa.gif	http://www.nasa.gov/images/ho...	GIF Image	4 KB	None	8/4/98 12:07 PM	5/19/88 11:38 AM	5/19/88 11:31 AM
bg_tile3.gif	http://www.nasa.gov/images/bg...	GIF Image	37 KB	None	8/4/98 12:07 PM	5/19/88 11:38 AM	5/19/88 11:31 AM
pasadena_21_t...	http://www.nasa.gov/images/pa...	JPEG Image	6 KB	None	2/22/00 8:32 AM	5/19/88 11:38 AM	5/19/88 11:31 AM
hawaii_18_thum...	http://www.nasa.gov/images/ha...	JPEG Image	7 KB	None	2/18/00 11:19 AM	5/19/88 11:38 AM	5/19/88 11:31 AM
hr.gif	http://www.nasa.gov/images/hr.gif	GIF Image	2 KB	None	8/4/98 12:07 PM	5/19/88 11:38 AM	5/19/88 11:31 AM
pasadena_18_t...	http://www.nasa.gov/images/pa...	JPEG Image	8 KB	None	2/18/00 11:20 AM	5/19/88 11:38 AM	5/19/88 11:31 AM
kamchatka_18.j...	http://www.nasa.gov/images/ka...	JPEG Image	80 KB	None	2/18/00 11:19 AM	5/19/88 11:38 AM	5/19/88 11:34 AM
fiji_21_thumb.jpg	http://www.nasa.gov/images/fiji...	JPEG Image	7 KB	None	2/22/00 8:31 AM	5/19/88 11:38 AM	5/19/88 11:31 AM
new.gif	http://www.nasa.gov/images/ne...	GIF Image	1 KB	None	6/24/99 7:32 AM	5/19/88 11:38 AM	5/19/88 11:31 AM
banner2.gif	http://www.nasa.gov/images/ba...	GIF Image	4 KB	None	8/4/98 12:07 PM	5/19/88 11:38 AM	5/19/88 11:31 AM
srtm_images.html	http://www.nasa.gov/newsinfo/s...	Microsoft HT...	12 KB	None	4/13/00 7:48 AM	5/19/88 11:38 AM	5/19/88 11:31 AM
maps.py?Pyt=T...	http://maps.yahoo.com/py/maps...	Microsoft HT...	15 KB	None	None	5/18/00 10:17 PM	5/18/00 10:17 PM

Figure 17.5 Cache files.

of someone doing the same over the network. One way this can be accomplished is if you are sharing your disk drive. Another would be through vulnerabilities that have from time to time been identified with both Navigator and Explorer. These include the Cache-Cow vulnerability, which affected Netscape Communicator 4.05, and the more recently discovered vulnerability for both IE and Navigator that involves using cookies to run JavaScript that can grab cache files and even html bookmarks. These kinds of vulnerabilities could allow a malicious Web site to grab or view information in the cache files that reside on your PC's disk drive.

When using Internet Explorer you can mitigate the risk of exposing confidential information in cache files by configuring the browser not to cache secure pages. In other words, if the page uses SSL with HTTPS then the browser will not cache the files to the PC's disk drive. This is accomplished by going into Tools/Internet Options and clicking on the Advanced tab. Scroll down until you find "Do not save encrypted pages to disk" and click on the box next to the option. This will prevent SSL pages from being cached to your hard drive. Figure 17.6 shows the Internet options screen with the appropriate option highlighted.

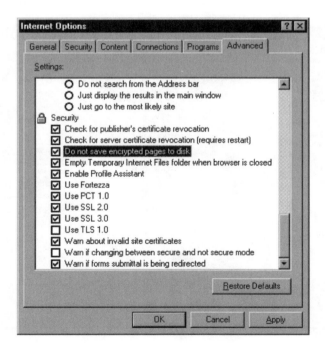

Figure 17.6 IE5 Internet options.

Another option is to simply delete the cached files before exiting Navigator or Internet Explorer. For Internet Explorer this can be done under Internet option. Referring back to Figure 17.4 you can see that there is a delete files button under the temporary Internet files section. Simply clicking on this button deletes all cached files. With Netscape the cache files are deleted by going into Edit/Preferences and clicking on the button clear disk cache. This screen is depicted in Figure 17.7.

With Internet Explorer, you also have the option of configuring the browser to delete cache files automatically when exiting the software. Referring to Figure 17.6, the option directly under "Do not save encrypted pages to disk" is the option "Delete temporary Internet files folder when browser is closed." By checking this option IE will delete the files cached to the hard drive during the browser session at the time the session ends.

Since most of the vulnerabilities associated with grabbing or viewing cached information over the network involves JavaScript, you should consider disabling the function. However, many reputable Web sites employ JavaScript for legitimate purposes, so there is a tradeoff with this option.

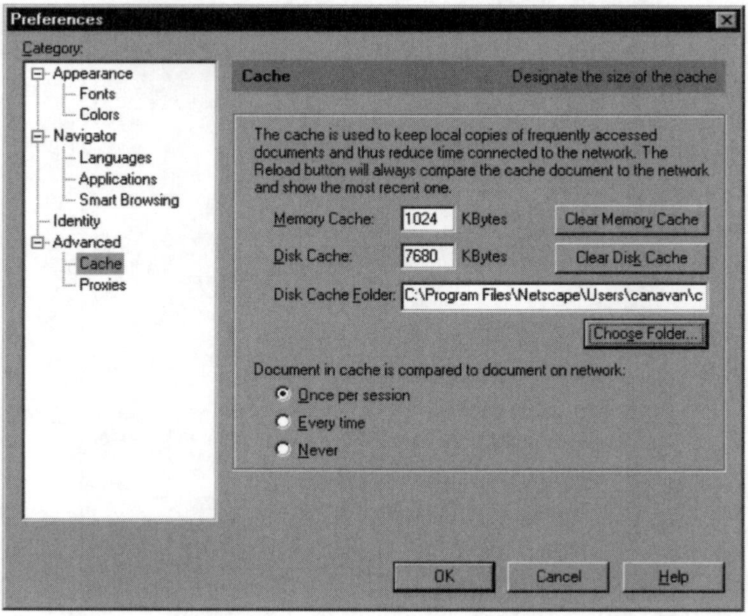

Figure 17.7 IE5 preferences.

AutoComplete

Another concern with using Internet Explore 5.0 in an environment where a PC might be shared with or used by others is the option of AutoComplete. The AutoComplete option can be found under Tools/Internet Options by clicking on the content tab. Figure 17.8 illustrates the AutoComplete settings box. The concern here is the option "user names and passwords on forms." If that box is checked, IE5 will store sign-on account information for those sites that require authentication, including Internet banking and brokerage Web sites. The risk associated with this is obvious.

Figure 17.9 illustrates how AutoComplete functions. The example again employs the Internet banking system of the fictitious Anybank Corporation. In Figure 17.9, IE5 has been configured to autocomplete user names and passwords. In addition, I have already logged into the on-line banking system using two different account numbers and have shut down and reopened IE5 to demonstrate the effects of AutoComplete. When I logged into the Anybank Internet banking system, IE5 recorded the account information. During subsequent attempts to log in to the Internet banking system I need only enter the first number of an account, and IE5 will display the entire account number for all accounts beginning with the number entered.

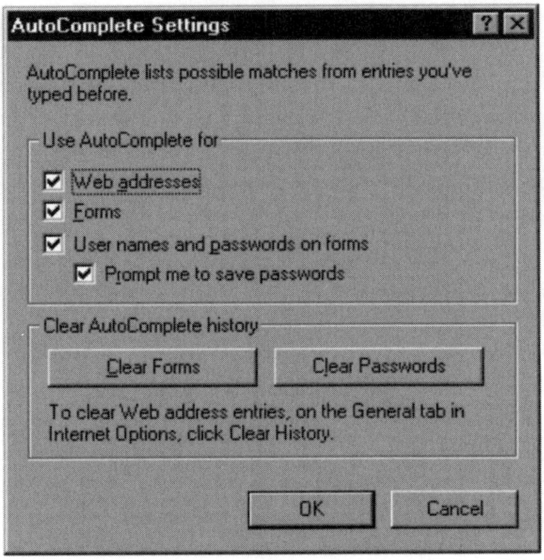

Figure 17.8 IE5 AutoComplete settings.

Figure 17.9 An example of AutoComplete.

In Figure 17.9 when the number 5 is entered into the account number field a drop-down menu appears displaying two account numbers, 55000037390 and 59001260504. These are the two account numbers that I previously had used to login to the Anybank Internet banking system. IE5 stored these account numbers and passwords and associated them with the Anybank Internet URL. When IE5 is configured in this manner, the end user need only highlight the account number, and the password is automatically entered.

Obviously, AutoComplete for usernames and passwords should not be enabled. This is especially true when working in an environment where PCs may be shared. I would also recommend against using the AutoComplete function on a laptop. If the laptop is lost or stolen, it could be used to access on-line accounts. If AutoComplete for usernames and passwords is enabled then access to accounts can be easily obtained. When IE5 was first released we found that AutoComplete was enabled by default. I believe that has since changed.

About the Author

John E. Canavan started his career in the IT field over 17 years ago working for Tymshare, Inc., a computer services and software company that created the Tymnet X.25 network. He is currently vice president for information systems and technology at Chevron FCU and an adjunct professor at Golden Gate University where he teaches in the telecommunications management program. He holds a B.S. in information systems and an M.S. in telecommunications management. He lives with his wife and daughter in San Francisco.

Index

DATE DUE

MAY 0 3 2004			
OCT 18 2011			
'JAN 07 2013			
DEC 12 2017			
GAYLORD			PRINTED IN U.S.A